Modular Programming in COBOL
Russell M. Armstrong

Functional Analysis of Information Networks
Hal B. Becker

Functional Analysis of Information Processing
Grayce M. Booth

Effective Use of ANS COBOL Computer Programming Language
Laurence S. Cohn

The Database Administrator
John K. Lyon

Software Reliability: Principles and Practices
Glenford J. Myers

Making Systems Work: The Psychology of Business Systems
William C. Ramsgard

D0812655

ROBERT E. KRIEGER
PUBLISHING COMPANY INC.

MALABAR
FLORIDA 32950

Making Systems Work

Making Systems Work

The Psychology of
Business Systems

William C. Ramsgard

*Drawings by
Rita Williams*

A WILEY-INTERSCIENCE PUBLICATION

JOHN WILEY & SONS

New York • London • Sydney • Toronto

This publication is designed to provide accurate and authoritative information in regard
to the subject matter covered. It is sold with the understanding that the publisher is not
engaged in rendering legal, accounting, or other professional service. If legal advice or
other expert assistance is required, the services of a competent professional person should
be sought.

*From a Declaration of Principles jointly adopted by a Committee of the American Bar
Association and a Committee of Publishers.*

Library of Congress Cataloging in Publication Data

Ramsgard, William C   1934-
    Making systems work.

    (Business data processing, a Wiley series)
    "A Wiley-Interscience publication."
    1. Business—Data processing. 2. Management
information systems.   3.   Electronic data processing
departments—Management. I. Title.
HF5548.2.R28   658'.05'4   77-5933
ISBN 0-471-01522-9

Printed in the United States of America

10 9 8 7 6 5 4

To my family

Preface to the Series

Business Data Processing: A Wiley Series is intended for practitioners in business/management applications of the computer. The objective is to provide a series of publications that will enable readers to improve their understanding and competence in the use of new computer technology.

Business data processing practitioners face challenging problems in keeping abreast of new computer technology. They are deeply involved in creating new application systems and in maintaining and enhancing existing ones, using the technology available to them. Under the pressure of this work, little time is left for learning about and becoming competent in new technological developments. But these practitioners recognize that not only their professional careers but also their personal fulfillment require that they stay abreast of technology. This series seeks to help them keep informed.

To the fullest extent possible, this series will draw on experienced practitioners as authors, so as to provide useful, practical information. Some books will be designed to aid junior level analysts and programmers upgrade their competence to reach the experienced practitioner level. Other books will be aimed at helping managers to broaden their knowledge on how new technology may best be put to use by subordinates. We expect that most of the books will be written for practicing systems analysts, designers, and programmers, to help them keep up with this rapidly evolving field.

In the past, this series has addressed a wide range of subject matter, including data base management, data communications, programming technology, organizational considerations, personnel implications, and application system design and development. Thus the series has addressed in the past, and will continue to address in the future, the breadth, complexity, and dynamic characteristics of the computer field.

The computer field abounds with controversy and different points of view. As Mark Twain said, "A man with a new idea is considered a crank until the idea succeeds." From time to time, therefore, the series will publish a book that challenges some accepted ideas, suggests novel approaches, and denigrates orthodoxy—but only when the author is a practitioner who has tested out his ideas and approaches. The book you are reading is of this type.

The computer field is an exciting place in which to work. For this reason, the problem of training, updating, and upgrading professionals in the field will be a continuing one. We hope that the series will be an effective tool in helping to cope with this problem.

RICHARD G. CANNING
J. DANIEL COUGER
Series Editors

Preface

For years the administrators of almost every organization have been on a paper binge. We have been creating for ourselves ever more reports, forms, and analyses. Experts at the National Archives estimate that the government itself has something over 700,000 business forms—but we're not sure because they're still counting.

It is not the purpose of this book to take the government to task. The deep, black pools of information waste in your own organization are far more important. Beyond the vast expenditures necessary to keep your paper mill moving, there lurk unnecessary loss of sales, lower competitive standing, and even business failure, strangely occurring in a computer age. In 25 computer years many a managing executive has moved from near collapse in a parched desert of no information to near drowning in a sea of unstructured data. The key to executive survival then and now has been simply to manage in the good old-fashioned way—by instinct! This book seeks to provide more realistic opportunities to use the information structure that you have to pay for to help manage your organization.

Warning! This book is not to be read alone or even in parts. Your organizational orientation has already built in a bias toward data processing, accounting, and various management training and review functions. In most instances you are directly inside or outside of the information processing system. When you finish the last chapter, pass the book on to your counterpart on the other side of that system. This may be difficult since you will find herein some realistic criticism of your own activity. But maximum benefits and even implementation of some new ideas will be best developed only when *both of you* mutually understand each other's problems. So check one box below and read on:

☐   ME   ☐   THE OTHER GUY

The first part of the book is dedicated to the identification of information problems that stifle your growth and opportunity. The series of tests presented in Chapter 2 is designed not to be definitive, but to help you develop a nontheoretical understanding of the problems that you have. You may declare that some of the tests are ridiculous, but each information evaluation test is a serious challenge for some organization, or part of it. Where previously you've had no bench marks for the comparison of your information systems, this book provides a sufficient number of assessment points for a broad reckoning of your information tools. The Appendix offers a separate and distinct test of the computer installation. This rating system (the Dragsmar Evaluation) has been applied in practice to many government and business facilities. This test is definitive and accurate.

The middle portions of the book concern the development of both an appropriately trained information staff and the education of a vital management task force who can better execute their responsibilities with information. Management by functions or management by technique has long been promoted by the various master's programs in business administration and by technical journals. Manager's time is a rare commodity. Perception of the organization is not a common talent; and since a true understanding of company activities has not always been available, the goal here is to establish an island of understanding. This island is populated by the manager and his systems analyst who together, understanding each other's problems, talents, and limitations, develop a common, usable structure of appropriate information. The rest of the island population of your organization can be made up of only two other groups. One group makes or sells your products. All the rest PROCESS INFORMATION for the doers and you. Common understanding will help bring your divergent organization forces together.

But even an awareness of information problems and a common understanding between managers and analysts will only curb paper pollution. The final chapters point the way to the objective, which is *to make your information system run like your business* while providing management with necessary controls and tools. Really—let's have the manager act *with information*. Three plans are developed to promote organization, then control, and finally mutual interdiscipline understanding. If applied, these three control devices will help carry your company into the future by appropriately reorganizing the data development structures. With information your organization can be superior.

The final chapter peers into the future, even beyond the time relative to the improvements the suggestions made here will produce. It is a world as different as tomorrow, where the business systems are NO SYSTEM and dramatic changes have taken place in electronic data processing job responsibilities. But tomorrow's people will be just as creative and individualistic as those who now are attracted to the truculent computer.

Many of the tales told in this book are completely factual, although names and places have been changed for obvious reasons. But I do wish to name the people whose efforts, support, and understanding make an undertaking such as this book possible. I thank each of them warmly.

Dorothy S. Gleisner, Ron Herrgesell, and A. James Andrews were supportive and helpful. Particular thanks are due Jack Cover for his comprehensive review, contributions, and suggestions. I would like to express very special appreciation to my mother for her dedicated efforts in typing and retyping the manuscript. Perhaps the greatest contribution has been the patience of my wife and children over 2 years of lost weekends, evenings, and holidays.

WILLIAM C. RAMSGARD

Baldwinsville, New York
August 1977

Contents

PART 3

Structured Systems

Making Systems Work

Problem Identification

As a manager do you feel that data processing is "above results"? Is this vital department in the organization measured on a scale different from that for all other functions?

It is the purpose of Part 1 to examine the effect that the information system has on the organization. In turn, we review the capability of key personnel and the attitudes of management toward a "technical" operation.

No matter what your personal role happens to be within the vast information processing cycle or the firm itself, Part 1 is designed to illuminate the challenges you must meet to make your organization grow.

CHAPTER 1

The Ecology of Information— the Pollution You Buy

THE ECOLOGY OF INFORMATION

In the last few years, it seems that everyone has suddenly become aware of what goes into the sewer pipe and what goes up the smoke-stack. Of course smokestacks were always there but now, perhaps because there are so many people, or so many smokestacks, everyone is concerned about what's happening to the environment and the impact of these changes on all of us in future years.

Something certainly can be done about the pollution. You'll get a good press each time you buy a new filter to purify the smoke or clean up the wastes going into the water system. But the cost is absolutely staggering. Each step taken to improve the environment lowers prof-its, reduces the return on investment, and does approximately nothing to improve your competitive position. Meanwhile your com-petitors may be doing nothing at all. Certainly your annual report will reflect in glowing terms the antipollution campaign that you put on, but the stockholders, it seems, seldom read that page.

The stockholders are concerned about earn-ings per share. Oh, they're happy that you fight the pollution fight, but since many of them live a hundred or a thousand miles away, your campaign really does nothing at all for them. Still, as owners of an organization which is interested in the welfare of the entire community, they have nothing to complain about. Progress and improvement, even without profit, cannot be condemned.

Now, while the new filtration and antipollution devices are necessities for the well being of mankind and the survival of your organization within the community, it certainly will not be to your credit to tell your stockholders and your board of directors about the pollution that you buy. That's right—you, as a top level manager, buy pollution, and you pay top dollar for it too. Inside your organization is a microecology of forces and activities that are not evident to the outside world. This internal system consists of people and information who do not produce any products and generally do not produce any profits. They exist to provide the services necessary to maintain your ongoing business and to measure the people who are actively engaged in producing your product and directly providing the profits. Unfortunately, in many instances the data, the communications, the reports, and the decisions they generate mire your efforts and cloud your goals.

If the interaction of management and information within your organization creates an environment that resembles Lake Erie, you, as a key executive of this organization, are a polluter and you are buying pollution.

A polluted atmosphere is one where normal living things are restricted in their growth and in many cases die. Pollution is dirty; pollution is an unsightly mess. Within your organization it is possible that we can find many different kinds of pollution, just as we find dirty water, and dirty air.

Just as we are bothered by unsightly messes, noxious odors, or very loud noises, just as we are being burdened by an enormous population growth which possibly will soon absorb all of our resources, we find the same dangers occurring within almost any organization. If pollution does occur within your microenvironment, a threatened species—the qualified manager—will not mature. And if the pollution becomes too serious, eventually the entire organization—your organization—will die.

Let's examine some of the different kinds of pollution that may occur within your microenvironment. To this end let's take a look at the microecology of your company.

The first question that we have to ask is, "Why do we find information pollution?" Why do we find an organization in danger of strangling itself with people, information, controls, and some of the most

Figure 1

cataclysmic procedural errors that have ever occurred? Size and volume are certainly primary contributors. Organizations frequently are bigger today than they were in previous years. Competition is tougher, and response must be quicker. The requirements of the marketplace are more stringent. Government controls, government regulations, and government requirements have demanded enormous amounts of information about our people, about our products, and about the way in which we conduct our business. Moreover, within this somewhat new environment, we find a tool which, for general business purposes, did not exist 25 years ago. That tool is the computer. And the computer is a generator of immeasurable quantities of what is called information. Here the pollution begins. Unless this information is proper, timely, and sufficient only to satisfy the needs of your organization, we begin to dilute and pollute the internal environment of the organization.

Let's take a look at how some of this pollution occurs.

POLLUTION TYPES

Some of it is like water pollution. The streams of our nation used to be clean and clear and filled with game fish eager to take the hook. Today most of these streams are poisoned with unknown substances, and the fish are gone. Years ago it was a simple undertaking to set up an organization to dispense a service or make a product. Today it's extremely difficult because of the competition, the size needed for success, and the information requirements.

Years ago you probably had a very clear stream of information about the product or service that you provided. Today that stream is no longer clear. Your computer system or systems are providing so much information, with so many different ways of evaluating (where a sale was made, how a service was provided, countless cost justifications for developing a new product or modifying or dropping an existing one), that soon no one can understand what the objectives and requirements of the business really are any more. People are so busy working their way through information they don't have time to think about what they are going to do with it. There's just too much of it, and gradually the qualified manager becomes drowned in data. Is your information stream so murky that it is impossible for your business to absorb appropriate data and then proceed on its way?

Some of your problems are like air pollution. Air pollution pollution is smoky; it's nebulous; it's indefinite. We know that something is there most of the time; we know that something is wrong—but we're unable to put our finger on it. Air pollution can be killing us, and we don't even know it. The information you receive and upon which you base your decisions can be just as confusing. Do you really know the content and meaning of the report you just looked at? Are you sure where the numbers came from? Are you certain that this is not just a manipulation of many different summaries from the computer, processed through the Accounting Department and resummarized for you into a few numbers that have been adjusted so many times that nobody is sure any more what they mean? Are you looking at 1-year, 3-year, and 5-year plans that may be 100 or more pages long, many of these pages containing 50 or more numbers? Can you possibly make use of all this data to determine clear-cut plans and directions for your organization? If you are not aware of the source, construction, and actual content of these summaries and plans, an invisible smog of worthless information is corroding the lungs of your organization.

Other problems may be compared to visual and noise pollution. Are your sight and hearing being bombarded by information which is used to measure sales or production activity? If you originally had three reports to adequately measure this activity, you will find that they soon beget thirty different kinds of reports to serve the same purpose, because the people who are in charge of these functions are desperately trying to control the somewhat uncontrollable environment. They're attempting to respond to demands of a marketplace which doesn't always function in a predictable manner. They are trying to respond to *your* pressures as you strive to have your organization perform in a more efficient manner. They therefore call upon the information system; they call upon the computer system to provide new types of reports indicating control. Your managers ask for (and you pay for) many reports attempting to evaluate varying circumstances, or reports offering persons in your organization guidance in controlling their microecology.

Since almost no one ever stops these shadow control reports, they come into existence and they proliferate by variation. As a result the computer system is soon so clogged with information that more people must be added to the organization simply to process all of these many reports. Then more people are added to supervise the processors. Inexorably, your environment becomes more polluted, and the structure gets more complex.

POLLUTION SOURCES

When pollution occurs, it is usually not very difficult to find the source. Let's take a look at the prime polluters within your organization. First of all we have the OPERATING MANAGERS, particularly the ones who do not know what they want. They don't know exactly how to control their environment. They refuse to admit that sometimes there are forces outside the environment which they cannot control, and they attempt to respond to today's conditions by changing the rules. Many of the rules of operation are reflected in various kinds of reports. Remember that these are not the people who make the product or sell the product. The operating managers supervise these groups. Yet these people keep changing the rules of information—changing the guidelines for the active, creative people so as to better respond to you and to the organizational needs. They do it by the proliferation of information. They do it by adding more reports, more variations, more information, and finally more people to process the information.

Another prime source of pollution is the DATA PROCESSING computer oriented people themselves. Here we have a group who are supposedly specialists in information. But they are really specialists in processing information with a particular machine called a computer, as opposed to being specialists in the use of this information. If these data processing people are not well controlled, or if you, as a user or a manager, harass them into quick responses, they do not or will not have the opportunity to adequately design and document an information tool. Then they may use the computer as a printing press, and you will begin to see illogically arranged, poorly designed reports. This is a case of visual pollution because you are not sure about the results that you are looking at. The picture becomes very murky and obscure.

Another prime pollutor may be TOP MANAGEMENT, because you frequently expect and pressure your organization to produce miracles. You yourself fail to recognize the complexities of the marketplace or the economy or the current situations within your organization. By living for and dedicating yourself to the next quarterly dividend, you may force your people to channel their activity toward very, very short responses. And because of this short response time, they, in turn, must demand quick responses in terms of information dedicated to the conditions of the outside environment. As this environment changes, they must make every effort to change the ecology of the organization. But one of their prime methods of responding quickly is to add new reports, new controls, new statistics, new measures, and an environment of overpopulation in information is reached. Then you're strangling on data and reports of activity two quarters ago and on good ideas and concepts meant for the marketplace last year. Your business data processing is strangling on short-term requirements. On the other hand, if you had a balanced general plan of information development for a long period of time, you could ease your manager's burden and your organization's problems and costs by not producing all these varieties of information. And it isn't the cost of the information itself that is so terribly damaging to your organization—it's the cost of processing it through your management hierarchy. Just like water pollution, just like muddying up a huge river, this immense body of information produced by the computer eventually destroys the ability of the game fish—the qualified manager—to adequately, actively function and perform to your expectations within your organization.

Finally, the MACHINES, the computers and the copiers are in themselves pollutors. But they're not the real source—they're only the tool of pollution. Actually, they are designed well—the copying machines can turn out thousands of copies an hour, and the computer printer, assisted by microfilm and mass storage devices, can produce untold quantitites of data already available and waiting to be reorganized for the umpteenth time into a new structure, a new format, to serve your organization.

SYMPTOMS OF POLLUTION

There are several different symptoms which you can look for to detect the existence of pollution within your organization. It is certainly worthwhile for you to be aware of potential problems within your microecology. Let's look at some of the evaluations you can make.

Data Quantity

Determine the amount of computer paper and the size of the clerical staff within your organization, and do some simple mathematics. How many cards are used per year by your computer system? How many are output cards, compared to the number of people in your clerical organization? How many sheets of paper are produced per year from your computer system, and how many people do you have to process these pieces of paper? How many copies are made on your copying machines during a year, and how many people within your organization do you have to process these copies?

Distribution

Obtain the distribution list for all of your computer reports. Don't be shocked if it's an almost illegible document. But be terrified if no one can produce a distribution list! Have someone summarize the distributions for you, and you'll find that a very few people receive a great deal of the computer information. Also, have someone summarize the reproduction uses made of your equipment, and you will find again that a very few people are using these services repeatedly. Even without any guidelines, a little human judgment will allow you to decide whether or not it is possible for some of these people to make use of all of the information they receive.

Time Movement

Is detailed information sent too high up in the organization? No manager can function with less information than his boss. Start following some of the movements of the computer data and reproduced copies of information. Many of these pieces of paper are following the flow of actual transactions. Find out how long it takes for an initial transaction to reach the person you consider the last one necessary to review this transaction. Is the time so long that the content and meaning of the transaction can no longer be acted upon?

Unit Record Equipment

This consists of the gray boxes which process punched cards over in the corner of the data processing room. These machines are the antiques of information processing from more than 20 years ago. They were in their prime before the first computer generation. No information processing application in the 1970s can justify their use! Why, then, do you have these ugly, slow, manpower consuming boxes? There may be several reasons such as the following:

1. The machines perform a step in a process, and no one in your organization understands what the steps are any longer.
2. Your organization hires analysts/programmers who are dedicated to carrying out computer work in small job steps. They don't understand or care about the unit record equipment, and they don't comprehend the gross requirements of the system.
3. Nothing is documented.
4. No one realizes that machines are inflexible. Since the work is done on *some* machine, this must be the optimum method. The people responsible for information processing have failed to recognize that machine information processing requirements have changed more rapidly than business requirements. One of the

most costly steps in the process is to have a computer wait for sorted or selected cards from unit record equipment.

5. There is no budget for conversion.
6. The operations data processing people think it would be impossible to get along without this equipment.
7. No one cares.

Report Content

Collect a series of reports about some large common function such as sales or employees. Include computer and noncomputer reports.

Are the column headings in some cases mysterious codes or jumbles of letters? Is there so much data about one employee or one sale that action exceptions can't be identified? Is the report unnumbered? Are the pages unnumbered? Pollution is creeping in on you if you answer, "Yes"!

The situation is worse—your organization may be struggling for breath—if you find that reports within the same function provide different results. For example, do sales by territory, by salesman, and by product all provide the same gross sales dollars? Does the number of employees processed by the Personnel Department equal the number of employees paid by Payroll? Don't be too shocked if the totals disagree. This situation is not particularly uncommon.

Summarizations

Like water pollution, summaries of data and report information seek to put considerable heavy content into a medium that may not be able to support it.

Occasionally organizations are run by an individual who receives only a one-page 8½ × 11 report a day. Maybe someone else can do it, but should you?

From the report information that you do receive can you tell:

1. What are the sources of data?
2. What data is included?
3. What data is excluded?
4. How old is the information?
5. How you might act because of this information?

Only management can answer these questions. Only you can determine whether you accept old, distorted, inadequate information. Only you can investigate, probe, test, and finally decide whether you promote and buy for yourself and others an environment of polluted information, cloudy decisions, and inapproproate actions while your organization—your microecology—attempts to deal with the future and the world.

CHAPTER 2

Tests for Pollution

Is it possible that some information pollution exists within your organization? We hope not! Still it might be both interesting and worthwhile to investigate. A *feeling* about how things are is just not good enough. We need to approach the information monolith with at least *some* organized measuring tools. . . .

Let's examine some definite ways that you can test your organization for pollution in a more specific and decisive manner. We recognize that your position within the organization provides the opportunity for or, conversely, limits the scope of your probe. Because of the possible range in your responsibility and authority we have developed three sets of general tests:

- Chief executive's test.
- Officer's or key manager's test.
- Interested manager's or user's test.

Incorporated in the tests are twenty-one separate evaluation approaches challenging the validity of the information structures in your organization. There are both variety and similarity between these questions. Because of the distinctiveness of your company, some questions cannot be appropriately applied for your test purposes, yet will be valid for others in a different work situation.

Most of these questions are, in fact, tests not only of the capability, but also of the credibility, of your overhead staff. And your overhead is consumed to a large extent by the financial, data processing, and specialized clerical people you employ.

It is important to recognize that the three sets of tests are not the application of high sounding theorical concepts. Rather they are aimed at the soft underbelly of the information system. The twenty-one questions are designed to strip the information processors of their professional ambiguity and examine the true value of their products. These EDP people are expensive and talented, but they are seldom tested in their own area of expertise. Do not anticipate excessive candor. Be tough and demanding. You are challenging some functions which have not always been held to accountability. And be honest—because several questions test you!

Scoring

Ask as many questions and conduct as many tests as your position allows. We suggest that you rate the results as either satisfactory or unsatisfactory. No quibbling! Tolerate no half answers. Divide the number of questions asked into 100, and give each question a point value. Score each satisfactory answer with the full question point value, and each unsatisfactory answer with a zero point value. Ask at least five questions. This is a harsh test.

An additional word of caution is necessary. A majority of the tests in this series are designed to provide comparison data. The assessment points established by the questions develop only a broad evaluation of your information tools.

This is admittedly somewhat of a Sunday supplement approach. But the problems exposed are present in almost every organization, and they need to be illuminated. What questions can you ask? What questions *should* you ask?

These tests provide a guide. The information processing staff will be heartened by your interest, yet dismayed by the challenges you present. The questions in themselves offer a threshold of understanding between information functions and the rest of the organization. Most of this book is dedicated to improving this understanding.

A definitive test of the Data Processing Department is offered in the Appendix. This test, called The DRAGSMAR EVALUATION, has been used widely in the United States and Canada to measure the quality of output from data processing and the capability of the entire department. As a test it varies extensively from the questions presented in this chapter. Many of its evaluations are related to factors beyond just information (data) and are restricted to the scope of one department. The Dragsmar Evaluation provides a special opportunity to quickly determine whether data processing can deliver a good product.

The three tests presented now are designed only to sharpen your awareness of the obscurities of the information processing function. Your reaction to these questions will also test your values.

Scoring The Results

100–80 Remarkable! Your organization is one of a very few that rate this well.

80–50 Problems and pollution exist within your information system. We suggest that you examine some of the remedies presented later as a start toward environment control.

50–0 Serious polluting exists in your data, information, and decision making structure. If your score is this low, your key financial, administrative, and DP people should be well aware of the inefficiency, redundancy, and stifling ineptness of the information process. If they do not realize these defects, they may be the cause of the clouds of uncertainty strangling the company.

THE FIRST POLLUTION TEST—CHIEF EXECUTIVE'S QUESTIONS

Question One

Is the information you buy crystal clear, or is it polluted? Most organizations have two prime sources of information and reports—data processing and accounting. Data processing may consume 2 to 3% of your budget and produce a wide variety of data. Accounting normally will produce the analysis, summaries, and evaluations of most functions, with small amounts of detail.

Determine whether the following are available:

1. Can the controller produce a list of the various analyses, statements, and summaries prepared by his group? This financial and statistical report function is the documented control boundary of your organization. If such a list is not immediately available, it is not possible to determine who controls what or how anything is

controlled. Where are the guideposts, and who are the traffic cops to police the machines, personnel, and assets your provide?

2.   Can the data processing manager supply a sample (one page is sufficient) of each report his machinery produces? The product of this very expensive computer function is *reports*. If he cannot show you samples, he cannot demonstrate his wares. How much of this volume of reports is inappropriate, inaccurate, untimely, or (even worse), duplicated? If the DP manager can't show you samples, you will never know—nor will anyone else—to what extent you are buying garbage. The victims of pollution are often unaware that they are being poisoned until it is too late.

As Dr. Lawrence J. Peter has said, "Because the computer's capability has far outstripped our ability to use it wisely, bureaucrats mindlessly make work for it by designing elaborate forms to collect vast amounts of irrelevant information."

If it takes longer than 1 hour for either the controller or the data processing manager to reply, consider the response unsatisfactory since you do not know what you are buying.

Question Two

Does someone understand the organizational objectives and functions well enough to provide the necessary information at the right time and in the right quantity to get the job done?

1.   Ask the systems manager (or someone he delegates) to make a presentation to you on a major information systems flow. Order entry or inventory control might be a good choice. Ask the systems manager to explain the basic flow of information from the start to completion of the process. Even if you are knowledgeable about data processing, pretend to be ignorant. Refuse to accept any DP "buzz" words or terms. The explanation must be in plain English. Keep asking *why* things are done in the way stated.
2.   Repeat the test with the controller. Ask him to explain the same system, and to relate how his review reports help to manage and control the process.
3.   Repeat the test a third time with the manager in charge of this function. After he explains the basic flow, ask him how he makes use of DP and accounting reports related to his function.

If the systems manager cannot explain the process in simple English, it is possible he either does not understand it or he is so technically machine oriented that he solves problems for the machines and not for the business.

The controller should be able to explain the process since he has financial responsibility to provide the proper controls. If there are no direct controls, he still needs to be able to explain the process to ensure that he knows that he needs no controls.

The functional manager should be able to confirm the understanding of the systems manager and the controller. Furthermore, he should be able to explain why DP and accounting controls aid his group.

A set of three satisfactory replies will indicate that you are achieving appropriate information and control goals. If the systems manager does not provide a satisfactory reply, some of your most expensive resources—programmers, analysts, and computers—are being inappropriately used. The man in charge of the information resources does not understand! In this case his computer operations can inundate you with paper pollution. A prime requisite of his job is to understand, or to employ people who understand, not just the computer but also the business function itself.

If the controller does not provide a satisfactory reply, he is driving your business vehicle through a fog. Watch out for a crash if he can't indicate where the controls are, or whether they should exist.

If the manager doesn't use the DP and accounting tools, your course is equally unclear. Either he is incapable, or the purveyors of the information and controls never completed their jobs and explained why the reports were provided and how they should be used.

Question Three

How many people do you employ? A simple question? Better try to answer it first. Ask Personnel for a count of people. The department may have a report covering this subject. No matter—after it has provided the data, call Payroll and find out why a different number of people were paid. This is one of the few areas where you, as chief executive, can ask HOW the number is derived. If explanations of categories and classifications become tedious, if you become slightly confused, if you are forced to apply your own definitions of what constitutes an employee, the fog may be setting in.

Understandable procedures for hiring and terminations with simple, clear explanations will be a satisfactory, adequate response. Unlike question 2, which was concerned with the quality of an information flow and the people who controlled it, here we examine the validity of the data itself. If the replies here are unsatisfactory to you, we may begin to wonder how your administrative, clerical, and accounting staffs handle anything as complex as GROSS SALES!

Question Four

How are key decisions made? How is the course of your ship charted? Identify an executive who has responsibility for key decisions in your organization. Such decisions must be vital to the organization, not referred to you for directive or "advice" and not rescinded by you.

Consider the results of this question unsatisfactory if you cannot name both an executive and the decisions for which the person is responsible. Authority and responsibility have not been delegated! If such delegation does not start at the top of the organization, no one below will delegate, and a "minor matters mentality" permeates your environment. Stagnation is in process.

It is not possible for you to answer this question objectively. At your next staff meeting ask your people to answer in typewritten, sealed envelopes the question, "What important decisions are delegated to my staff members and not later modified by me?" Afraid? Indeed, you may well be disturbed by the replies.

Question Five

How many reports do you receive, and do you use them? An answer of five or less indicates you've been reading your *Harvard Business Review* but is unsatisfactory. There is no magic number of reports, nor any set of vital statistics which by itself will keep you continually informed on the internal condition of your organization.

Remember that your organization is much like a living, growing organism. Products and people are consumed, and parts are continually changing. Without your constant vigilance and review, ineptness, inconsistency, and inefficiency will disrupt and destroy your objectives. If you do not have a general plan to review, *in various levels of detail,* the financial and functional information systems, consider your reply unsatisfactory. You are not keeping in touch with reality.

Question Six

What action have you taken in the past month based on the reports you received? Critical information will cause you to act. If the information you received produced no actions on your part, there are three possibilities:

1. It may have been mixed and stirred into meaningless pap by your subordinates.
2. It may have contained voluminous detail impossible to digest.
3. It may not have been the information needed for you to exercise control.

Credit yourself with a satisfactory reply if you can remember two decisions, based on these reports, which you made in the past month.

Question Seven

When do you receive the monthly financial statement? If it reaches you by the end of the third day after the accounting closing, consider your reply satisfactory. Any period longer than 3 days indicates cloudy financial and data processing procedures. You are buying pollution.

NOW CHECK YOUR SCORE, OR TRY SOME PARTS OF THE SECOND POLLUTION TEST.

THE SECOND POLLUTION TEST—OFFICER'S OR KEY MANAGER'S TEST QUESTIONS

Conduct any test designed for the chief executive that your authority and responsibility allow. In addition you may try the following.

Question One

Is the filtration system running properly? Each organization has one group, and many have two groups, dedicated to maintaining the purity, clarity, accuracy, and completeness of its business systems. These groups are your internal and external auditors. Consider your answer satisfactory if you provide the external auditors with some time to conduct operational audits (examining how clerical processes function) and no more than 5% of their time is spent verifying cash as part of the financial audit.

If you have a staff of internal auditors, consider the reply satisfactory if at least 75% of their time is devoted to operational audits. This group of internal auditors is perhaps the single most important control within your organization. From their intimate observations of all levels of information flow and organizational interaction they can supply valuable insights, suggestions, remedies, and, to a great extent, the necessary pollution controls on day-to-day routine systems.

The Institute of Internal Auditors has prepared the following statement on the nature of internal auditing:

> Internal Auditing is the independent appraisal activity within an organization for the review of the accounting, financial and other operations as a basis for protective and constructive service to management. It is the type of control which functions by measuring and evaluating the effectiveness of other types of control. It deals with accounting and financial matters but it may also properly deal with matters of an operating nature.[1]

Question Two

Conduct a report and information inventory of a function that is your responsibility. Select an area such as sales analysis, labor control, or purchasing for your study. Hold separate meetings with all the managers, work group leaders, and an accounting and a data processing representative. Ask each person in the function to bring a copy of *every* report he or she receives.

Review each report. How is it used? Does the recipient understand every item in the report and its proper use?

Are you buying pollution? Only you can decide whether the replies are satisfactory, based on the following:

1. The knowledge and understanding of the information by the users within the functional group.
2. The amount of report duplication through carbon copies or different versions of the same data.
3. The utility of the reports to the function.
4. The number of times the accounting or DP representative must explain the purpose or detail content of the report.

Accounting and data processing costs are incurred, to a great extent, in producing these reports. It is not necessary to determine at this point the cause of unsatisfactory replies. Perhaps the supervisors have not received sufficient education related to the tools of their jobs. Perhaps the accounting and data processing people believe that they play no part in continuing employee education. Perhaps you haven't provided time for either. No matter—at this point you need only determine whether you are buying pollution.

[1]F. A. Lamperti and J. B. Thurston, *Internal Auditing for Management,* Prentice-Hall, Englewood Cliffs, N.J., 1958, p. 387.

Question Three

"I can get it wholesale!" Unfortunately these stirring words also apply to the volume of computer data you receive. In question 2 we were concerned whether you bought pollution through less than optimum use of report content. Here we want to find out whether you are a wholesaler. The question applies primarily, but not exclusively, to computer reports.

Are any of the reports used in the functions just reviewed too voluminous in detail? Are only the totals used? Does the recipient select only a standard portion of the report for his use? Consider your reply unsatisfactory if one report in five is not used entirely. Consider your reply unsatisfactory if one report in eight is a complete register of all transactions and is used only occasionally for reference. Remember—what you get, you pay for!

Question Four

Evaluate the impact of the data processing group on your organization. Call the data processing manager and ask, "How many programs do we now have, excluding utilities?" The answer, to be satisfactory, should be 1500[1] or fewer.

Well organized systems and programming will easily capture all information systems appropriate to automate. Although each organizational environment is unique, the problems and solutions of various businesses are generally quite similar. More than 1500 basic programs (excluding edits, sorts, and uniquely identified versions of the same program, that are run at different times) indicate poor systems planning, fragmented processing, and low grade solutions per program. An exception must be made for autonomous divisions using a central computer system. Increase the base of 1500 by 10% for each geographically separated, generally independent division of your organization.

If the answer is more than 1500 basic programs, you have just uncovered a prime source of pollution. While many devices exist to measure the efficient use of computer hardware, there are only a few rating systerms for evaluating an entire Data Processing Department. As a completely separate evaluation technique you will find the Dragsmar Evaluation in the Appendix. If the reply to question 4 is unsatisfactory, we suggest that you make use of this particular type of evaluation and probe deeply into the DP function in your organization.

[1]See question one in the Appendix for variation of between 500 and 1500 programs—depending on your firm's size.

Question Five

Can your data processing staff support the constant changes in your environment? Sales policies, purchasing requirements, government regulations, and the like force continued maintenance of computer programs. Such maintenance requires the full time efforts of two programmers and one system analyst for every 75 to 100 programs. If you do not have this minimum staff, you are not adequately meeting the requirements placed on your organization by the changing business environment. Your reply then must be unsatisfactory.

Question Six

How long does it take to completely process a key transaction? How long does it take to completely process a sale for a brand-new charge customer? How long does it take to change a price or a rate of pay? Consider your replies satisfactory if you believe that the existing clerical, administrative, and computer processing fulfills your organization requirements and takes no longer than 3 days. Any key transaction process requiring more than 3 days limits management reaction time for vital situations.

Question Seven

Determine how well your manager of systems understands how a key function works. Pick a function with a large clerical content within your area of responsibility and ask the manager of systems to meet with you and explain the various inputs and reports. He may use a representative to explain the support he provides. Concentrate on *how* the process works as related to the service he provides. Does he understand the objectives of the function? Can he talk intelligently about procedures, forms, work flow, and the relationship of this function to other parts of organization?

If "yes" is the answer to all these questions, consider the reply satisfactory.

This man is one of your key pollution fighters. It is his job to be aware of interrelationships between people and paper and to maintain minimum levels of information costs. If his replies are foggy, no one else can be expected to produce clear-cut solutions based on interrelated information systems.

NOW CHECK YOUR SCORE, OR TRY SOME PARTS OF THE THIRD POLLUTION TEST.

THE THIRD POLLUTION TEST—INTERESTED MANAGER'S OR USER'S QUESTIONS

Conduct any part of the first two tests that your authority and responsibility allow. In addition you may try the following.

Question One

Can you obtain a brand-new computer "file" report in 5 or fewer working days using a report generator? A file report is one which makes use of data already in the computer in one set of records. It can include totals, simple mathematics involving numbers already in the record, selection of certain records, and a sequence determined by you. An example of a file report might be the following listing: "all female employees in the western office in sequence by years of service." A report generator is a previously written set of instructions used as a framework for this request. Hopefully this type of request can be completed by data processing in just a few days. If it takes longer, these people are wasting dollars to write a unique program, and the reply must be considered unsatisfactory.

Question Two

Select two or more reports related to the same subject (sales, number of customers, value of inventory, etc.), and determine whether the totals agree. If they are in agreement, the answer is satisfactory. If there is some disagreement and you don't know why, the reply is unsatisfactory. If *you* understand why the totals or data are different, contact every recipient of any of these reports. These people may not see all of the reports, but they should be able to explain properly the data included in or excluded from each report they receive. Failure to do so constitutes an unsatisfactory reply, since people are then taking actions and making decisions on an unknown base of data. Pollution is seeping into your system.

Question Three

Select an accounting or financial report sent to you. Ask the accountant or controller what actions he expects you to take with this document. A reply of "Just for your information!" is unsatisfactory. If, on the other hand, the reply indicates that the report enables you to take some control action, politely ask, "How?" If the accountant's or controller's answer seems hazy, you have identified a pollution source.

Paper and reports are absorbing his time and yours without clearcut purpose.

Question Four

Review the clerical functions in your department. Do you have a posting machine and tub files? Do you have drawers of punched cards? If you stack all of the computer reports in your department in one pile, is it taller than you? Any "yes" answer indicates a stifling drudgery and lack of ability to respond appropriately and efficiently to business demands. Such a reply is, of course, unsatisfactory. Seldom can card handling, filing, or working with massive computer printouts be economically justified.

Yet, time and again, we find people going through motions, filling in forms, and completing meaningless rituals. These expensive inefficiencies dilute the ability of your people to apply their energies toward more fruitful objectives for the time invested.

Question Five

Is any one person in your department spending 50% or more of his or her time transcribing data? A negative reply is the satisfactory one. Work applications creating a need for massive rewriting can almost always be automated with improved performance and accuracy.

Question Six

How is a computer processed key number (employee number, customer number, inventory number) verified? If it is checked by the machine, your reply is satisfactory, since your systems people recognized the advantages of machine checking and were able to overcome the resistance of stubborn old-line management. Lack of a self-check number system causes great dissatisfaction among the group that uses the data. It can also cause some awful messes. If your key numbers are not self checking, this probably indicates a lack of insight and capability within the systems group. It might, however, demonstrate a lack of essential understanding of business information processing by the manager who made the final decision establishing such a system. This may build fog into the information flow.

Question Seven

Select the most important calculation which the computer makes for your department. Ask the systems manager or his representative to explain how the machine does it. If the explanation is rapidly forthcoming and clear, you have received a satisfactory reply. If not, a machine has now taken over part of your operations. Furthermore, the computer people may become angry if you press them for additional clarity. We live in an age which respects machines that think and is suspicious of people who try to.

NOW CHECK YOUR SCORE before moving on to the pollution fighting techniques described in the next chapter.

Figure 2 **The accountant moving through the financial cycle.**

CHAPTER 3

Remedies for Pollution

If you have scored your organization on the internal pollution rating system, you probably agree that steps should be taken to purify the information atmosphere. It is now obvious that some of the investments made in data, reports, and information production are not providing appropriate returns.

There are positive actions which can be taken to improve the environment. Some of the suggested remedies are quite brief and easily defined, and the results are measurable almost immediately. Other approaches require more time, effort, and, in some instances, bullheaded persistence to accomplish satisfactory results.

Six individuals or functions can provide most of the necessary cleansing effect on the information system in your organization. These six are as follows:

- Yourself, as a top level manager.
- The systems analyst.
- The director or manager of data processing.
- A data control function.
- The auditor.
- The requestor/user.

YOURSELF, AS A TOP LEVEL MANAGER

First. Develop a plan to review the activities of the Accounting, Auditing, and Data Processing Departments. Budget 1 hour per month of your time for each 1% of gross sales consumed as expense by these functions. If, for example, the expense of these departments is equal to 3% of gross sales, then budget 3 hours.

Use this hour to meet your managers personally. Do not expect or accept written reports. Review activity (not accomplishments) since the last report. Ask about internal controls. Never ask "What?" or "How?" or recommend. Just keep asking, "Why?"

This interest on your part is the most important pollution fighter available to eliminate the fog and stagnation within your organization.

Second.   Examine and evaluate your own concern about the development cost of a data processing system, whether new or revised. All too frequently grossly inefficient systems are left unchanged, since the suggested development costs for improvement are expressed in the expensive unit "man-years." The term "man-years" troubles most managers as they consider both start-to-finish time and cost. It just seems as if the total is *too much!*

Yet what do you invest *today*? Count all of the analysts and programmers in data processing. The total is at least part of the number of man-years you are investing every year in information processing!

In some organizations (not yours!) the information development people never present for approval any project which may take longer than 6 months. From experience they have learned that management will rarely, if ever, approve apparently long-term efforts. We find that in such organizations pollution appears in the form of many small job steps which inefficiently fragment a major system. But this is the only way to get the job done when management will not commit the long-term resources necessary for modern and appropriate information processing.

Examine your own "man-years threshold." Where do you draw the line? Don't force the developers of ideas or projects to sell you pollution because your concepts of man-years of cost are inappropriately low for building information systems.

Third.   Have a sample of *every* new or revised data processing report sent to you. This review process will curtail frantic fumbling by your subordinates as they strive to develop control information. Since they know that you will see what they are asking for, they may spend a little time to clearly think about what they want and how to use it, rather than writing something in haste and then taking it back to data processing again and again for editing and revision. You don't have to look at these reports; just receiving them is all that is necessary. It might, however, prove to be an interesting information source for you to find out what is going on down below.

THE SYSTEMS ANALYST

"Nurse."

"Yes, doctor?"

"How long have you worked with me in the operating room?"

"Six years, doctor."

"And at how many appendectomies have you assisted me?"

"Oh hundreds, doctor."

"Well, I am sure you know the procedure as well as I do. I'm a bit tired today, so I want you to operate!"

If that seems ridiculous to you, why have you let exactly the same thing take place in your Data Processing Department? The best computer operators frequently become programmers. The best programmers frequently become systems analysts. Worse yet, you may have that common hybrid, the analyst/programmer. What is he? Is he the dedicated programmer who makes the machine hum? Is he the dedicated generalist who makes the business run? He *can't* be both!

The key person, therefore, is your manager of systems. He must be a man who understands forms, procedure writing, clerical methods, *and the business,* in addition to the computer. If he is a computer man, he speaks fluent "DPese" and staffs the organization with people who understand a machine and are loyal to it, and not to the organization. The manager of systems is a prime pollution fighter. But if you find that his knowledge, understanding, and communication are oriented inward toward the computer, provide him with the appropriate education. If that doesn't work, think about replacing him.

More than any other individuals, the systems manager and his systems analysts are the key to pollution-free information flow. Later chapters are devoted to the analyst's training, his customers, and his tools. But this man needs a supporting directive from top management to move into the future.

Once you have satisfied yourself of the capability of your systems manager, give him the following directions.

First. "Build data bases." In other words, collect all the data about each major portion of the business into one set of computer records. This is not difficult, and only a few sets of data are needed. After you have established data base records for employees, customers, specifications, inventory, accounts payable, and accounts receivable, there is little else vital to your day-to-day operations. This base of approximately six sets of records contains almost all of the data needed for the clerical, accounting, administrative, and management staffs to guide the business. This structure of a few major records simplifies and clarifies information processing to a degree that allows you to understand and manage the organization.

The sometimes maligned data base is a prime tool for the analyst and the information system. As such, we will explore, in depth, the nature and use of the Primary Data Base in Chapter 12. Its development is mandatory for efficient pollution-free information processing.

Second. "Make the computer run like the business." Direct that major programs be written to update all necessary records at the same time. This will stop the Accounting Department's month-end closing blues. Also, it will place you in a position to interrogate the records *now* to find your business position *now*.

Perhaps this directive seems a bit unusual. Most people believe that the information system (especially if it is computerized) and the accounting system already operate like the business. *They don't*!

When you ship a customer order you may:

- Reduce a gross back order.
- Reduce an inventory-on-hand quantity.
- Change the customer credit position.
- Update the customer accounts receivable.
- Update sales history.

At the time of shipment, status in each of the above situations, and perhaps others, should have changed. Within the physical business, the status changed at the moment of sale! All the records could and should have changed at the same time. Yet it is most likely that only at different times in the next day, week, or month was each of these records brought up to date. In short, your information system usually does not reflect the current business status of the organization. *It can*!

DIRECTOR OR MANAGER OF DATA PROCESSING

The person holding this position is much like a factory manager. His responsibilities include machine tools (computer hardware and supporting gear), design and sales staff (analysts and programmers), a physical plant (the computer room facilities, environmental controls, etc.), engineering personnel (the software group), and labor troubles (everybody).

Experience and ability will help the DP director or manager to apply appropriate managerial skills to his divergent groups. This is a complex job. Furthermore this individual is torn in many directions by irate users and by constant new demands for service.

The manager or director of data processing must therefore depend on capable people within the functions he supports. He must be first and foremost an administrator. Although he may provide value judgments which could affect the efficiency and worth of changed or new systems, he should rely on his systems analysts, for his own systems experience (if any) was probably obtained many years ago. Unless he is well versed in current systems application technology and the *present* information processing requirements of the business, the DP manager can become a polluter.

On the other hand, he can be a pollution fighter through the intelligent application and administration of his available resources. He has three prime tools which will aid the fight. One or even two may be in use today, but certainly he is not yet employing all three.

We therefore suggest that you do the following:

First.   Direct the DP manager to develop a *charge-back system* for all data processing services. Users or managers will exercise greater caution with new requests when they find that such requests incur expense to their budgets. They may even eliminate some reports when they discover the cost of each one.

A charge-back system will help prevent clogging the information system with unused reports, but it will not make any system better. Inefficient existing systems may continue because it is too costly to revise them.

Some suggest that the charge-back system incorporate only computer production runs. All development and testing are absorbed by the Data Processing Department. This argument has some merit, since it allows redesign of inefficient operations without penalizing the user for the acquisition of more efficient equipment or newly designed systems capable of accommodating newer techniques.

One danger in a charge-back system is that the user/customer may insist on inefficient and inappropriate information products. Since he is paying the bill, he refuses to accept appropriate constraints. In effect, he insists on buying pollution.

Hopefully, such a user can be dissuaded by appropriate management control (remember that you are now reviewing *every* report) and stringent budgeting.

Second. If you do not have a tool like the ANS COBOL report generator, direct the DP manager to buy or lease a *report generator*. This extremely useful tool consists of a computer program that will extract and format data from the computer records. It does not require a programmer. The requester can have his report the same day. Some of the commercially available packages are so simple that a clerk can handle all necessary setup work.

This type of package frees your organization from the overloads and technical whims of the programmers. As long as you require a charge-back of computer time, each user will pay for what he gets. Therefore he is likely to use this tool carefully.

Third.   Direct the DP manager to set up a *Reports Book*. This is a set of samples of every computer report or its latest revision and is an invaluable tool throughout your organization. As new managers are hired or transferred, they can review this book for all of the available standard computer reports appropriate to their functions. Data processing people will also use this book to prevent the creation of duplicate reports.

Like the Primary Data Base, the Reports Book is a vital, essential pollution fighting tool. The systems analyst and the organization cannot move forward together successfully without it. We will discuss its construction and function in detail in Chapter 13.

Each of our first three pollution fighters (yourself, the systems analyst, and the director of data processing) can be trained and directed toward positive, definable actions designed to cleanse the information system. Each of the final three pollution fighters (a data controller, the auditor, and the requestor/user) must manifest a daily attitude and routine job accomplishment which will enhance the organizational objectives through information control. Let's now examine an appropriate posture for each of these three pollution fighters.

DATA CONTROL FUNCTION

A data control function with various titles is beginning to be found in more and more organizations. As the information system has grown more complex, it has become necessary to assign to a person the full time responsibility for the technical aspects of file organization. An information system is built on bits and pieces of data. What moves, how it moves, when it moves—these need to be controlled. And, in fact, as the technical complexity of the system grows, we may require a departmental or divisional employee who acts as the interface (the person who understands) between his own departmental needs and the services that the information technical processing system performs for him. Data control pollution fighting may take place on three levels. Staffing should match organization size and needs *and* the complexity of the systems. The following may be needed:

First.   An *information manager,* reporting to the systems manager. It is the job of this individual to look primarily inwardly at data processing and the various administrative and financial functions. It is his responsibility to:

- Standardize all organization coding and nomenclature, including the Chart of Accounts and a "data dictionary".
- Direct analysts and programmers to existing computer files and prevent the redundant building of new files.
- Encourage and control the building of data bases.
- Control the DP Reports Book.
- Maintain a file of all DP financial reports.
- Control documentation.
- Supervise and control data and report flow.

Note that some of these duties may seem to be the prerogative of other functions, such as accounting. Typically we find, however, that these functions are dedicated more to daily activity and objectives then to the necessary constant restructuring of information controls like the Chart of Accounts. It is therefore more practical to make this restructuring and data framework control the responsibility of an information manager.

Second.   A *data controller,* reporting to the information manager. It is the job of this individual to control the flow of data into the computer. Furthermore, he should check the correctness and distribution of the reports coming out. It is not unusual for the Data Processing Department to receive twice and process twice the same data. Neither is it unusual for a long-running program to go bad because of a rare untested condition, use of an older version of the program, or input errors. The data controller is a necessary internal policeman.

Users are faced with a proliferation of dreadful reports. Poor and inadequate editing of input data, inappropriate management of file data, bad timing, and lack of review of output all contribute to the problem. When a barber cuts your hair, he always asks, "Is it all right?" Much more expensive computer output is never checked. A well designed system will provide automatic program checks for consistency, accuracy, and appropriate data ranges. Yet we do not want simply to detect errors after processing. Human controls can save time, money, and reputations by reviewing inputs too. To give users faith in the integrity of the system the positive actions of a data controller must be applied to the information system.

Third. Multiple data specialists. This job exists in larger organizations where the data controller is forced to turn inward toward the computer to complete his function. The data specialist(s) then become the necessary link between the system and the function. The data specialist works for and is in the department or division where he is the interface. In larger systems it is this man who provides the validation of inputs, timing, and output. Without this function the system will lack integrity, cause confusion, and generate distrust. Therefore the need for this type of person is real. Even with a data controller staff, mistakes will take place. Like any group of human beings, not all these persons are perfect. Don't be discouraged if some errors get by them. They will still save you the equivalent of their annual salaries every week.

The following incident is true. Only the names have been changed to protect the guilty.

The Chief came into Hugo's office looking sterner than usual.

"Hugo, where are those quarterly corporate dividend checks? They were supposed to be in the mail yesterday."

"Don't worry, Chief, we're keypunching the message for the check stub right now." Hugo smiled and continued, "We'll have the checks done within the hour."

"They better not be messed up like the last quarter," barked the Chief. Hugo stopped smiling. "I don't trust the computer. Last time it nearly cost my job to explain that your printed dividend rate of $1.00 per share was supposed to be 10c per share."

"But, Chief, that rate per share is just part of the president's keypunched message. The computer didn't do it."

The Chief got very red. "I don't like the idea of putting up the president's message on every stub, but even so you didn't even proofread it, and besides . . . ."

Luckily for Hugo, Lynda walked into the office at that moment with the

Figure 3

new quarterly dividend message punched into cards. The Chief stopped in midscream.

"Lynda, let me read the message. We've got to get the checks run right away." After a short pause to read the cards, Hugo said, "It looks O.K. to me, Chief. Here, you read it."

The Chief took the cards. "The dividend rate is correct. O.K., get the checks out. You're a day late now!"

Three weeks later Hugo was in his office talking with Lynda when the phone rang. Hugo listened for a minute, gave two one-word responses, and hung up.

"Wow, is the chief boiling. I've got to see him right away in the president's office."

Hugo rushed into the president's office and found the Chief redder than usual and J. P. scowling.

"Hugo, look at J. P..'s check for the quarterly dividend. Mrs. Hasp, our largest stockholder, called this morning and wanted to know if she could cash that dividend check. Do you see what is wrong?" The Chief was yelling!

"Umm . . . no, Chief, I . . . ."

"LOOK AT THE DATE!"

"Oh," said Hugo, "it's April 1, 1472."

"That's right! That's 20 years before Columbus discovered America!" The Chief was screaming again.

"And the bank won't cash them?" Hugo asked.

"They haven't noticed it yet. But that's not all! You spelled J. P.'s name wrong!"

"But, Chief, don't you remember you proofread the message with me in my office when . . . ."

Hugo didn't finish the sentence because the Chief had just turned redder than catchup and was making strange hissing sounds.

Neither man ever forgot the incident. It should not have happened. Yet both had jobs which did not normally call for the careful checking, editing, control, and review expected of the data controller function.

A data controller might not have caught the errors. Then, again, perhaps he could have prevented the whole unpleasant incident.

For day-to-day peace of mind you can't do without an official data controller to review these situations.

INTERNAL AUDITOR

QUESTION: What do auditors do?

ANSWER: They count cash!

If you are satisfied with that answer, you shouldn't be. Today is the coming age of the internal auditor. He has discovered the computer; now you should discover him.

The internal auditor is becoming knowledgeable about and resourceful with computer information systems, their development, their usefulness, and their impact on the organization.

Today the auditor is not dazzled by the monstrous machine, the flashing lights, the clatter of equipment, the mountains of paper, and the scurrying personnel. Rather, he understands computer files and data organization. He can determine whether the record base is adequate and appropriate and can even provide necessary file and field limit constraints.

He can audit the computer room! Are there too many reruns? Are programming and operations standards adequate, and are they followed? Are output reports understandable?

He can start at the beginning of the process. The auditor can participate in feasibility studies. He can help with plans, estimates, conversion schedules, standards, and so forth. In short, the internal auditor can bring *reason* to the sometimes frantic systems development function.

Finally the auditor can, if you are willing to support him and listen to him, bring enlightenment and necessary modernization to existing systems. This individual is one of the few who crosses departmental and functional lines. He can suggest new uses for data, he can propose better controls, and he can stop waste.

While you expect him to detect defalcations, also expect him to analyze existing systems. The auditor should review the system and find the duplicate invoice payments, the unnecessary clerical work, the unused reports. He should analyze the existing reports to determine whether inventory is too high, or production runs are too short. Let him suggest appropriate controls. The internal auditor can and should do more than count cash and declare that present rules and policies are ignored or followed.

The internal auditor's professional organizations are impelling him toward a larger role in effective business controls. It is your turn to involve the auditor early and deeply in systems development. Force him to commit himself. Keep him trained. Insist that he remain independent.

REQUESTOR/USER

The final pollution fighter really consists of a group of people: the requestors of information and the users of information within the organization. That category, of course, includes just about everyone. All of us, therefore, must develop something in the way of a formal ongoing approach to this nebulous group. A later chapter is dedicated to the education of these persons whom we call requestors/users.

SUMMARY

Information pollution is a problem never completely solved. It will take constant action and vigilance on your part to keep it under control.

Never expect information, data, reports, and the computer to solve all your problems. Your human evaluations and judgments are necessary to keep everything in perspective. Many of the controls that we suggest will keep your environment clean because they will control the human tendency to make the information system only slightly better, regardless of the cost or effort incurred. The common mini-improvement approach really creates fog. Much work is done, but little is changed.

Of course, It is a natural human tendency to get involved in day-to-day routines and forget vital organizational objectives. *You* must force this insight, by your own action and controls, and by demands upon the Systems and Data Processing Departments to maintain a proper perspective. *You* must cause a better system to exist by creating positions and providing support for routine control functions such as auditing and data control. These two groups will operate successfully with short-term daily goals of making the organization work more appropriately in a systematic and smooth fashion.

As controlling management, *you* are the key to a successful fight against internal information pollution.

Education of Technical Staff and Management

Any organization is made up of people who perform only one of two functions. The first group makes, sells, or disseminates a product or service. The second group processes information, either as a creator or as a user of data.

Each firm's universe is clouded by functional disciplines, a variety of management theories, and sometimes inadequately trained personnel. In Part 2 we are concerned with the development of an appropriately trained information staff. Additionally we seek to develop a well educated management task force which can execute its responsibilities *with* information.

Special consideration is given to the systems analyst, the manager, the user, and that unique individual, the chief executive officer.

Finally we will examine the somewhat complex systems development cycle from the points of view of both developer and user.

Throughout Part 2 it is our objective to promote common understanding so as to bring divergent organization forces together.

CHAPTER 4

The Systems Analyst, Doctor of Business

"**D**r. Pierce?"

"Why, Miss Dunning, I saw you just last week."

"That's right. I told you I didn't feel well, and my ears hurt."

"And I sent you to Dr. Conroy, the otorhinolaryngolist."

"Yes, he took some wax out of my ears. He was able to solve the problem in a few minutes."

"Good," said Dr. Pierce with a smile.

"And also my back was bothering me, if you remember."

"Yes, I remember. For the back I sent you to the osteopath, Dr. Cover. Did he help?"

"Well, the pain is gone, but I have to return for six weekly treatments. I don't mind though—he has warm hands."

"Oh, yes," said Dr. Pierce with a knowing grin. "I went to medical school with him. He always made a hit with the nurses. Well, mmm . . . . enough of that, Miss Dunning. Since we took care of your ears and the back problem is on the mend, why did you come here again today?"

"I came back, Dr. Pierce, because when I saw you last week, I also told you that I just didn't feel well—all over! It's not my ears, and it's not my back. Nothing hurts now, but I still don't feel well. What can you do?"

Dr. Pierce frowned deeply. This was the kind of problem he hated. He was accustomed to dealing with parts of the body. And since his own specialty was thoracic surgery, he relied on a quick diagnosis and referrals to take care of his patients. But when someone, like Miss Dunning, just didn't feel good—Dr. Pierce frowned again.

The Organization

Your business organization is surprisingly like the human body. It has particular specialized functions. Each of these functions requires unique care and treatment to make it operate properly. When any part fails to work according to required minimum standards, action must be taken to repair the malfunction. Although a specialist may be called in, we hope he will maintain a proper perspective and evaluate the impact of his actions on the entire organization.

Miss Dunning's back problem may be only a symptom of a more serious situation. In this case treatment by the doctor, without some awareness of her total physical condition, could aggravate a grave basic problem.

How does the systems analyst make a business organization "feel good"? Can he or she separate the product or service that a business dispenses from its employees, inventory, marketing, advertising, accounting, or other functions? Each new system must take into account the fact that it is related to the entire organization and must integrate with the whole. Changes, modifications, and minor repairs to the information process and flow cannot be made unilaterally. Any medication has the potential of causing a reaction somewhere else in the corporate body. Nor can business prescriptions and directed courses of action for improvement be presented in the sometimes dictatorial fashion of a medical doctor. In the application of business systems, analysts do not have the control that the medical profession exercises. When a doctor says, "Take my advice or go to another doctor," he can exercise prerogatives not available to systems analysts as they develop and implement systems.

Let's examine now the type of characteristics that we might hope to find in a business systems analyst.

What is Needed

The many people who fill a position titled systems analyst possess a wide variety of diverse backgrounds and skills to apply to the adequate completion of the job. It would be ideal to find a blend of three major sets of characteristics in the systems analyst. These distinguishing attributes can be acquired in a business environment, but also require a basic inherent quality that can only be classified as aptitude.

BUSINESS GENERALIST

The *first* necessary characteristic of a systems analyst is that he be a BUSINESS GENERALIST. He must have an understanding and appreciation of each function within the business organization. It is equally important that he be fully aware of the interrelationships and interactions between functions. A basic understanding and awareness can be taught at the university level, but appreciation will come only through actual experience within a business organization.

Vital skills which can be taught include data processing, production, marketing, auditing, and especially accounting. An academic background in such subjects provides the systems analyst with the appropriate basic foundation of knowledge necessary to apply his talents to any type of organization. Accounting is particularly emphasized. Training in accounting teaches that a structured, orderly approach is possible in any situation. It instills an awareness that a single transaction may have many results. It preaches control, organization, and coding. And, unlike any other area of instruction (including data processing), it relates to the entire organization.

Vital skills which must normally be learned by the systems analyst relate to the peculiarities of the organization, office management techniques, and interfunctional relationships.

Within "peculiarities of the organization" we find that the analyst must learn the following:

1. Jargon of the business ("spiffs," "1099s," "shelf-life," etc.).
2. Jargon of the organization. Within each organization terms such as "region," "territory," "gross sales," and "available inventory" have been defined internally. Furthermore, many products, clients, and internal processes may be internally identified in such a way that only direct personal experience and time will provide the key to understanding.
3. Business systems in use. Is the accounts receivable system open item or balance forward? Is the cost system standard or direct costing? What is the nature of the sales incentive system, the credit policy, the depreciation method, the regional warehouse stocking plan, and so on?
4. Data processing systems in use. Some knowledge of the hardware and software configuration is required. Disk packs are quite dramatically different from head per track disks. Other aspects of data processing, such as real-time processing, teleprocessing, intelligent terminals, time sharing, languages, spooling techni-

ques, and compiler aids, all have some impact on the ability of the analyst to respond.

"Office management techniques" encompasses many of the traditional skills of the systems analyst. Sometimes these skills are acquired in a formal manner through university training. Usually, however, they are learned on the job, since their use and acceptance relate, at least in part, to the personality of the organization itself. Some analyst tools developed on the job are the following:

- Work sampling.
- Work measurement.
- Policy writing.
- Procedure writing.
- Flow charting.
- Forms control.
- Forms design.
- Duplicating methods.
- Reproduction methods.
- Office machines.
- Office layout.
- Organizational structure concepts.

These tools and others are part of the analyst's "bag of tricks." Few are actively and continually used at one time. Usually the analyst finds that the requirements of a long-term effort demand the extensive use of one or two such tools at a time. And the analyst will develop as his job provides the opportunity to flex all of his muscles—to use all of his tools—within the business environment.

"*Interfunctional relationships*" covers the most complex, most difficult learning situations that the analyst must deal within the organization. The flow of data, the flow of information, from work station to work station and from department to department, is more complex than a flowchart can ever express.

Therblig, the new analyst at A. L. Gall Insurance Inc., had discovered a major flaw in the flow of information. Betty in the premium accounting group was processing premium payments and then mailing the checks to Marie for deposit. Marie sat only 29 feet from Betty, but the mail system in the company took 2 days.

At their next meeting, Therblig suggested to Betty, "Why don't you carry the checks over to Marie? She is only a few steps away. We can improve cash flow tremendously in. . . ." Therblig never got to finish. Betty had begun to sniffle and had then jumped up and ran to the ladies' room.

Therblig planned to discuss the situation with his boss at their meeting the next morning. When he returned to his office, however, he found a note to see Mr. M. Portant, the general agent, immediately.

Therblig's keen senses detected serious trouble as he walked into Mr. Portant's office and was greeted with, "Therblig, why are you upsetting my sister-in-law with some nonsense about her husband's first wife?"

Of course, Betty and Marie do not necessarily have to be people. They can be entire departments such as Payroll and Personnel or major functions such as manufacturing and sales. These situations and rivalries exist to some degree in every organization. They impede progress, and stifle optimum systems development. But they are tolerated and, in fact, sometimes encouraged because of the background and interests of management.

So what must a systems analyst be? He must be the business generalist who has some understanding of the classical role of each function within the business, and the jargon, peculiarities, and interrelationships that never fail to exist.

At this point the systems analyst is much like the general practitioner, who has a broad knowledge of all aspects of the body, and the internist, who is keenly aware of the functions of all organs and their relationships to each other. But the analyst must be more.

CREATIVITY

The *second* vital characteristic of a systems analyst is CREATIVITY. In the medical profession it is the expert diagnostician who applies all of his formal training, coupled with practical experience, to determine the nature of and suggested remedies for an illness. The systems analyst as a doctor of business must also draw on his training and background. The analyst, however, cannot as readily resort to a bank of prepared and researched prescriptions. He faces problems that the doctor does not encounter.

Upon diagnosing a business problem, the analyst must provide for the following additional complications, which modify his remedy:

- Limited resources of the organization.
- Time available to provide a solution.
- Personalities involved.
- Organizational interrelationships.
- Previously tried or known suggestions.
- Resistance to any change.

Now the systems analyst must become a salesman and a showman. He must develop, demonstrate, sell, implement, review, and modify his plan. More often than not, these actions take place in a hostile environment. The corporate patient never stands still and is never very agreeable to the whole process of change.

The analyst is a person of alternatives. The business problem solutions which he purveys must generally be sold to higher levels of management. They must encompass sufficient problem definition to provide his customers with a strong confidence in the solution proposed. And to a great extent this confidence is developed by the presentation of alternatives. The development of these alternatives requires a formal background of business training, skills learned on the job, and a strong dash of *creativity*.

The creative analyst is one who consistently builds on what is already available, to develop something new. But all too often analysts have not adequately met the challenge of the problem and the organization by offering the clear-cut, unique alternatives which will grasp the attention of the people involved.

Many business problems require a strong dose of applied imagination but unfortunately receive instead—applied data processing! The good manager is quite frequently described as a person who is "always in control of the operation." This operating manager wants creativity that supports his operations and reduces his risks. He does not want creativity that will make his present operation obsolete. He prefers and supports creativity that reinforces *his* plans and ideas.

The analyst is faced with a Gordian knot. His position within the organization requires the constant development of alternatives. He knows that the history of civilization is essentially the record of man's creative ability. Modern business is admittedly dependent on imagination to meet the dynamic changes in society and the marketplace. Yet the internal resistance to change is stifling.

Upon the presentation of a dramatic new concept or idea every analyst has encountered complacency, rationalism, negativeness, dogma, inertia, minimization, and the like. And even systems analysts have reluctance to present ideas, for they fear that people will laugh at new ideas.

The analyst's sword to cut this knot consists of his trained and learned business skills and a diplomatically applied ingenuity.

Can the analyst learn to be creative? Can this great vital resource be developed? The answer is a resounding "YES!"

Some time ago Dr. J. P. Guilford conducted a federally financed project at the University of Southern California for a period of 4 years.

In a summary of findings on creativity, Dr. Guilford concluded:

> Like most behavior, creativity probably represents to some extent many learned skills. There may be limitations set on these skills by heredity, but I am convinced that, through learning, one can extend the skills within those limitations. The least we can do is remove the blocks that are often in the way.

Some of the stimulators that we might use to promote creativity in ourselves and others are as follows:

- Checklists—write down all possibilities.
- Brainstorming—this works even if you try it alone.
- Analysis—break it down into parts.
- Synthesis—take parts and form a whole.
- Association—what is almost like the thing in question?
- Ideals concept—reach for the ultimate.
- Modify—change meaning, color, odor, and so on.
- Substitute—use another ingredient, person, process.
- Rearrange—interchange components.

Creativity requires that you *don't* "follow the leader"! Your mind and imagination are like a babbling brook. It is a never ending challenge to develop and maintain a useful imagination. Dr. George Washington Carver was able to think of over 300 uses for the peanut. Have all the optimum systems been developed? We will see there is no end to progress if we can apply a broad outlook and admit that the things we know are infinitesimal compared with the unknown.

All that stands between ourselves and great systems is our own lack of vision.

BUSINESS STRATEGY

The *third* and final vital characteristic of a systems analyst is a strong sense of and ability in BUSINESS STRATEGY. The previously defined vital characteristics of being a business generalist and of creativity must at some time be applied to real-world problems. Now the analyst, our doctor of business, must begin to use a myriad of skills. In addition to systems techniques, he is also in the people business.

Knowing and understanding people is just as important as achieving excellence in all business and systems methodology. Application of the system solution and satisfactory implementation can never be accomplished in a vacuum. The analyst must elicit cooperation and, in fact, enthusiasm among all levels of the organization in order to derive any measure of success. In this profession and also in many others, we find people with knowledge who are unable to state their ideas. At the same time we find others who exhibit great skill at expressing themselves in an interesting and understandable manner, yet they may not say anything important.

Although a glib tongue may be an asset, the analyst should study and promote three of the most vital skills of business strategy. These skills are motivation, salesmanship, and perception.

If one skill in business strategy stands out more than the rest, it is *motivation*. First, let's define the word. Motivation is a process by which we develop in an individual (or in a group of individuals) a mood which stimulates him (or them) to satisfy some human need. Anything, then, that makes a person act on his job in a direction for his own long-term benefit and the good of the organization is motivation.

Unfortunately, some of our most basic analytic tools, such as work simplification, are nonmotivators. Some of our best programs for reducing costs and increasing productivity are nonmotivators. Why? Because people generally enjoy performing work where the complexity of the task is a challenge or is equal to their skill. Employees are deeply concerned about the constant changes which may make them obsolete or dehumanize them into an impersonal role. Making work simpler does not motivate the employee. Cost reductions frequently mean people reductions.

Management and analysts have often attempted to motivate employees and subordinates by some of the following methods:

- Authoritarian approach—simply ordering them to perform a task.
- Monetary approach—offering more money to do the job.
- Paternalistic approach—the employee will identify with the job or program, and no other motivation is needed.
- The "stick and carrot" approach—do what I want and I will reward you; if you don't, I will hit you.
- "Snow job" approach—since management is smarter than the employees, we can persuade them to do what we want.

It is necessary that the analyst recognize that he needs people to get the job done, and especially to get it done well. His success comes *with* people. He cannot motivate anyone in the organization if the need he is appealing to is already satisfied. Nor can he expect to motivate all the people, all the time, and all in the same way. It is necessary to appeal to a hierarchy of needs. It is necessary to understand people (including the boss) well enough so that he can properly approach and motivate them.

As a doctor of business, the analyst, the motivator, has a number of means at his disposal. A few of the most important appeals that he can make are as follows:

- Intellectual motivators, such as a desire to learn, to satisfy curiosity, to develop creativity.
- Financial motivators of both the direct and the indirect types.
- Psychological motivators, such as a person's wish to improve, self-respect, or pride in a job well done.
- Social motivators, such as recognition, enhanced work reputation, and a sense of being part of the team.

The key to successful system implementation is to appeal to the proper human need to motivate a particular person. Flexibility breeds success when you motivate, for if one approach fails to get results, you must try another way.

Somewhat inseparable from motivation is a second skill necessary in business strategy. The analyst must possess some competence in *salesmanship*.

The analyst is sometimes so deeply involved in a system he has developed and so enthused about its benefits that he forgets to sell it. But even with the best of wares it is necessary to arouse interest, demonstrate the product, and explain its benefits. As he sells his system, the analyst finds that he becomes a focal point and interpreter between the system, the organization, the management and the human beings to whom he is directing his selling campaign.

Much of what an analyst does automatically involves change, or doing new things for the first time. Any first-time activity is always difficult.

Recently I was helping my youngest boy with a Cub Scout woodworking project. Andy picked up a rough board and put a large sliver into his hand. I said, "Andy, let me pull it out."

He shied away, saying, "No, it will hurt and then it will bleed."

I explained that pulling it out might hurt, but certainly it was also painful now. And besides he couldn't work on the project or even play until something was done. Andy finally agreed with me and then pulled out the splinter himself.

In our business systems environment we are always picking up splinters. Specifications must be revised, a new form layout prepared, procedures reworked, and whole new systems developed. Let's take a leaf from the professional salesman's book and apply ourselves to selling systems.

Getting through to people is difficult. Some of the techniques the analyst might use are:

- *Practical persuasion.* Develop your systems presentation in the most basic terms possible. Assume no previous knowledge on the part of those present. Avoid the use of any technical terms, or, if they are essential, explain them carefully. An intelligent customer never buys a product he does not fully understand.
- *Practical commitment.* An analyst's natural enthusiasm frequently drives him to oversimplifications and unrealistic conclusions. Avoid any direct statements or claims in a controversial area. Only two things are not controversial: a demonstrable fact and a necessary truth. Sell only systems which you can deliver. Gain a reputation for being on time and within budget.
- *Showmanship.* How many dull meetings have you attended? Spark up your presentations with slides, foils, and models. Stand up and use the blackboard. Force leading questions; even plant them in the group.

  You have only a few chances to present ideas and hold the floor. Make your presentation as interesting as a national park. Put in some hot springs of fire and earnestness. Include some tall, snow-caped mountains of interest and aspiration. Stimulate your presentation, and enhance it with spouting geysers of enthusiasm.

  Make your presentation enjoyable in addition to being factual. This will afford you the opportunity for further chances to sell other products. Everyone enjoys a good, solid, professional show.
- *The ideal product.* Give the customer what he wants. Remember what every businessman and every leader in your organization wants:

  a reputation as a leader, turns in merchandise, better use of capital, better qualified help, a competitive advantage in the marketplace, and so on;

  and he wants less:

  competition, taxes, union trouble, government regulations, lost sales, red tape, inventory, downtime, rapid change, chiseling, and so on.

  Respond to the wants of these people, interpret them, and sell to them.
- *The human element.* Getting through to people is difficult. We have especially difficult problems with systems since we represent change and a complex technology. Humility has never gone out of style; do not be a

DP "know-it-all." Build a case with hypothetical situations and phrases such as "Let's suppose . . . ." Interject the possibility of alternatives with "I wonder if . . . ?" Prove that your mind is not a maze of irrefutable electronic circuitry by occasionally pondering out loud: "I often think . . . ." The customer will listen to you if he can relate to you and you can make him care.

- *Closing*. The most important part of the sale is the closing. After you have made a clear and effective presentation and given an exact picture of the system and its value, the final step is to gain agreement. Always get a commitment for a next step. It may be another presentation, a further evaluation, or the development of a budget and project outline. Whatever it is, agree to some action within a specific period of time before the group leaves the room.

Many ministers make the mistake of urging people to believe what they already believe. What is needed is emphasis on action instead of on belief.

Finally, the skill of *perception* is absolutely vital to business and the overall success of the analyst. Yet it is unusual to find anyone who views the organization as a whole. Each functional manager looks inward toward his own set of responsibilities. The chief executive officer frequently looks outward only toward large customers, the marketplace, financial resources, and community organization and functions.

There is an old story about three blind men who come upon an elephant in the forest. The elephant touches the first blind man with his trunk. The man yells, "A snake has me—help!" The second man finds a leg and says, "I'm coming, but big tree trunks are in my way." The third is brushed by an ear and cries, "I'll help too, but I'm behind a giant leaf."

Many people in the organization choose to wear blinders. But the analyst is in a unique position to cross departmental lines, to follow transactions, and to evaluate the entire process. Perception of the objective and goals of the organization is the rare but necessary talent that separates the amateur from the professional.

FINAL DIAGNOSIS

Most organizations are filled with people who are specialists of one type or another. Through formal training, experience, habit, and organizational limitations they conduct their business affairs and make their decisions based on restricted horizons.

Into this environment strides the systems analyst—the business generalist. The professional analyst is the diagnostician, the man who can evaluate and prescribe for a business problem on the basis of its signs and symptoms. The expert analyst is a general practitioner who views the organization as a complete entity, understanding that one part is not isolated from the rest. He knows that any problem and any solution have some impact on the entire corporate body.

Finally, the systems analyst must be part psychologist and sociologist. He treats the human feelings, wants, desires, and attitudes of each customer and respects the vital interrelationships between groups and the organization and himself.

The system analyst, in short, is a doctor of business.

CHAPTER 5

"The Computer Made Me Do It!"

In Chapter 4 we examined the vital traits necessary for the successful systems analyst to complete his job. The analyst, we learned, needs to be a business generalist, develop his creativity, and practice the very important tools of business strategy.

If we remember the group of blind men encountering the elephant, we clearly recognize that there is more than one way of evaluating a situation. Each of the men standing at one part of the elephant can make his own analytic assessment of the situation, but the combination of "snake," "tree trunk," and "large leaf" does not, when synthesized, form a whole elephant. Without the development of an overall perspective, we remain lost in our individual investigations. Such a perspective does not arise from a intensive study of any part of the whole. The man at the trunk of the elephant can become a trunk expert but never know that the part belongs to an elephant. A programmer can be an expert with files or software and yet never know a great deal about the business organization he supports.

Into the business world's paradoxical environment of desired total perspective and actual exhaustive detail we bring a new candidate for the position of systems analyst. He may be a recent college graduate vaguely conversant in seven computer languages (three of them obsolete), or he may be a topnotch programmer, ready to leave his old job for more money across town.

Other candidates for the position of systems analyst may be capable administrative, financial, or engineering people within a function who assume input-output control positions in their departments. This "data control" type of post often grows into some statistical work, reports design, and even systems design within the function. These people then naturally gravitate toward a systems analyst position. But they, like many topnotch programmers, are experts only in the elephant's trunk.

Worst of all is the far too frequent situation of an organization that has no systems analysts. Programmers become, through promotion (i.e., time in grade), that hybrid, destructive force in the organization called analysts/programmers.

How can all of these individuals be trained? What course or institution exists which will supply the ingredients required to produce that necessary business magician, the systems analyst? The answer is, "No such course or institution exists!"

The training and development of a systems analyst is a process that takes time, planning, and money. It requires the application of resources and instruction as varied as the demands we place on the analyst himself.

What happens when the systems analyst is not properly trained? Training for most business skills can be measured by the quantitative results we obtain. A secretary writes a specific number of words per minute of shorthand. A sales manager beats his quota. An accountant produces financial statements on time and calculated correctly. In each case the success of the activity is measured by the results. Not so with systems development, because here the key word is—"DEVELOPMENT!"

The systems effort must provide the most appropriate way to reach the desired objective. We must ask these questions: Will the results achieved be worth the trouble? Have we studied the problem well enough to *completely* understand it? What alternatives are possible?

These can be much tougher questions than you first might imagine. Actually, they are more difficult, in many instances, than the original problem presented. Yet all too often these questions do not receive the time and attention they deserve.

Let us now examine a common set of circumstances involving systems, data processing, vendors, users, and, most importantly, people. Each person in this situation contributes according to his or her position, interest, and abilities. If the solutions are not the correct ones, the problem doesn't get solved—in fact, it may become worse.

The following scenario *has taken place* in your organization. Unfortunately it has happened there more than once. For the sake of understanding, a variety of names and functions have been provided. Select and insert the most appropriate options for your situation.

Early Tuesday afternoon, Al Paca, the (manager, controller, vice-president) called Fred Rill, the DP manager, on the telephone.

"Fred, I think we need your help. We're running overtime every week trying to process (sales orders, inventory transactions, claims, factory job cards, policies). Perhaps your computer can do something for us."

"Let me see what I can do, Al. We've got quite an overload here with the conversion, but I think Miss Meric is nearly done with her part of the project. She is *quite* good. We moved her up from programming just last August."

Arrangements were made, and within a week Miss Meric had met with Paca and had discussed the problem and obtained statistics on the volume and the reports required. Miss Meric did not interview anyone else, since Al Paca as (manager, controller, vice-president) was the acknowledged expert on the subject—he had been with the company 31 years! And, besides, he reminded Miss Meric of her father.

After reviewing the findings, Rill decided that his machine capacity was not sufficient to handle the job. The volume was just too great for the existing computer configuration, and the conversion had not really provided all the extra capacity they had anticipated. So he called George Reed, the computer salesman, for a consultation.

G. Reed was not at all surprised. He had been with Monolithic Computers for 9 years and had worked with Rill most of that time. He did his job well. Most of the visits he made to the company were "missionary" calls. He didn't try to directly sell Rill. Instead he talked with all the officers and department heads who could give him a few minutes. He gave them free literature, occasionally offered "free" executive courses, and suggested frequently how other Monolithic Computer customers had used the computer equipment to solve their problems. In fact, just the other day, Reed had been discussing the situation with Al Paca.

Rill arranged for Miss Meric and Reed to meet with him. At the meeting Miss Meric outlined the project requirements. Reed in turn suggested (more core, point-of-sale equipment, CRTs, upgrading the system). Rill was concerned that the increased costs of equipment (even ignoring development costs) would cause Paca to reject the proposal. At this time Rill felt that it would be best to call in Paca before going any further. Al joined the group a few minutes later.

"Al, do you know Miss Meric and George Reed?"

"Yes, Fred, Miss Meric has been extremely helpful in evaluating my problems and needs. And Reed, of course, has told me about the other organizations with this problem."

"Fine," replied Rill. "Now Miss Meric has a solution which we would like you to see."

After a brief presentation of the proposed system, Paca grinned happily. "That's just what I want. When can it be started?"

"Well, Al, that *is* a problem," Rill replied. "You see, this system requires additional computer hardware we don't have today. That is why Reed is here. He'll explain what is necessary."

With a great deal of confidence and understanding, Reed then presented his equipment proposal for (more core, POS, CRTs, upgrading the system).

"You know, Al, that this type of change is going to cost ($1000, $10,000, $100,000) more each month in rentals," ventured Rill.

"I don't see that as a problem, Fred," replied Al. "If Reed's equipment works as he proposes, we will get more savings than that in personnel and paper cost reductions. You get the proposals ready for the Executive Committee, and I'll handle the justifications."

"Fine, Al, that is just fine," Fred purred. "This is a tremendous opportunity for out company and your group, Al, to stay in front of the competition and to be front runners in DP innovation. I guess, then, we can adjourn the . . . . Yes, Miss Meric, what is it?"

"Well, before we break up, Mr. Rill, I thought that, well, I . . . umm. . . ."

"Yes, Miss Meric?" Rill said somewhat shortly.

"Well, Mr. Rill, if we are concerned about cost, I just read the other day about exactly the same kind of rental equipment being offered by Unicorn, Ltd. And it was quite a bit less for the monthly rental."

"Oh, yes, of course, Miss Meric, I saw that ad in the paper," answered Rill. "But we have had some disasters trying to work with off-brands. You can't get service, and they don't offer the type of support that Monolithic can give us."

"I might mention too," offered Reed, "that we have a series of announced upgrades coming soon for the equipment I propose. The new releases will substantially outperform Unicorn."

"Besides," chimed in Al Paca, "Reed and Monolithic understand exactly the needs of my group."

G. Reed smiled (mentally), and the meeting adjourned.

Before we go to the Executive Committee, let us examine the actions and motivations of our participants. Each, without question, has been acting quite honestly and capably within the arena of his jurisdiction.

Al Paca, the (manager, controller, vice-president), has had a long successful career with the company. He understands his people and the business. His present position, however, has removed him far enough from the mundane organizational transactions that he is not completely cognizant of the activities of his people. He *is* aware there is a growing clerical overload.

Reed has explained what some other companies have done. But Paca does not understand data processing very well.

Fred Rill, the (manager, director) of data processing, worked for Monolithic many years ago. The company had hired him away from Monolithic to run its first installation. As it grew, so did Rill's position. Today he acts as an administrator for large groups of operators, programmers, and analysts. He is somewhat remote from today's technology and depends extensively on his departmental experts. No one in Rill's department (in fact, no one in the company) is responsible for a "system" without the computer.

George Reed does his job well. In sales terminology he spends most of his time "in courtship" with the customer by establishing warm personal relationships at all levels of higher management. George has the opportunity to "suggest" what is available and what others are doing. At times he has "sold" a system before anyone in the Data Processing Department knew of a need. He has been most successful when he can create the image of working for the company and not Monolithic.

Miss Meric is perhaps our weakest link. Her experience up to this time has been almost entirely in data processing. She was hired as a programmer trainee because of her brilliant math background at college. With her excellent work record she passed quickly through the programming ranks to a point where some promotion was necessary. Miss Meric had the ability and aptitude necessary for the in-house software group. Her easygoing personality, poise, and conversational competence also made her a systems analyst candididate. Miss Meric selected systems. Assigned to a senior analyst, she frequently continued to program since the conversion overload demanded all the programming help that Rill could muster. Miss Meric, like most of the analysts, had received no formal training of any kind. She simply did what her predecessors did.

Miss Meric's mistakes? She thought (and many senior analysts would do the same) that Al Paca understood the systems, the clerical activity, and his needs. Therefore she did not interview anyone else concerning the work load. Actually, Paca was a capable administrator who had assumed charge of this group years ago. He made policy decisions but never was involved to any extent in the routine clerical function. Miss Meric failed to find, therefore, that 10% of all data had been prepared solely for Paca's predecessor and now was not used by anyone.

Failure to visit with other members of the department besides Paca also caused her to miss the fact that (forms redesign, revised work flow, work simplifications, employee suggestions, or a much less sophisticated system) could have drastically revised the need for new hardware by eliminating unnecessary steps. Her lack of any general business background and her shallow but highly technical data processing exposure allowed her to choose only a DP solution to the problem. This course of action was encouraged by Reed, who generally was not aware of, and certainly did not desire, any other solution.

Let's now briefly watch what happens at the Executive Committee meeting. This group is made up of the senior organization officers and meets one morning every month to provide policy and planning direction.

Paca and Rill have been allocated 15 minutes to make a proposal. Reed has prepared five copies of seventy-six page proposal made up of generally "canned" paragraphs organized to fit the situation plus pages of hardware specifications. Rill has brought a one-page capital expenditure request form, and Paca a one-page budget change authorization.

As Paca and Rill join the meeting, they find the Executive Committee engaged in acrimonious debate. The committee is 45 minutes behind schedule and deeply engrossed in a proposal calling for $800 to carpet the lobby and receptionist's area. Discussion is heated, and Paca and Rill are concerned as they watch the proposed carpet reduced to linoleum for the sake of economy. Everyone on the committee speaks to the subject.

The chairman finally obtains approval of the reduced amount for floor covering. Noting that Paca and Rill are waiting, he suggests that the committee skip the next two items temporarily and instead discuss the new computer proposal.

General agreement is murmured, and Al Paca takes the floor to explain his needs. Since his presentation is brief, only a few Executive Committee members have stopped thinking about the linoleum and found the computer item in the agenda. By the time Rill is already explaining the economics ($1000, $10,000, $100,000) per month and the hardware functions of the new gear. Rill mentions Monolithic by name several times, as well as the comprehensive proposal prepared by Reed. Rill concludes by reminding the committee that they have had three copies of the complete proposal to read and that Monolithic prices may rise very soon.

CHAIRMAN: "Thank you, Mr. Paca and Mr. Rill. Does anyone have any questions? Mr. Rudder, do you have any observations?"

Mr. Rudder is the only man on Executive Committee who has the slightest understanding of data processing. There are many questions he could ask. He distrusts the round figure of ($1000, $10,000, $100,000) per month. Won't there be some costs during the period of change? What about forms and people to staff the job? Are Paca's justifications and Rill's time estimates realistic? The Data Processing Department certainly has a terrible record for meeting deadlines. But Rudder does not know where to begin. As he read the proposal, he hadn't understood many of the terms. The question (more core, POS, CRTs, upgrading the system) would require technical discussion with Rill that was beyond him. And certainly no one else on the committee would understand. It would be better to say nothing.

MR. RUDDER: "I have no comment to make."

CHAIRMAN: "Does any other member of the committee wish to comment on the proposal?" [No response.] "I assume, that you are all in agreement with Mr. Paca's budget change request and Mr. Rill's capital expenditure request?" [Heads nod in agreement.] "Fine. Let's now move on to the next item on the agenda."

Figure 4   **Designed by the computer department.**

Figure 5   **What the user really needed.**

Could all of this possibly happen? It has occurred time and time again. The technology of the computer has been used relentlessly to automate existing trouble situations rather than to find the problem.

No one ever asked the proper question: "HOW CAN WE REDUCE THE WORK LOAD?"

Each person in our scenario, using his formal education and training and work experience, assumed the question had to be, "HOW CAN THE COMPUTER SOLVE THE PROBLEM?"

So many systems are designed by a data processing oriented person with 80-column card vision that it is sometimes difficult to find "good" systems. And we can define a "good" system as one that satisfies the user in a time frame and with a capability consistent with his needs and at a reasonable cost. Hardware need not run efficiently in a "good" system, nor need every loophole and circumstance be covered.

Automation is for speed. Automation handles massive volumes of redundant detail. And automation is generally inflexible. As a system is designed, it is essential that an analyst use his perception and understanding of the organization and its requirements and not over-structure a disorganized world. As systems expert A. G. Waterman succinctly says, "You can't automate a mess!"

As an actual example of the problem, why did a very popular magazine send the following card to each new subscriber?

PLEASE NOTE!
Thank you for your subscription order.

To serve you in the most efficient manner possible, we are converting our Fulfillment System to one that employs the most modern automated computer available.

Because of this, delivery of your first issue may be delayed. You will, of course, receive the full term of the subscription you ordered.

Was it over optimism on the part of the DP people or their management, or just a lack of proper perspective, that caused spectacular problems in a major federal agency in Washington, D. C.? As reported by the news media, the following happened:

> Since the computer was installed 3 years ago many mistakes have occurred. Before it was caught 3 years later, the machine issued extra paychecks to some employees and free savings bonds to others. It gave salaries to people who resigned, were on leave without pay, or had never reported for work at all.
>
> It also gave employees W-2 forms listing income below their real pay, thus potentially granting income tax deductions."

How could this go on for 3 years? Where were the controls? And we've all heard about the fantastic water bills, utility bills, tax bills, and others sent through government systems. Students in California don't get their Veterans Administration checks to continue school! New York City sends parking violation summonses to people who haven't been in the city in years! Read today's paper. Someplace you'll find an article on the latest "computer goof."

But in almost every case the computer did not goof! It is the people trained in data processing but ignorant of how to solve business problems who goof. It is the people trained in business problems but lacking an understanding of the complexities and restrictions of data processing who goof.

Put them together, mix them with the constantly changing circumstances of the real world, give them time to simmer in their narrow expertise, and then read about the latest computer stew in tonight's paper.

The plain truth is that many computer applications are simply not practical. Even when a proper need is justified, the DP hardware oriented group may frequently design a system which is far too ambitious and sophisticated for the human beings who will do the job. It takes a well oiled, coordinated, ambitious team to get a system moving. It must be guided by a unique individual. A jack-of-all trades? A magician who can pull rabbits out of a hat? No! A systems analyst.

CHAPTER **6**

Magic School

Systems appear to be poorly developed for zillions of the darnedest reasons. Problems arise because of the differences between what the system does and what someone wants it to do.

Everyone wants a functional, inexpensive system. Yet we have relatively few such systems. As we noted in Chapter 5, what people identify as "the problem" often isn't the problem at all. It is merely a symptom of the problem. Until the real problem is understood in sufficient detail and with a proper dash of perspective and business understanding, proposing a solution is simply shooting from the hip.

When systems go wrong, the place to start an evaluation is with the systems analyst. Should you first ask, "Is he capable?" No! Rather you should ask, "Is he trained?"

"Miss Lane?"

"Yes, Mr. Rhodes."

"Is my report for Vice-President Barkley ready yet?"

"Not quite, Mr. Rhodes, but I am on page 2."

"Miss Lane, you've been typing that report since yesterday afternoon. I have to have it for Mr. Barkley for the Sales Committee meeting. What's taking so long?"

"Ooohh, Mr. Lane, don't shout at me! When you hired me away from my dancing job, you never told me I had to type."

The performance you get from your systems and from the people who design them is directly related to the quantity and quality of training and systems education that they have had the opportunity to acquire. An employee operating unit record equipment or a computer for the last 10 years does not have 10 years of data processing experience. What he has is 6 months of experience repeated 20 times. As for information and systems design experience—he has none!

We all want good systems, meaningful information flow, and exciting involvement in our daily work environment. All this is possible. But it takes training. It takes time. It takes money. It takes a qualified systems analyst trainee. And it takes a plan.

How shall we select qualified systems analyst trainees? Consider our success so far. We've read about the half-used computers at the Social Security Administration DP operation. We've wondered about overpayments to welfare recipients and underpaid Medicare claims. Just be thankful that your own organization hasn't made the papers with its systems fiascos.

Certainly these situations indicate that existing selection processes for analysts are fallible. Some organizations select trainees based on company-wide aptitude tests. Some take 4-year or 2-year DP graduates. Many trainees are selected by the Peter Principle. Others have arrived at their positions through unique circumstances. The following is an example;

Some years ago Dick Brandon was conducting a seminar in Washington, D.C. As he evaluated the attendees, Dick asked, "How many analysts and programmers do you have in your shop?"

Each participant replied with a reasonable count until Dick came to a man who said, "Approximately 1000 analysts and 3000 programmers."

Everyone was astounded! Dick then probed and learned that this man was in charge of some major installations for the Department of Defense. "How," Dick asked, "do you select some people to be programmers and others to be analysts?"

"That's easy," was the reply. "The enlisted men are made programmers, and the officers become analysts."

Since the selection of trainees is not yet refined, we should take two actions. Today neither step is taken often enough. What we must do is:

1. *Train* the analyst trainee.
2. *Cull* the trainees who fail to meet our standards.

Let's examine an extensive training program designed to develop that rare individual—the magician of complex business puzzles—the creative systems analyst.

ACTIVITY ONE: GENERAL BUSINESS UNDERSTANDING

No person joining your company from college or now performing a task within an existing clerical function has anywhere near the comprehension of the nature of the business to immediately become a systems analyst. Assign the analyst trainee to work with the manufacturing clerical process, if you produce a product. If you sell a service or are a retailer or a distributor, assign the trainee to a key sales person. The assignment should be for a period of at least 3 months. This is the school of hard knocks. This is where your business succeeds. This is where the action is.

At the end of 3 months the trainee will appreciate the jargon of the trade, the demands placed on people, and their day-to-day problems. This assignment will put a few practical clouds into his blue sky.

Now require that he explain in explicit detail what he has learned in these 3 months. If you are satisfied, *keep him in this position until he provides some practical suggestions* to improve the function. If he is to be an analyst, he *must* be creative. If at the end of another 3 months you do not have the suggestions, fire him, for the required bubbling springs of innovation have not developed.

ELAPSED TIME AT THIS POINT: 6 MONTHS.

ACTIVITY TWO: BASIC SYSTEMS ANALYST TRAINING

Many vendors in the education market offer a "basic" course. It usually is 3 to 5 days in length and covers a wide variety of subjects. Such a course will generally include the following in a "broad brush" presentation:

1. The systems approach and types of studies.
2. Definition of a problem.
3. Data gathering.
4. Interviewing techniques.
5. Qualitative data analysis.
6. Quantitative data analysis.

7. Controlling data input and output.
8. Internal DP controls.
9. Backup and security.
10. Documentation.
11. Logical system review.
12. Economic system review.
13. Hardware.
14. Software.
15. Data communication concepts.
16. Data base concepts.
17. File organization concepts.
18. Selling systems.

This type of material is also available on video tape. The tape may offer more thorough, paced development of each subject. The group seminar, on the other hand, provides greater opportunity for questions, detailed explanations, and the interchange of ideas, problems, and understanding.

TOTAL ELAPSED TIME AT THIS POINT: 6 MONTHS AND 1 WEEK.

ACTIVITY THREE: TRAINING FOR SYSTEMS WITHOUT THE COMPUTER

A great deal of functional improvement, waste elimination, and information flow within an organization does not require automated data processing. Often data processing is used simply because the analyst lacks training and awareness of any other types of possible solutions.

The DP function is a very positive action of recording and moving information, using a specific array of tools. The computer is applied particularly to many jobs with high clerical contents of work and slow movements. Automation is prescribed inappropriately for many of these situations because the habits, training, and depth of business understanding of the analyst cover only the narrow band of DP knowledge.

Non-DP training courses will generally include the following:

1. Work measurement.
2. Work simplification.

3. Manuals.
4. Effective writing.
5. Indexing and coding techniques.
6. Forms design.
7. Office machines.
8. Charting.
9. Records management.

TOTAL ELAPSED TIME AT THIS POINT: 6 MONTHS AND 2 WEEKS.

ACTIVITY FOUR: PROCEDURE WRITING TRAINING

Although we agree that there are many ways to skin a cat, we must make one exception. Telling people how to follow necessary work steps in a constantly changing business environment with frequent personnel changes is a most difficult job. Fortunately, the problem was eliminated some years ago by Leslie H. Matthies when he wrote *The Playscript Procedure: A New Tool of Administration*. With only 175 pages of easy reading the analyst can learn the simplest way yet devised to write procedures. This book is a "must"!

TOTAL ELAPSED TIME AT THIS POINT: 6 MONTHS AND 3 WEEKS.

ACTIVITY FIVE: INFORMATION TRAINING

Basic training is now complete. The budding analyst has acquired some feeling for the nature of the business and a primary understanding of the systems tools available to help get the job done.

The trainee is by no means ready yet to design a system. The first 6 months of "firing line" experience were invaluable. Yet he was never exposed to the myriad of complex, interrelated support functions necessary to keep the sales or manufacturing people free to devote full time to their objectives. Now is the time to deepen his knowledge and understanding of the business.

The next step, then, is exposure to the monolithic information structure, and the conformity exercised (but not necessarily required) to get the job done. Ideal areas for assignment during this period of training include:

1. Policy writing or updating.
2. Designing or updating the Chart of Accounts.
3. Forms design.
4. Office supplies purchasing.
5. Data processing forms control and distribution.
6. Data processing tape control.
7. Data processing scheduling.
8. Financial statement preparation.
9. Financial analysis.
10. Budget preparation.

The activity five assignment should be for a period of 6 months. Ideally it will consist of two 3-month tasks, each with a different department or function. Most of the suggested areas can use another set of hands. Many have been long neglected or never even worked on at all.

During these assignments our budding analyst will experience the frustrations of dealing with complex and varied situations, unreasonable demands, and out-of-date and inappropriate rules, regulations, and forms. He will learn of the ignored, misunderstood, or unknown actions of one department or function as it deals with its problems and the other parts of the organization.

He will begin to understand the purpose (or lack of it) of the massive flow of information and regulation that is methodically and meticulously prepared—yet frequently neither analyzed nor acted upon. He will learn that great effort is spent on preparation but little time on interpretation.

Any analyst will become frustrated with such an activity. But here we have two excellent checkpoints to measure the trainee's potential, two prime guides to indicate his future value and capability.

First, did the trainee do a good job in his assigned task? Did he make every effort to learn about the function and then apply himself? His performance must be more than adequate. Since we expect an analyst to provide appropriately detailed, documented, and controlled methods *at all levels,* he must be able to tolerate detail and function well with it. His business systems of the future cannot be expected to direct others to perform appropriate and meaningful work unless he himself can carry out adequately some routine tasks. It is not very important what the work is. It is important that he understands the work and how human beings relate to it. To gain this knowledge he must perform his assigned task well. His total success will come only in a real-world environment.

The second demonstrable (and even more important) requirement is that the trainee provide some suggestions for the improvement of the functions where he has worked. He should have witnessed enough to question actions, question reports, even question the entire system. There is always a better way! His ideas may be too costly, they may be impractical, but he should not be satisfied with what he has seen. Complacence is no trait for an analyst!

After 6 months the trainee must be performing well in the job assigned, bombarding you with suggestions for improvements, and strongly exhibiting frustrations if not allowed to proceed with his proposals. Anything less, and you have the "GIGO analyst." The person who will automate a mess. The person who may make things go faster, but seldom make them go better.

Only if the trainee does well in both tests should you proceed to the time and expense of activity six.

TOTAL ELAPSED TIME AT THIS POINT: 12 MONTHS AND 3 WEEKS.

ACTIVITY SIX: FIRST ASSIGNMENT

Under the watchful eye of a senior analyst or the manager of systems, assign the trainee to review, document, and design a new system for a complete subprocess. Some possibilities might be in the following areas:

1. Order entry.
2. Payroll calculation and payment.
3. Credit memos.
4. Accounts receivable.
5. Receiving.
6. Production order writing.

The area he is assigned should have a defined beginning and end. It should not encompass the activities of an entire department, such as Production Control or Payroll. It should not be something as volatile as sales analysis or as complex as general ledger. Instead, start the trainee with a necessary activity in the organization comprising a large number of steps, considerable detail, and a need for improvement. You will certainly be able to find one such area.

Now the analyst has the opportunity to try his wings. Can the fledgling fly? Can he find the beginning of the chain of events? Can he understand and document each step in the process? Does he know why each action takes place within the existing system? Does he know the results of these actions? Is he well enough versed in the activity to be able to step in and perform almost any task in the routine? Does he have a feeling for the legal and organizational requirements of the system?

If you have been replying with a litany of "yeses" to the above questions, we need to ask only one more set.

The next questions are as follows: Did the trainee design a feasible new system? Is he able to put the pieces of the puzzle together in a new way that is appropriate, economical, and possible? Will the function now run more smoothly? Will the people do more meaningful work? Is his system controllable and measurable? IS IT PRACTICAL?

If you are still nodding "yes," you have the systems analyst you need. Many people can make things work. This person can make them work better.

TOTAL ELAPSED TIME TO THIS POINT: 18 MONTHS.

The basic training is now over. We have a proven analyst ready for more complex tasks. This part of the program is not simple. First you must identify three or more areas where the new analyst can learn. He must be assigned to people who will teach. Moreover, he must be measured.

His college, relatives in the company, articulateness, good looks, good figure (females), friendliness, and even willingness do not count. What does count is the ability to grasp a situation, think logically, weigh alternatives, offer creative suggestions, and then sell the ideas.

Expect no more than one good analyst in every three tries. Use the people who don't quite make the grade as supporting analysts and for other information processing related positions. But let only the few who pass all your tests design large new systems.

The training, moreover, can never stop. Keep the new analyst up to date. Keep him informed. Keep him active within the educational circles of his profession.

The following activities describe programs to use, or to avoid, in his continuing education. These recommended seminars may serve for general education, as refreshers of the broad brush techniques learned in basic courses, or for the development in depth of knowledge required for a new system.

ACTIVITY SEVEN: CONTINUING EDUCATION

Now that our analyst has been through trial by fire, it is wise to promote and polish his talents. This can be done by having him attend seminars offered by various professional organizations. He should attend a minimum of two such education sessions each year. If this seems expensive, read your newspaper tonight and find the latest "computer goof" which was really the fault of "cheap" systems training. You may then calculate the cost of a cheap system to your own organization.

Here are some courses, seminars, or workshops available today in the marketplace. Each of them will enhance the ability of your analyst.

1. *Business communications.* These programs demonstrate how to do a better job of communicating through the spoken and written word. Topics usually include oral communications, interviewing techniques, effective writing, and perhaps procedure manual writing.
2. *Personal communications.* This type of program is designed to demonstrate methods of improving person-to-person communication in the workplace. Emphasis is placed on personal evaluation and the development of improved communication styles and selling ideas.
3. *The systems survey.* This popular course is designed to show how that very vital "systems perspective" applies to evaluating present systems, identifying problem areas, and developing new systems as they are needed. Necessary topics include planning the system survey, survey tasks, survey priorities, and formulating systems recommendations.
4. *Corporate systems planning.* This type of course is designed to show how systems and user management can cooperate in reaching corporate goals. Topics may include long-range planning, corporate objectives and systems priorities, and utilizing corporate resources.
5. *Documentation.* This seminar has as its objective the development of basic concepts of fact gathering and analysis. The program may include systems survey initiation and fact gathering, analysis of data, techniques of charting systems, and systems improvement through flow-chart analysis.
6. *Decision making.* This vital type of training seeks to improve decision making ability through actual practice. Some of the material may include the decision making process, realities in

the corporate environment, decision tables, and management by objectives.

7. *Designing forms that work.* This type of workshop teaches proven design techniques to improve the utilization of forms and increase their efficiency.

8. *Standards of documentation.* This is a popular offering, but attendance should be restricted to those who have the opportunity to exercise some control over the organization standards. Either a classroom presentation of multiple methods or a round table of actual experience provides the same benefits.

9. *Systems reports.* This basic type of instruction, which is frequently difficult to find, emphasizes the fundamentals of report preparation so that reports can be easily read and understood. Material covered may include oral presentation techniques, written presentation techniques, and formats for readable reports.

10. *Effective Writing.* The objective of this type of workshop is to show how words can be made to work effectively on paper. These sessions usually offer a structured series of learning situations which give repeated opportunity to use the English language in predictably successful ways.

11. *The psychology of systems.* Offered in many forms, this type of seminar teaches the skills, attitudes, and techniques needed by everyone who works through people to get a job done. Topics may deal with resistance to change, motivating people, the psychology of working through people, and the care and feeding of the Systems Department customer.

12. *Human resource management.* The objective of this type of session is to help the attendees develop skills and understandings that will enable them to make better use of the human resources available to them. This type of course emphasizes developing an understanding of human dynamics and personal managerial styles.

13. *Developing systems.* This very important type of course helps the analyst learn how to define objectives through mutual agreement with management, resolve key problems, and build effective systems/user teams.

14. *Performance evaluation and control of EDP systems.* Much like the evaluation system suggested in the Appendix, this type of workshop offers a training situation to develop effective information and control systems for EDP. Suggestions may be offered to improve the return on systems investment, improve project per-

formance, and improve operations performance; perhaps the analyst will be called upon to design a performance evaluation system of his own.

15. *Records management.* This basic information pollution fighting seminar teaches the essential features of a well organized records management program. Records discussions include retrieval, retention, creation, and utilization.

16. *Project control.* Perhaps the most commonly offered seminar is a variation on the theme of project control. In this type of seminar the analyst can expect to review material on establishing the climate for project control, development of a plan, project control mechanisms, progress reporting, and auditing.

The contents of some of the programs suggested above are partially redundant. Such repetition is both necessary and beneficial, however, since we recommend only two such general courses each year.

ACTIVITY EIGHT: ASSOCIATIONS

The systems analyst cannot be left to operate in a vacuum. He must refresh, renew, reinforce his ideas. He must learn of applications completely unrelated to his present job requirements, for frequently this most creative person can derive a useful application for you. It is therefore most beneficial to have your analyst join two professional societies.

He should join first the Association for Systems Management. This organization places him in contact with his own kind. Its resources, "dedicated to the advancement of information systems knowledge," are invaluable. In addition to the publications, reference works, and seminars, he will be able to draw upon the entire body of systems knowledge within the community. Someone he meets will have encountered his problem before, and he will find that almost everyone in the Association for Systems Management is willing to be helpful.

Your analyst should also join a professional organization closely related to the basic interests of the functions he serves. He might join:

The National Association of Accountants.
The Administrative Management Society.

American Production and Inventory Control Society.
Management and Operations Research Society.

Or you might review the *Encyclopedia of Associations,* Volume 1, published by the Gale Research Company, Detroit, Michigan. Here we find that it takes over 1400 pages of fine print to list and briefly explain all or most of the known organizations.

Whatever organization, in addition to the ASM, your analyst joins will keep him in touch with the world of reality. He needs to understand the problems of other disciplines, for without this knowledge even the best analyst will begin designing systems for the computer and not for people.

Membership provides education that would be cheap at ten times the monthly meal and meeting price.

ACTIVITY NINE: SPECIAL SEMINARS

Courses oriented toward special subjects such as point of sales, online, general ledger, OS, managing the (X) function, and word processing should be taken by the analyst when you plan to develop a system related to a particular machine, function, or concept. He should take the course *before* you *decide* on the project. The seminar may not only enlighten you both but you may also change your mind about the whole project.

It is most probable that, if you have planned a project, someone, somewhere, is now offering a course on the subject. Avoid courses, workshops, and seminars with titles that have as the first word "advanced" or "senior." This type of session is normally a repetition of the "basic" course material and cannot provide in 3 or 5 days the in-depth material now required by the analyst. After his "basic" courses as outlined in activity two and activity three, send the analyst only to specialized sessions.

One final word about training the analyst: The good systems analyst understands Pareto's law, which says that in any set or collection of objects, ideas, people, or events a few within this set or collection are more significant than the remaining majority. For example, 20% of your (sales, clients, purchases, inventory) accounts for 80% of your (dollars, bad debts, inventory movement).

The same is true of analysts. Only a few are really good. So don't train the people who "need it the most." Don't follow Parkinson's law by educating your worst people. Follow Pareto's law and spend your educational resources on the best prospects.

Figure 6

CHAPTER 7

Yin Yang

For countless centuries the ancient Chinese principle of yin-yang (or yang-yin, if you will) has served to remind man that for every action there is a reaction. For every part there is a counterpart. Every time we say, "There are two sides to every story," we are yin-yanging!

We have discussed appropriate training programs to enlarge the systems analyst's horizons. But a system is not developed in a vacuum, nor does it work in one. Equal responsibility for the success of the system information flow is shared by at least two others, the requestor and the user. Many times, but certainly not always, the requestor and the user of a system are the same person.

Usually the requestor and the user (hereafter called RU) have little trouble in defining goals. But the fatal error that RU often commits is to try to jump from understandings and explanations of simple systems to decisions about more complex systems. The data processing world is replete with examples of great leaps forward in hardware development. But business information processing has not maintained the same pace. All too frequently the human side of the system seems to be standing still or occasionally even regressing.

In your own organization you, as operating manager or user, have experienced this problem environment as RU and the systems analyst meet. Is is very probable that RU will have the following complaints:

- The information systems do not provide the data that we really need to get the job done. It is therefore necessary to continue or (worse yet) *start* subordinate micro information systems to fill the gaps.
- Computer systems cannot be modified to accommodate the additions, deletions, or changes required in the everyday business world. When changes are made, the process takes too long and is too expensive.
- The information and reporting produced by the system are not in a simple, usable format. The level of detail is not appropriate to RU's needs.
- New systems cost far too much to develop. They are always late. They frequently cost too much to run. It seems that, in regard to times and costs, data processing is usually far too optimistic.

And while RU complains about systems and data processing, the systems analyst has a complaint about RU. The analyst justifiably and vigorously states, "He doesn't know what he wants!"

Actually the grumbling by the systems analyst is a little more involved. In dealing with RU, the analyst frequently finds a lack of cooperation and RU involvement. He finds that RU makes unrealistic demands for information and sets impossible deadlines—or perhaps fails to provide proper lead time. He finds that all too often RU is critical of the systems development effort while at the same time refusing to get involved in solving his own problems!

Perhaps the worst of all the problems that the analyst faces is the unending string of changes forced on him as the system is developed. Many of these changes could have been avoided if RU had realistically understood the systems capabilities and the information required by the analyst to support RU's function—or even the intense effort required of the requestor/user to get the job done.

Up to this point we have placed the burden of a system's success on the analyst's shoulders. We have showed that the analyst must be a business generalist who has an understanding and appreciation of each function within the organization. He must also possess strong creativity, meeting tired old problems with fresh solutions. Finally, the analyst must be a strong practitioner of business strategy by applying the psychological tools of motivation and salesmanship, coupled with perception of the whole organization.

Even if the analyst has these skills, RU may still have valid complaints, unless the analyst provides some very basic tools and checkpoints. These prime working tools for the analyst will be discussed in later chapters. Here let us address ourselves to RU, for he is also part of the problem.

A requestor/user who has little or no understanding of information systems, data processing, and the other activities in the organization serves as the all too common germ that breeds discontent. We live in an age of specialization where credit, transportation, inventory, claims, personnel, auditing, data processing, and most other functions each develops its own set of standards, attitudes, and communications. In our complex society this is an understandable development. But good systems rely on the flow of information. Therefore problems of nonunderstanding and noncommunication must be addressed within the business environment. Means must be devised to overcome the language and understanding barriers within the organization. Your business does not run through the activities and successes of one function. It achieves and grows by the constant intermixing and blending of its resources.

The blend can be made smoother as the functions improve their understanding of one another. And since we've gone to great lengths to train the analyst about the business, it is most appropriate that we teach the business something about data processing and (just as important) about itself.

John Dewey once said, "We only think when we are confronted with a problem." Let's prove John Dewey wrong. Let's build into the organization an understanding of systems and data processing, as well as an appreciation of what the guy in the next department does. Problems can be diminished, and profit, growth, and efficiency enhanced, as the levels of mutual understanding are raised.

EDUCATION IS THE WAY

Our minimum requirements to develop the basic level of business understanding consist of two in-house courses. The first course is called Information Awareness; the second, Participatory Systems. Each course should be organized to change job behavior. We can't completely eliminate RU's complaints about data systems. And we can't completely eliminate the analyst's cry, "He doesn't know what he wants!" But we can take giant strides toward the improvement of these problem areas.

INFORMATION AWARENESS

Energy! Where does it come from? Just about everyone understands what happens in the many methods we use to make energy.

First you *put in* coal, oil, uranium, or water; then through a *process* you convert the material to an *output* of electrical energy. There are three major steps involved:

- Input.
- Process.
- Output.

The same is generally true of information. Just taking two numbers, adding them, and arriving at a total exemplifies the three elements described. So let's outline a simple course of instruction centered around the three functions—input, process, and output—to develop a basic "information awareness".

Before we begin to outline a course, let's examine our basic requirements. We need to make sure that we have the following:

- *An objective.* Our objective is to acquaint the class with the rudiments of information handling within the company.
- *An instructor.* Our instructor should be a systems analyst and not a data processing specialist. He must be able to relate the world, the company, and the information to each other, not just to the computer.
- *A class.* The material should be appropriate for all levels of personnel who use information. Clerks, secretaries, and managers can be equally comfortable in this course, for it is intended to develop understanding rather than to train for fulfillment of a function.
- *Materials.* Every card, tape, form, or method described must be physically handled by the class, illustrated, or worked on as a practical problem. Notes should not be taken, since no one ever reads them. "Touch and do and learn" is the rule.
- *An outline*

   A. *Input*
      Cards
      Tape
      Disk
      Forms
      Interviews
      Microfilm
      Microfiche
      Recording devices
      POS

   B. *Processing*
      1. Hardware
         Terminals

    Data communications
    Time sharing
    Copy machines
    Transcription devices
    Reproduction machines
    Collators
    Microfilm readers
    Common office machines
    MICR
    OCR
    Word processing
    COM

2. Software
    Programs
    Automated files
    Data base
    Playscript
    Policy manuals
    Numbering systems
    Check digits
    Filing systems
    Forms design

C. *Output*
    Detail reports
    Exception reports
    Record retention
    Report utilization
    Report cost

Now the instructor/analyst should select from the outline the areas which directly relate to his organization. Emphasis should be placed on the inputs, processes, and outputs already in use in the company. Nothing, however, should be dropped from the outline. In fact, the new and different devices and methods constantly appearing in the marketplace should be covered. Do not present "How we do it," but rather present "How it can be done."

Next prepare a series of 90-minute sessions, offered once each week. Use as many weeks as required to cover the material. Hold each session for only 90 minutes, since many supervisors will feel that a 2-hour session causes an employee to be away too long. Less than 2 hours is generally more acceptable to management.

For each session schedule one hardware vendor to make a presentation. Use your own vendors and also those who do not currently do business with your organization. Almost none of the vendors will pass up this opportunity, especially those trying to break into your company. You will be amazed at the variety of equipment, features, and information processing opportunities not offered by your current set of vendors. And these salesmen all have fresh ideas. Perhaps some will be useful to you.

Finally, as soon as the class is completed, start with a new group. This 90 minutes a week can become one of the most potent salves to heal wounds incurred in organizational strife.

At the end of the first course the requestor/user will be able to express himself somewhat intelligently in conversation with the analyst. He will no longer fear the unknown. To some extent, RU will understand the myriad of choices available as the information is processed. By designing just one form, he will begin to appreciate the limitations of columns of data, abbreviations, symbols, and the like. By writing one simple procedure, he will experience the difficulties of describing work actions with words. In fact, the most telling lesson comes as the RU class exchanges forms and procedures and then tries to follow fellow students' intentions and instructions.

Communicating and mutual understanding promote good business. And, except for those who spend all their time making, selling, or dispensing the product or service, what else do your employees do? They process information! So, rather than simply train each new employee to blindly follow the actions of his predecessor, let's begin to teach him different ways of handling *his* product—information.

Participatory Systems

The place: a cave just outside Egypt.

The time: many centuries B.C.

The characters: two cavemen named Co and Bol. As Co approaches Bol's cave, he sees Bol running to the woods, picking up branches, running back to the front of the cave, and then throwing the wood on something as bright as the sun.

Co is astounded! The wood seems to disappear, and since Bol does not seem to be afraid, Co walks nearer, but cautiously!

"Bol, what are you doing?"

"Oh, Co, this is my latest invention. I call it fire!"

"Hmm," replies Co, not getting too much closer.

After watching the "fire" for a long time, Co gets up to go hunting. "You know, Bol," he says as he walks away, "I don't think your new invention will ever make it. All it does is consume wood!"

The first in-house course, Information Awareness, provides the foundation of terminology, tools, and techniques of processing information. As with the production of energy, we have now brought the class attendees to a level of understanding which recognizes that data and information also go through the steps of input, process, and output. But, like our cavemen with their fire, we must appropriately match activity with needs to get a good performance.

PARTICIPATORY SYSTEMS

It is the purpose of the second segment of instruction to broaden RU's level of knowledge to a point where rationally discussed decisions about systems can be made by the requestor, the user, and, in fact, management. Then let's add management to the RU formula and call the group RUM (requestor/user/management). Better systems won't help anyone if those who manage them continue to ignore principles, treat symptoms, or allow themselves to be pushed around by technical expertise.

For the course entitled Participatory Systems we need the following before we begin:

- An *objective*. Our objective is to acquaint all levels of RUM, particularly the decision makers, with a *practical* understanding of the cost of a new or revised system and its effect on the organization.
- An *instructor*. The sessions will be conducted by the same systems analyst who taught Information Awareness, but this time he acts as a thought provoker, discussion leader, and questioner, rather than an instructor.
- A *class*. The class will consist of the same group that attended Information Awareness. The information and understanding disseminated in the Participatory Systems course will be appropriate and profitable to everyone. Add to the class managers who already possess the information provided in the first course. Also add managers whose pride would not allow them to attend a first, "basic" course.
- *Materials*. All that is required is the *firm* understanding of the class that everyone can participate in the discussions, regardless of his position. And *everything* in the way of information that is currently processed is open to debate.
- *Outline*. The Participatory Systems course is divided into four sections called:

    Interdiscipline training.
    Development through participation.
    Be practical.
    Control.

Each section consists of presentations, discussions, and, where possible, class problems. Every effort should be made to avoid a lecture note-taking situation. Make this course a real-world shirt-sleeves experience.

The interdiscipline training and the development through participation sections will be treated in this chapter, since they approach the final level of yin-yang. The last two portions of Participatory Systems, that is, be practical and control, will be outlined in the following chapter.

Interdiscipline Training

One of the most difficult concepts to convey to the class is the idea that the entire organization *does not* revolve around their individual functions.

The importance of each function is perhaps appropriately proclaimed in every professional journal. All of them demand more time of the top executive to support the critical nature of their work. Few journals recognize formally the equally vital need to keep the entire organization moving through the activities of other disciplines. It is necessary to develop some degree of this understanding within the class. The instructor/analyst hopefully has the required amount of organizational perception. Now we must build some of this perception into the class. The systems its members work with in the positions of requestor, user or manager can seldom be just for themselves.

Three activities are recommended to promote this interdiscipline understanding:

1. Ask the class to list on a sheet of paper, in order of importance, all of the vital functions they perform for the organization's success. How do they contribute? A discussion of each list will provide a fine medium of common understanding.
2. Ask the class to list on a sheet of paper each duty performed without inputs from any other person and without outputs to any other person. We expect that the lists will be very short or, more probably, nonexistent. Almost all activity is, then, the result of interactions between persons and groups.
3. Present a series of guest lecturers who will describe the major functions of the organization. Run this series as the business runs. Start with the person who makes the sale or provides the service, and end with the treasurer. Do not let the speakers provide platitudes and generalities. Keep asking them, "How is this

done?" The class will soon catch on and assist. When you've got enough basic information, start asking, "Why?"

Some of the long-term employees who act as class participants will resist this section of the course. But this is the group in the company that we need most to challenge. These people are most set in their ways. After 10 years of service, the longer the tenure, the more they have forgotten. Especially work with the older group to enlarge their horizons. Help to keep them flexible in a changing world!

Development through Participation

Earlier we discussed some of the common complaints expressed by RU about information systems. Basically two of the four friction areas revolve around output. The requestor/user says, "The information in the report is not complete (or the way I need it, or what I really need to get the job done)."

The men in the boardroom sat glumly and waited. The superintendent of insurance was due at 2:00 P.M. to announce his decision. He might decide to take over GLEECO, or he might declare the company bankrupt.

"After over 40 years of solid, profitable automobile and homeowners underwriting, how did this happen?" mused Mel Stormer, the controller. Overall business had been profitable until skyrocketing costs of automobile parts and medical care—the two chief items in claims against GLEECO—rose even faster than prices generally.

New systems had been developed. The company *had* responded dramatically with extensive policy and internal reporting controls after that vast insurance fraud on the West Coast. Perhaps, as Gernick, the systems manager, had warned, they were putting out last year's fire!

Yet things had happened so very fast. Since the old reporting systems blended the results of almost 3,000,000 auto policies with those of 800,000 homeowners, it was difficult to detect the source of trouble. Then, too, it wasn't until the first quarterly report of 1976 that management finally admitted the trend which the operating departments had been signaling for 6 or 7 months. Underwriting losses were staggering.

"Maybe," thought Mel, "we should not have put Gernick down so hard when he requested money to develop detailed management reports by line, by state, by category." Sure, the mandated reports had been costing a bundle. Yet how much more could have been saved, and even this big mess avoided, if they had had the proper reporting systems to get the job done. Gernick's pilot project alone had cut their losses over $2,000,000 in the last 6 months. This small project had identified New Jersey as a dismally unprofitable state, and GLEECO had immediately pulled out.

"In recent times," Mel reflected, "GLEECO had been the Cinderella of the insurance industry, becoming one of the largest auto insurers in the land." Investors had bid the stock up to fantastic prices. This morning, however, it had been selling at less than $2.00 a share, and Cinderella had turned into a pumpkin.

Everyone jumped as the door to the boardroom opened. The room had been completely silent for over 5 minutes. Everyone tried to interpret the stern look on the superintendent's face as he took his seat.

Could management have influenced the superintendent of insurance's decision, or even his need to act? Perhaps. They certainly could have acted earlier in a more decisive manner.

Can a RUM group influence the present system? Definitely. The board of GLEECO cannot be expected to act without information, and RUM isn't expected to do detailed systems investigation and design, but we do expect all of its members to participate!

This portion of the Participatory Systems course is the section which will aid the class in (of all things) participation.

Economic Threshold.   Determine *when* each person will become involved by holding a class discussion. Does the class care about any change which will save $1.00 per year or 5 minutes per year? No? Well, then, what does count? Everyone should test his own individual and organizational feelings on the subject.

Facts Threshold.   By now the class recognizes from the first part of this course and from the previous Information Awareness course that various departments have different names for the same thing: Engineering, Production, and Sales may each have its own numbering system for one and the same set of products. Also, even good managers and leaders may be quite rusty about the exact details of work going on every day. Discussion should center on who should provide data and suggestions for the basic fact gathering. In this section, group discussion is the teacher.

Design Threshold.   Discuss the following: Shall a consultant with wide experience design a new system? Or our computer salesman? Or the system analyst? Whose system is it? What if it crosses departmental and functional lines?

Prohibition and the Vietnam War were not popular, they were not supported generally, and both finally were brought to an end. How far can we go in diluting the systems objectives to make everyone happy?

Figure 7   **Crossing departmental lines.**

How does the class feel about any department's system which gives other departments no choice but to do a job to support it? How should they feel about *any* system that forces them to do certain tasks?

This entire section of the course is meant to build an awareness of responsibility. Requestor/user/management *must* assume a portion of responsibility for the system—for its development, its implementation, and its execution.

SUMMARY

At this point we have completed the Information Awareness course and one-half of Participatory Systems. Has RUM learned a little about systems development and his own business? We hope so. We further hope that lectures by vendors and company managers will open the door to new ideas, variations of opinion, and an understanding of the necessity of participation in information systems development.

Now let's finish the Participatory Systems course by exposing a talent present, to some degree, in every human being—it is called COMMON SENSE!

CHAPTER 8

Common Sense

Grandma used to give everyone spring tonic whether or not he or she needed it. And Grandpa changed his long johns twice a year, no matter what.

How much wonderful data is collected, sorted, and reported daily in the business world and never used? The answer is that more unused (and in some cases useless) information is produced than we dare think about. A little later we will offer a specific method of coping with this monster of too much data already in existence. But here we are interested in stopping—before it starts—the juggernaut of new reports and systems.

Like Grandma's tonic, information systems are frequently created not by RUM (requestor/user/manager) but by just R or just M or, even worse, someone who is no part of RUM. A whole discipline called operations research has grown up, developing wonderful concepts no one can understand or will use. Why? Well, one prime reason is the failure of its practitioners to relate their specific talents to the actual needs and capabilities of the people who operate in the real-world environment.

Frequently R and M read or hear about information concepts or practices which are successful or supposedly successful elsewhere. Just as Al Paca wanted a new system (Chapter 5) because it was successful elsewhere, we find people doing the same thing in every organization. There are new trends, there are new ideas. But does management by objectives (MBO), or teleprocessing or a 4-day work week or perpetual inventory or PERT work for everyone? The answer is, "Of course not!"

Many new ideas are developed and programmed, and procedures written and implemented, by people who understand the business and the computer, yet give hardly a thought as to how the information in question will be utilized. Unbelievable? No, it happens all the time.

Up to this point the Participatory Systems training has taught RUM about the business (interdiscipline training) and about the necessity of making any new venture a cooperative one (development through participation.) Now we arrive at the most vital part of RUM's development. It is the section of the training called . . .

BE PRACTICAL

Although their points of view are quite different, RUM and the analyst bemoan the same lack of practicality as they meet each other and the information system. To RUM, the inflexibility of an established system supporting his changing environment is disturbing. The analyst, in turn, is vexed by RUM's discontent plus his own frustrations as he tries to firmly structure a constantly mutating organization.

In this section of the course we will attempt to bring about a more harmonious relationship between RUM and the information system and the analyst. Group discussion should center around two questions:

1. Is the system worth the effort?
2. Is the system worthwhile?

To answer the first question let us examine the relationships between cost, the current status of the organization, and the complexity of effort required to get the job done.

The following discussion outline is suggested:

1. Review with the class the individual economic thresholds it established earlier.
2. If we are currently financially successful, shall we bother with a change or a new system now? Isn't it more important to expend our energies toward a profit rather than to improve how we do

this? In addition to generating heat, this question may generate light.

3. How complex is it to create or change the system? Here is an opportunity to share with the group a vital lesson. No change is simple. Computer programs, procedures, forms, and the like require massive amounts of effort to modify or create because of the level of detail demanded. Use the following problem to illustrate the point in a most enjoyable way.

THE PROBLEM

You are an explorer who wants to be the first person to drive his family car to the North Pole. You stop at Nord, Greenland, 450 miles from the pole, and pick up Isam, a native Eskimo guide. Isam is intelligent, speaks English, and has never been in an automobile in his life. With Isam, a little luck, and the old car you finally reach the pole.

After parking the car facing open water at the edge of the ice flow, you ask Isam to take your picture planting a flag at the pole.

Just then disaster strikes!

You are bitten by the rare white thrashing mosquito. Instantly you are paralyzed from the neck down. In 3 minutes it will become impossible to speak. Both you and Isam recognize immediately what has happened. Your only hope is to get back to Nord within 24 hours for the serum. But while you can momentarily talk, you can't even turn your head, and Isam was never inside an automobile until yesterday.

THE REQUIREMENT

The key is in the ignition. Write the exact instructions you would orally give Isam so he can drive you to the serum.

THE RESULT

What will happen? Some will start using technical terms like "ignition," "brake," "clutch," and so forth, that Isam won't understand. Others will drive straight ahead into icy water. By the time the class participants get done laughing at each other, they will begin to understand that writing directions for people (procedures) or writing for a computer (programming) requires an immense effort of concentration and exacting detail. If you miss one tiny point, the result won't work right.

Figure 8   **The white thrashing mosquito strikes.**

In order to answer the second question, we need to discuss whether or not the entire proposal for a new or changed system is *worthwhile*. Cost, complexity, and effort required to get the job done are not issues here. Ultimate value to the organization is the question.

In order to be worthwhile the proposed system must certainly be feasible. Is it possible with organization, direction, sufficient finance, and controls to make the system happen? The Club of Rome had talent, time, and money, yet missed the mark when forecasting the resource use of the world. Can you incorporate enough data into your organization's management information system (MIS) to make it work?

Is it possible to organize a system to control your business environment, your competitors, your salesmen, or your Payroll Department? The answers run the gamut from "no" to "maybe" to "yes."

Of course, even if the proposal can be classified as feasible, is it marketable? Many good systems, many badly needed systems, have died an early death for lack of popular support. An all-volunteer army is a great idea—but it needs people. The people living in Northern Ireland all want peace. But is it humanly possible to satisfy the various factions in a peaceful way? The production control manager wants to control inventory. But that requires locking up the storage areas and using requisitions. Management agrees. Factory supervision, on the other hand, is measured by output and refuses to take the time to make innumerable separate trips to the storeroom to fill small requisitions and make out a four-part form. Management again agrees. It supports the goals of inventory control *and* output. In this environment the system, no matter how sophisticated, will never work.

Rather than enumerate an endless string of evaluation characteristics relating to the worthiness of a system, let's examine a common new management tool, perhaps already discussed in your organization. It is called skills inventory or human resources.

A skills inventory consists of collecting information about the past and present skills of each employee. The information is then organized, coded, and filed for the employee. When a new position is created, a job vacancy occurs, or a special temporary need arises, the most appropriate candidates can be selected through a review of their records. Such a system is supposed to increase employee moral, since they understand that their records will now be reviewed each time an appropriate job is open. Furthermore, needs can be filled from a pool of employees already experienced in organizational methods and philosophy.

On a small scale the system has always existed. You know the people who work for you! You may have copies of their employment records in your file. Moreover, day-to-day contact with them provides a constantly updated, critical understanding of their abilities. But on a larger scale we have a problem locating the right people for the right job.

"Well, Chief, how did the conference go?"

"Fine, Hugo, several other VPs of Personnel were there. Even Cahsion was there."

"Old L. C.? Why, I haven't seen him since he left us 3—no, 4—years ago. What's he doing now?"

"Well, L. C. has my job over at Bland Electric. He spent hours telling me about his new skills inventory system.

"You mean, Chief, a system where we record the education and past jobs of the employees?"

"More than that, Hugo. A skills inventory can cover career interest, geographical preferences, things like professional licenses and certificates, and even significant achievements made by the employee."

"Oh, sure, I've read about some of that in the trade journals. I'm surprised L. C. had enough brains to get a thing like that going. He never showed that ability around here. What kind of results is he getting?"

"I'm not sure. The whole system is a bit behind schedule, but he's going to use it to avoid some of those sticky seniority problems they had last year. Why, L. C. told me the union almost won an election that time!"

"Say, you know, Chief, maybe it would be a good idea for us to develop a skills inventory. Remember the trouble we had in April finding a CE with an ornithology background to design our new line of birdhouses?"

"Yes, that's the job for which we finally hired Taber."

"Right."

"Chief, why don't I get some of those trade journal articles together, and we can sit down with Armstrong and come up with something ourselves?"

"Sounds fine, Hugo. Go to it."

"Porky" Armstrong, the systems manager, put down his *Computer World* and answered the telephone. As he expected, it was Hugo calling again about final arrangements for their meeting to discuss a system. Porky had decided to bring Gary Husk to the meeting because he had considerable systems experience. Although Gary had not been with the company when the existing payroll/personnel work was developed, he had maintained the system as new modifications were requested. Porky had asked Hugo to also bring Miss Miller to the meeting. She worked in the Personnel Department and had recently been through the "Information Awareness" and "Participatory System" courses. Also, she was a bright girl.

Hugo, of course, had to ask the Chief whether Miss Miller could come.

"Porky, the Chief gave his O.K. Miller will be there too."

"Fine," replied Porky, and he hung up.

The meeting got off to a brisk start with an excellent presentation by Hugo, summarizing the published material he had collected.

"A lot of people are doing this sort of thing now. In fact," continued Hugo, "the Chief saw old L.C. Cahsion recently at a meeting. L. C.'s got a great one going over at Bland Electric. I think if we send out a form and ask everyone to fill in the information, we will be able to do the same thing in a short period of time."

The Chief nodded in agreement.

"Well, I've read a bit about skills inventory and human resource files," said Miss Miller. "It takes a bit of effort to get one started."

Both Hugo and Gary Husk started to talk at once. Finally, Gary got the floor.

"You know, fellas, we already have a payroll system and a personnel system on the computer. They both contain a lot of data. In fact, they repeat a lot of the same information. And, besides, you have other records and files in your department. I think we ought to review your objectives and uses of such a system before . . ."

"Now, look," broke in Hugo, "we pay for every bit of service we get from your department. Besides, I think it's up to us to decide when . . ."

"Hold on now," Porky tried to slow things down. "Miss Miller, you've been in Gary's classes and have an understanding of data organization. Why don't we start by examining the existing computer files—Gary can help there—and you can survey the existing personnel records. This might be the necessary base from which we can start, if the Chief and Hugo agree."

"Sounds good to me," said Hugo.

"Chief, why don't I coordinate the survey efforts, and we can get together again in a few weeks. I'll summarize Gary's and Miss Miller's information, and then we can sit down and develop this thing."

"Sounds fine, Hugo. Go to it."

A week later Hugo broke into the Chief's office with a sheaf of papers in his hands.

"Chief, you won't believe this. I've found, so far, that we write the employee's name on seventeen different records, and his gross pay in eleven places, and. . . ."

"You got this from the skills inventory survey?"

"Yes, Chief, but I guess that's not really important. We are identifying all the different pieces of information we already have on each person. It just surprised me to find gross pay in eleven places. We'll be ready to meet again next week. You know, I found we have quite a bit of stuff already on everybody. But it is just not all together."

At the second meeting Hugo summarized the survey work and presented to the group a list of the information and its sources currently available. He also offered a form he had prepared which each employee would fill out for additional new information.

Porky was the first to speak.

"Hugo, this is a fine job. I am concerned, however, about a couple of things. First, how are we going to prepare a set of records for you? Second, I'm concerned about the extent of the information you want in this skills inventory."

"You guys are always talking about millions of bits or bytes or something like that," replied Hugo. "What's the problem?"

"I wish you would attend my class, Hugo," said Gary. "Today in our company we have two separate sets of records for you, one for Payroll and one for Personnel. They both contain much of the same information, and neither one has room to take much more data—certainly not anything like the size of your skills inventory. In fact, a lot of the same information is repeated again and again even in your clerical files."

"That's right. When Gary and I put our survey results together for Hugo, we found the same pieces of information repeated again and again. Why, gross pay is recorded. . . ."

"Eleven times," Hugo finished Miss Miller's sentence. "But so what? All we need is a new file."

The Chief nodded in agreement.

"You know," Gary explained, "a new file is not all that simple or even appropriate. If we repeat all the necessary basic data for skills which is already in the payroll and personnel records, we will be wasting space. . . ."

"We pay for it," interrupted Hugo.

"And," continued Gary, "there is not enough room to add to either existing record. So we must build a completely new record."

"Why don't you just sort them all together?" asked the Chief.

"Well, each file is organized in a different way and. . . ."

"O.K., don't get too technical, we'll take your word for it," said Hugo.

"This situation of more than one set of records is terribly expensive and confusing," said Miss Miller. "When a girl gets married, we have to change no less than seventeen records. We never get them all to agree. I didn't know, until I helped Gary with this study, how many times we repeat the same thing! If we create a human resources file, the maintenance problem will only get worse and the confusion greater."

"You're beginning to sound like you belong in Systems," Hugo told her.

Porky decided this might be the time to suggest the major systems revision he had long hoped to get started. But before he could open his mouth, the Chief spoke.

"Miss Miller, I'm sure you are correct. But I know from long experience that it would take us and Data Processing 2 years or more to combine and refine all our records. In the meantime it seems that we need a skills inventory. But I'm concerned, as is Porky, about the quantity of information that you want for each person, Hugo."

"Every piece of information can help us, Chief," answered Hugo. "I can get one big report back with all this information on it *and really use it* for promotions, transfers, and job training. Besides, look at the time we'll save by not having to interview people and by avoiding grievances."

"Oh, Hugo!" Miss Miller was exasperated. "You'll get a pile of paper higher than your desk. It will be worse than the payroll register. You can't make sense out of that much data."

"How about the past technical training information you're collecting?" asked Porky. "I was a cook in the army, but I can't imagine how this item will help to evaluate my worth to the company."

"Or hobbies and skills," chimed in Gary. "If I can operate a ham radio, or have a home woodworking shop, it doesn't qualify me for a different job."

"The language skills is the one that bothers me," offered Miss Miller. "I speak French. The form even asks for a level of proficiency. But so what? We don't have any clients or employee situations that require anything but English."

"But when we need a new secretary . . . ," Hugo started.

"When we need a new secretary, we post the job in the company paper and allow anyone to try," said Miss Miller. "We already have skill test results in the girl's file. But no way can we determine if she is ambitious and appropriate for the job. She's got to be interested in the change herself. Even if we had a girl completely classified, we still have to do the same thing for every job so that we understand its exact content.

"In fact, the situation is even more involved. We have been trying to get a girl for Mr. Young for 2 months now. Nobody wants to work for the old grouch."

"Well, I don't know about Mr. Young, Miss Miller, but the rest of what you say makes sense. It seems," continued the Chief, "that we in Personnel may have a good theoretical idea, but we need to study the possible methods of application and our objectives in much greater detail before we get into this sort of thing."

"Well said, Chief. Why don't I collect some materials for a. . . ."

Let's leave Hugo and his next study at this point.

The group has achieved far more than most in the examination of a new system. With some feeling and understanding for processing information, its members have begun to ask, "Is it worthwhile, to have such a system?" A human resource file sounds as good as motherhood. Who could be opposed to it? Yet many systems are built without RUM asking, "How will we make use of it?"

Hugo's total printout would have made an impossible system. Even ignoring the data processing problems, it is still dangerously impractical. On too many occasions RUM assumes that an information system, simply by its creation and use, will make things better. Sometimes this is true, but more often the system per se improves nothing.

Only the practical application of a worthwhile system can make improvements in an organization.

The class should review the type of problems just presented. Then the application of a completely new system in the organization should be evaluated. Some suggestions are as follows: point of sales (POS), a factory job cost system, integration of all lines of insurance into one policy base, an open item accounts receivable system—or just the opposite of any of these.

THE TRAP

A most inviting pitfall awaits RUM in discussing any new system with the systems analyst. The mechanical method of processing data becomes the subject discussed, rather than the objectives of the system itself. Such discussions are frequently encouraged by the analyst since he is more familiar with handling data. Such discussions are *directed* if the systems analyst is really computer oriented and trained and not a business generalist.

Systems exploration and development meetings frequently fail to question motives and objectives at the appropriate early stages of discussion. Everyone seems to forget to ask, "Is it worthwhile?" since everyone is so busy talking about how to do it.

The common complaint voiced by RUM was, as you recall, "The information system is not practical to my needs!" What RUM forgets, and the analyst too, is that the *goal itself may have been impractical.*

Systems that don't quite meet RUM's expectations have often been composed of 1% of effort devoted to goals, objectives, and results and 99% of effort directed toward methods to get there.

AN ESCAPE

The very difficult, but most necessary, way of avoiding an impractical new system is for RUM to question his own ideas. Such questioning can be reinforced by the analyst to the extent that his own abilities as a business generalist and the company's political environment allow.

To avoid the trap of a new impractical system or a new impractical modification the requestor-user-manager need ask only one question: "Why?"

WHY should this be done or not done?
WHY is it done at all?
Why is it done in this manner?
Why is it done there?
Why does this person or group do it?
Why is it done at this time?
Why will my way make it better?

In the classroom environment of a Participatory Systems course RUM will ask the question, "Why?". Here RUM will have the opportunity to be reasonable in discussing an abstract problem. Once done in a classroom, RUM and the analyst may have at least a chance to openly discuss, question, and probe new systems or changed systems in the real world.

It is sometimes difficult to be *reasonable!*

CONTROL

The final segment of Participatory Systems relates to RUM's fourth complaint. Remember that RUM was frequently concerned that systems development projects were too costly, took too long to develop, and even were not the exact desired product.

The final part of the course can help each of these problem areas. First review in necessary detail the basic project control requirements of a plan, the development of estimates in time and money for both systems and user requirements, the establishment of checkpoints, the setting of deadlines, and so on.

It will not be difficult to itemize and explain project control. It will not be difficult for the class to accept project control. The one vital (and frequently omitted) part of the development of a project is concerned with where this control should be concentrated. This vital part consists of *pilot program.*

Any new system, any information stream modification, in fact even a forms design change must be tried in the real-world environment. It is simply impossible for even the best qualified systems analyst and the RUM team to foresee all the consequences of a change.

Development of a system is somewhat like having your portrait painted. While you may choose the artist, the amount of time it takes to paint you varies with his temperament, the time you make available to him, and the length of time you are able to sit still. Project management control features will help you to understand how the artist is doing. Ear, neck, nose, and other features can become checkpoints. Shading, proportion, line, and other details, on the other hand, cannot be easily quantified and checkpoints applied. Furthermore, you may hate the completed portrait since you feel it does not look at all like you.

The problem could be solved by supplying a pilot portrait (a photograph) which you ask the artist to copy. He probably won't do that since it might violate his artistic principles. But the system or the change you want is not exactly art. It should be a hardheaded application of practicality and reason to a business situation. It is possible in every new development to test the ideas and methods involved on a small scale.

Again remind the class that a successful system is not a successful computer program. A successful system provides appropriate information to human beings or better methods of getting a job done. A new insurance form, factory job ticket, incentive system, or even skills inventory can be tried with a small group, paper and pencil, and a copy machine. If the proposed system is a data base with a wide variety of information, a typewriter will serve to produce sample reports.

Figure 9

Nine times out of ten, a pilot program will provide new insights into methods and problems. Before expensive programs have been written, procedures worked out, and thousands of forms ordered, you have a chance to get the bugs out. Keep asking, "Why?" and the opportunity may even arise occasionally to stop a good idea, but a bad application, before it's too late.

CONCLUSION

The Participatory Systems course is a forum for bringing divergent organizational forces together.

Here is an opportunity to build common understanding and mutual respect. As ideas are translated into specifications, everyone becomes more aware that upstream requirements are to be considered, that an appropriate and not a "blue sky" system is to be developed, and that the systems analyst (SA), the requestor (R), the user (U), and management (M) constitute the SARUM to cure the problems and get the job done.

Homer expressed the same idea 2600 years ago when he said in *The Iliad:* "You will certainly not be able to take the lead in all things yourself, for to one man a god has given deeds of war, and to another the dance, to another the lyre and song, and in another wide-sounding Zeus puts a good mind."

CHAPTER 9

The CEO-
A Special Case

DEVIL: "Name, please?"

EXECUTIVE: "Where am I?"

DEVIL: "You just had a heart attack in your office. NAME, PLEASE?"

EXECUTIVE: "McGrath. Why is it so hot here?"

DEVIL: Wait until you get inside. What did you do in life, Mr. McGrath?"

EXECUTIVE: "I am chief executive officer of McGrath Enterprises."

DEVIL: "Answer the question, McGrath. As a CEO what work did you do?"

EXECUTIVE: "Well, that's hard to answer. I am responsible for many things."

DEVIL: "Down here you had better learn to use the past tense and to be more specific."

McGrath noted that the walls of the room were suddenly glowing red hot.

EXECUTIVE: "It's really hard to describe the work I did. May I have time to think about it?"

DEVIL: "Lots of time."

As McGrath heard this, the floor disappeared and he suddenly began tumbling downward.

Chief executive officers, politicians, prison wardens, hospital administrators, shop foremen, union leaders, presidents, and prime ministers function entirely or in part in the role of top manager. The literature of management is filled with stereotyped characteristics of the manager. A list of his distinctive functions generally includes such items as the following:

- Planning.
- Organization.
- Motivation.
- Direction.
- Control.
- Integration of effort.

Every manager, at any level, must possess the ability to carry out these functions. But the skill level and the quantity of top managerial activity vary extensively with different jobs. Take, for example, the positions of factory foreman and corporate controller. Both jobs would normally be classified as managerial. Yet in most instances each position will require that the incumbent perform a series of routine tasks having no managerial content at all. Only part of the job is managerial. Even less may be classified as top management functions.

One distinctive feature of a top management function, performed at the foreman level or by the CEO, is that the activity *is not routinely reviewed* by a higher authority. Regardless of the source of inputs of information, or the application of managerial duties, the resultant decision activity is not evaluated at a higher level. The decision activity stands! This is a top management decision, without consideration of the operating level at which it was made.

Another distinctive feature of the top management function is the lack of almost any type of formal documentation of plans and policies. The CEO generates very little paperwork directly from his desk. Long-range plans, budget proposals, capital expenditure requests, acquisition studies, and new policy proposals flow *to* this position. With the stroke of a pen he will modify a word or delete a paragraph or scribble an incoherent phrase which can completely alter or confuse months of work. But little original written work ever emanates from the CEO himself. His reasoning remains a mystery to lower levels as they rewrite their presentations another uncountable time.

The successful individual who climbs the management ladder to the rarefied atmosphere of the CEO's office will find that there are no longer any routine tasks to perform. And none of the CEO's daily activity is reviewed by anyone. It would seem, then, that at last we have found the position in the organization where Henry Fayol's "plan, organize, coordinate, and control" activities can be pursued full time with quiet and effective deliberation.

More recent studies of top management activity universally proclaim that these functions never take place in a calm, unruffled, intellectual atmosphere. The CEO's primary activities do not include conceptualizing long-range plans or making broad policy decisions or formulating precise objectives. The top person in the organization does not know everything that is going on. Furthermore his life becomes more complicated than ever before as he reaches the top of the pyramid.

The people who develop information systems must recognize a special case, a special problem— the CEO. Information systems developed for the chief executive cannot be equivalent to any other type of organizational systems, since this person, once he assumes the position, becomes unlike anyone else. First let us examine the individual holding the top position. How does he work? How does he make decisions? Can we supply inputs to his needs? Does he, in fact, *want* information inputs to his daily routine? Later we will look at some possible methods of assisting this most harassed of all organizational executives—the chief executive officer.

EDUCATION

Up to this point we have indicated energetically that education is the way to develop better information systems to solve *real* problems. In particular, Chapters 7 and 8 outline an in-house education series called Participatory Systems. The CEO has risen above the level of understanding offered by this course. After all, he controls all of the many functions presented in the class!

Education has never been an adequate measurement to indicate how well a manager will perform. The success of a CEO cannot be predetermined by the grades he received in school, the number of degrees he holds, or the universities he attended. Livingston[1] argues:

> Academic achievement is not a valid yardstick to use in measuring managerial potential. Indeed, if academic achievement is equated with success in business, the well educated manager is a myth.

This might be true in view of the problems encountered by management scientists of practically every stripe. Almost without exception they complain of the lack of attention and understanding applied to their programs by the CEO. Certainly the offerings of management science can be varied, extensive, relevant, and at times even cunningly presented in layman's terms. Operations research people tender exten-

---

[1]J. S. Livingston, "Myth of the Well Educated Manager," *Harvard Business Review*, January–February 1971, p. 79.

sive, penetrating financial models. Corporate planners project the business and its needs far into the future. Economists prepare comprehensive but frequently inconsistent market simulations. Social scientists provide insights into the needs and goals of our society. And last, but certainly not least, computer specialists (scientists?), more than any other group, have had the reason and the tools to break down the "old man's" door and thrust upon him new, vital insights for better management.

Armies of capable people plan, develop, and execute immensely expensive programs to assist the CEO. But he never seems to use them! Look at that most ambitious system development called the management information system (MIS). This all encompassing series of interlocking systems, files, and programs obviously offers the top man unique, fingertip controls of his own organization. Systems planners spend considerable time during the development phases of an MIS creating ports of special inquiry specifically oriented toward top management's needs. Designers of well structured, completed MIS find, over and over again, that these portions developed especially for the chief executive go completely unused. Even more often, the systems designer never knows whether his special constructions had any impact at all on the CEO. At that level the presentation of the system was left to the designer's boss, or even someone a step or two higher up the ladder. This person knew the chief would never sit still for a couple of hours of technical presentation. Even if he did listen, even if he had extensive EDP education, there is little use of any management information system by a chief executive.

The problem of appropriate employment of available systems tools is often discussed in terms of motivating the user and selling the system. But the chief executive is like no other information customer. How many standard data processing reports does he receive? A most common answer is a somewhat mystifying, "None!" Considering the variety of data facts available to him, this seems astounding. Are the traditional management science disciplines more successful than data processing? The answer again is "no." Although their methods develop less routine results, management scientists boast an equally dismal record of success with the chief executive.

As I was leaving the coffee machine, I spotted my old buddy Thurgood coming out of "heaven." That's what everybody called the executive wing of the office. He had a pile of papers, folders, and graphs under his arm. Thurgood surely looked like the kind of guy who belonged in operations research. His suit was rumpled, his thick glasses were halfway down his nose, and that premature balding spot added the final touch to the general picture.

But today something was wrong! His face had a glum look, and he was watching his shoes so intently that he would have walked right by me.

"Hey, Thurgood, what's the matter?"

"Oh, hello, Hugo, I didn't see you."

"I know. I watched you walking down here from "heaven." You look like you got fired."

Thurgood stopped and bought himself a cup of tea with double sugar, double cream. "It's not that bad, but almost. I had to present the second stage of development of our financial model for next year to old F. A."

"And he didn't like it?"

"I don't know!" Thurgood blinked. He always blinked when he was nervous. "I needed at least an hour just to explain how the model works. It's quite complex with . . . ."

"Yes, yes, I know, Thurgood, you've told me."

"Well, I was just beginning and I showed F. A. my project schedule. I need another 12 weeks to test, refine, and make sure that the model runs perfectly correct."

I'd heard about F. A. and could begin to imagine what was coming. "I'll bet he didn't like your schedule."

"You know what he said, Hugo? Do you know what that man said?" Thurgood was blinking rapidly. "He told me he didn't want the financial model so perfect; he wanted it next Friday! He just doesn't understand."

It is possible that there is a ring of truth to the operation researcher's complaint that the chief executive does not understand. Yet many chief executives do have appropriate backgrounds of education coupled with experience which should make them eager to use management science tools.

Formal business education programs, particularly those leading to MBA or MPA degrees, do indeed examine almost all modern business techniques. But such sequences of academic training are preoccupied with problem solving and decision making techniques. This emphasis often overdevelops the individual's analytical skills, while leaving undertrained his ability to take action and get things done. Also the academic programs ignore the talents necessary to *find* the problems that need to be solved. Yet the basic understanding is there. Every year the CEO is a more intelligent person. Success, however, is not dependent on education. It overwhelmingly depends on how well the chief executive can find and exploit the multiple opportunities available to him. Management science techniques, MIS, and standard data processing methodology apparently do not meet the chief executive's opportunity standards.

A clue to the Data Processing's Department's dilemma with the CEO can be found in the writing of C. Jackson Grayson, Jr., Dean of the School of Business Administration of Southern Methodist University and, for 16 months, chairman of the Price Commission in Phase II of the Economic Stabilization Program. Dean Grayson has done research and written a book on management science. Yet in his position as chairman of the Price Commission he ignored the use of management science tools in every instance.

Among the reasons given for using absolutely no management science tools were shortage of time, inaccessibility of data, long response time, and invalidating simplifications. Most strikingly, this is what Dean Grayson[2] had to say about the shortage of time.

> Although I thought about using management science tools on many occasions, I consistently decided against it because of the shortage of time. Management scientists simply do not sufficiently understand the constraint of time on decision making, and particularly on decisions that count, and the techniques they develop reflect that fact. They may write about time as a limitation. They may admonish managers for letting time push them into a "crisis" mode. They may recognize the constraint of time with a few words and comment on its influence. They may say they, too, experience time constraints. But their techniques are so time consuming to use that managers pass them by.

Does all that sound familiar? Sure, we've heard it before—many times. The chief executive's well justified criticism of the turtlelike development of all DP systems is well known. The man in this position just cannot wait. He is not like department heads, section chiefs, even vice-presidents. He's the CEO. How does he manage without our scientific help? Probably he manages in much the same ways as Tutankhamen of Egypt in 1344 B.C. or Nero or the firm of Scrooge and Marley. All of these old-time managers made use of the same general source of information—word of mouth. They acted out complex, intertwined, but fragmented and interrupted days. And they seemed to like it that way.

If data processing and the other management sciences are going to respond successfully to the CEO, we had better understand that his needs are different from those of all other individuals in the organization. And the ways we may be able to communicate with his needs are also quite different.

The CEO won't wait for us. Can we then compile a full enough understanding of his decision process to anticipate some of his requirements?

[2]C. J. Grayson, Jr., "Management Science and Business Practice," *Harvard Business Review*, July–August 1973.

THE NATURE OF THE CHIEF EXECUTIVE OFFICER

Success in any field of endeavor requires concentration, repetition, extensive training or thorough practical experience, and, normally, the development of special skills. Engineers, doctors, musicians, sports stars, tool and die makers—all normally work within narrow fields where intensive training coupled with experience makes them experts. Salesmen, accountants, and programmers similarly develop distinctive capacities. Such career path concentrations beget accomplishment and oftentimes prosperity. The daily employment ads in the newspapers enumerate lengthy experience and education requirements for most well paying jobs, demonstrating our society's continuing demand for expertise.

But what are the duties of a chief executive officer? It would be fair to assume that he has risen to his position, at least in part, because of exceptional ability in some particular discipline. Certainly as CEO he cannot continue to exercise this expertise in the same way. His field of interest and control has abruptly expanded to include financial concerns, legal matters, marketing, public relations, maintenance, employee training, and the many other functions which exist in almost every organization.

According to long-held theories, the CEO spends a good part of his time in monastic seclusion, developing the long-range plan, probing the financial model, or fine-tuning the management information system. Individually, practitioners from operations research, corporate planning, and data processing notice that such concentrated efforts do not normally take place. Their observation seems to be supported by much in-depth research into the actual workings of the CEO position. In other words, the managerial activities ascribed to the CEO are not executed with the same pattern of concentration and repetition that is associated with success in almost any other field. The work pattern of the chief executive is far different from that of his subordinates.

Considerable empirical data has established the special character of the chief executive's work activity. The CEO earnestly seeks action rather than reports. He enjoys and promotes oral communication. Most importantly, any encounter with this man can be best described by one word—brief!

An early study of managerial work was conducted by Sune Carlson in Sweden in 1951. In an examination of the work patterns of company presidents, Carlson determined that, while the executives averaged about 1 hour of time alone each day, this total time was broken into four or five periods of 10 to 15 minutes each. In other words, there was seldom time to start a new task before another interruption occurred.

Carlson's study made use of the diary technique. With this investigative method the subject records how his time is distributed among known job factors. Using simple preprinted forms, the manager can record events quickly. In 1954 and 1957 Tom Burns published the results of two other diary studies. These studies, verified by many others that followed, indicated that middle and senior managers spent a high proportion of their time in conversation.

In a major study conducted in 1967 by Rosemary Stewart the problem of fragmentation of work was strongly illuminated. Stewart's extensive program examined the activities of 160 managers for periods of 4 weeks. During the periods of the study the managers' time was so divided that they averaged only nine periods of 30 minutes or more without interruption. Some 60% of the total time was spent in oral communication.

Mintzburg carried on research on five chief executives in 1967–1968. Among his findings he characterized the activities of managers as brief, fragmented, and filled with considerable variety.

In short, study after study indicates that individuals who perform top management functions (i.e., activities generally not reviewed or documented) are constantly interrupted and seem to accept and even prefer this mode of operation. Managers go from activity to activity without prior planning. These activities average from 3 to 10 minutes in time; only rarely are they of longer duration.

Generally it appears that the top manager responds to the needs of the moment. He is a real-time responder to stimuli. He reacts rather than acts. The planning process is quite the reverse of what we suppose it to be. Furthermore, chief executive officers basically work from their own mental plans. Little or nothing is written. Long-range planning is virtually impossible as the CEO concentrates on today, the daily job, and on oral communication. The top manager works, lives, and breathes in real time. No wonder he sometimes appears to act abruptly and to make decisions in small increments. No wonder he can't wait for the development of the next program or the absolute finalization of the latest OR project or MIS. His world of action and activity is *today!*

The leader of any organization fulfills many roles. Current research diminishes none of them. The content of the job of chief executive officer has never changed. It is the method of job accomplishment which is frequently misunderstood.

Depending on the individual's previous experience and training, we still expect the CEO to fill, in varying degrees, the following roles: figurehead; leader; spokesman for the organization; negotiator with government, industry leaders, unions, and chief customers; focal point of communication horizontally and vertically throughout the organization; and finally the firm's representative to the outside world.

Regardless of the functions performed by the manager, research pointedly indicates that managers strongly favor oral communication. Reports, written documents, and mail are of course all handled to some extent by the chief executive, but telephone conversations, planned and unplanned meetings, and informal encounters seem to be preferred. In fact, averaging the oral communication time of the three studies cited demonstrates that 74.6% of the manager's total time is spent in such oral situations.

The evidence suggests that a wide ranging variety of information passes through the chief executive. Because of his unique opportunities through peer contacts, customers, and the general marketplace, he can collect a great deal of information normally unavailable to his subordinates. Inside his organization intelligence gathering is even simpler, as he uses the power of his position for both formal and informal contacts, which he normally may sample on a daily basis.

In one organization the president routinely queries a janitor: "What's going on today, John?" This janitor has a unique set of duties taking him from major conference rooms through a variety of offices to the president's office. This is a completely illogical pattern in terms of efficient work accomplishment. But John always spends 5 or 10 minutes at the end of each day chatting with his friend, the president.

This type of contact is by no means unique. A top manager continually seeks information from a wide variety of sources. With it he can develop a matchless collection of knowledge relating to business pressures and trends, plus a unique understanding of internal operations and outside events. Much of this basically oral collection of data is current and is not available anywhere in written form. The chief executive must therefore somehow organize and develop his own information system, constantly fed by varied, but brief, contacts.

The characteristics of the CEO's position (i.e., brief contacts, varied contacts, and oral communication) seem to indicate that few scientific principles are exercised in managerial work. With all of the data processing and management science tools at hand, we have done little to improve the work methods or habits of the chief executive.

In *The Nature of Managerial Work* Mintzberg[3] examines the ac-

[3]H. Mintzberg, *The Nature of Managerial Work*, Harper & Row, New York, 1973.

complishments of the management scientist in the fields of production and data processing. He indicates the ineffectiveness of these tools as he comments:

> The management scientist . . . has done virtually nothing to help the manager manage. The reason is simple. Analytical procedures cannot be brought to bear on work processes that are not well understood. And we have understood little about managerial work. Hence management scientists have concentrated their efforts elsewhere in the organization, where procedures were amenable to quantification and change.

FILTERING

Our very large, formal, precise computer systems provide much in the way of useful data and exception reports for the middle manager. Operations research, long-range planning, modeling, and other techniques provide aggregated abstractions of the future world. But the chief executive officer is a person very much interested in today, not in computer history and not in management scientists' assumptions. In fact, he feels far more secure with his own understandings. They are certainly more current and viable than any computer program or 12-month long-range project.

Because he is not supported by his formal information organization, which is not in concurrence with his operating style, the CEO relies on orally acquired data, stored in his own mental data base. Contrary to data processing's hopes and desires our MIS inside the computer is not the most important set of information within the organization. The prime data lies within the manager's head.

The location of this most essential information then poses a difficult problem for the chief executive and for the organization. Only this one person possesses the key information required to correctly evaluate a great many situations and make important decisions. Because so much of this information has been acquired orally and is not documented, it is extremely difficult to disseminate to subordinates. But if it can't be easily dispersed to the manager's staff, the delegation of tasks becomes difficult. Top managers are frequently accused of failing to delegate authority appropriately. They, in turn, complain of the lack of time available within the working day to get the job done. Both problems are generated by the chief executive's thirst for varied oral communication. Managers must either assume for themselves a considerable number of undelegatable tasks or spend a great deal of time disseminating information and understanding. Meanwhile the chief executive isolates and burdens himself as he establishes the fact that the nerve center of the organization consists of his personal values stored in his mental MIS.

Without diluting the formal roles and functions attributable to top management, we find that a series of operating characteristics portray the CEO's daily activity. They are as follows:

- Brief activities.
- Oral communication.
- Variety of information inputs.
- Little or no documentation.
- Emphasis on today's world and activity.
- Small interest in management science, MIS, or standard processing tools.
- A mental MIS of information and values.
- Difficulty in delegating because of this mental data base.

Figure 10 expresses the information processing characteristics of the chief executive operating within his daily routine. Because of the brief, varied, and primarily oral contacts that he maintains, a great deal of heavy information never passes through the collection sieve to his personal MIS. This includes the extensive detail plans of the various management sciences. The pieces of information which do manage to pass the filter generally are retained, to some extent, within his personal data base. The compilation of this variety of data into a priority sequence is difficult. The CEO must necessarily maintain a high tolerance for ambiguity. To a great extent managers must rely on judgment and intuition. Responding to today's oral inputs does not provide long-range planning opportunities or well thought out controls. Because of the nature of the input, one of the inherent problems of the top manager's personal data base is that it will result in shallow problem evaluations.

The information released from the CEO's personal data base is far from adequate and is often confusing. Much of the information which the chief executive has personally collected is far more valuable to his subordinates than to himself. He is the first to hear of internal problems which may affect many divisions. He normally is the first to learn of outside opportunities to which his organization should respond. Subordinates depend on him for important information, and frequently they cannot make effective decisions without it. All too often, knowledge of advantageous challenges is not transmitted downward. In some cases even explicit, necessary guidelines are not shared. If the manager does not illuminate the objectives of his personal data base,

Figure 10   **The chief executive's filtering system.**

his subordinates will be unable to comply with the goals and plans he has kept to himself.

Of particular distress to subordinates is the theory X type of manager.[4] He conducts all of the management functions discussed but in different proportions from other managers. The operating characteristics of his information collection are consistent with those already enumerated. His personal data is, however, far more mysterious. Subordinates do not question his motives, ideas, or pronouncements. When his comments, orders, or remarks are somewhat cryptic, no one dares ask for any explanation.

[4]See "The N. Chamberlain Organization" in Chapter 11.

J. Edgar Hoover once wrote on one agent's personnel record: "Give this man what he deserves." The staff was thrown into deep consternation. What did Hoover mean? What should it do? Its solution was to give the man a transfer to the post he was seeking and at the same time present him with a letter of censure.

POSSIBLE SOLUTIONS

The complex personalities and management styles of chief executive officers do not lend themselves to straightforward solutions. Little could be done to improve the lot of J. Edgar Hoover's subordinates. It may be, in fact, that top management is not a profession. It certainly cannot be described in terms of a systematic, analytically determined set of procedures. The job is as distinctive as the person who holds it, and his attitude toward the position functions.

Since we are concerned with information, a possible approach may be to acquire an understanding of the chief's information collecting, retention, and dissemination techniques. If the foregoing descriptions seem to fit your chief executive to some extent, perhaps we can find better ways of reaching him with our analytical tools.

ONE MAN'S SYSTEM

Because the chief executive is the real data base for much important information, systems design should be based on his unique needs and interests. The analyst cannot design for this position by following the information systems development patterns used with most business functions.

"Good morning, Henry."

"Good morning, Mr. Browbeater."

"What was it you wanted to see me about, Henry?"

"Well, sir, as you know, we have been developing a corporate MIS for some time, and we've got to the point where we can now process individual data requests." Henry warmed to the subject as he continued, "We now want to structure your needs into the system."

"How long has this project been going on, Henry?"

"Oh, about 26 months, sir. Now, if you could just answer a few questions for me. First, what reports do you receive on a regular basis?"

"None!" the chief replied crisply. "How many people are on this project?"

"About twelve to fifteen, but we expect to be finished in another year or so."

Henry suddenly regretted that he had said "year or so." He continued quickly, "Mr. Browbeater, can you describe some of your standard daily work routine?"

"I have none!" the CEO replied with a grimace. "Now, Henry, let's discuss how much this MIS is really costing me."

In the field of systems development for top management, Henry's problems are not unique. Let's visit the advance projects programming team at Heterodyne, which is just a short distance down the industrial park from Henry's company. The group is drinking coffee and discussing options in its new cost analysis system.

"Well," says Debbie, the project leader, "I think we have summarized, segregated, and compared the raw material, component, packaging, shipping, and total costs of the products in every way possible."

"Did Mr. Bellweather ask for anything else?" Tony asks.

"I'm not sure," Debbie shrugs, "but then I don't get to talk to him very much."

Everyone laughs, since no one in the advanced projects group has *ever* talked to Mr. Bellweather.

Very few systems have ever been designed with the chief executive officer supplying his list of requirements beforehand. Features for top management are normally built in by the systems team with little realistic understanding of the CEO's work characteristics.

The systems study for the chief executive's needs should evaluate his information sources. Because of the unstructured nature of the chief executive's job, it is difficult for top managers to describe the speculative varied inputs which continue through each day. At the same time the systems analyst cannot readily adapt the manager's ambiguous sources to his structured computer environment.

What are the chief executive's sources of information? What trade associations does he belong to? What types of information do they prepare? What magazines, newspapers, and technological reports does he read? Does he receive any standard reports? Does he leave his office frequently for company tours? If so, where does he go? Who does he talk to? What is the nature of the meetings he attends outside the company? Who calls him on the phone? Whom does he call?

The chief executive will never open his door all the way and allow the analyst to become privy to every source of his personal data base. After all, knowledge is power. Some CEOs will have no part whatever in an internal program to intrude on their private world. In a certain number of organizations, no one would dare ask to share in such an understanding.

Yet,where the chief executive is mature enough and bold enough to disclose his daily working characteristics, it is possible for systems and particularly management scientists to routinely capture some of the information required. By organizing and structuring the market trends, trade organization data, new competitive information, and new technology that interest the chief executive, it is possible to help. Management science and data processing can apply their disciplines of dedicated research and comprehensive organization to seek out additional sources of information. It certainly is not possible to capture all the different sources of data, but by using information theory techniques we can monitor an extensive part of the chief executive's world. We can save and return to him his most valuable commodity—time!

THE STRATEGY ROOM

Further opportunity to develop contacts with the chief executive officer will take place in a special environment called the Strategy Room. ("War Room" is an ominous sounding name.) This enclosed, locked room might contain the following:

- Wall size maps of the organization's regions and territories with company facilities identified.
- Comparative arrangements of the firm's products next to those of leading competitors.
- Graphs of major sales and financial trends, also wall size.
- List of the major orders of the day.
- List of the major expenses of the day.
- Pictorial display of major industry and economic trends.
- Section reserved for presentation of the "report of the day."
- "Alternatives board."

Necessary staff will be assigned to maintain all charts, graphs of trends, and economic statistics on a daily basis. In some situations chalk boards should be used to demonstrate the timeliness and changing nature of the data.

The Strategy Room, if used by the CEO, creates a nerve center where at least some of the current pertinent information is routinely available. When the chief executive disagrees with or adds to the data, we have the opportunity to determine *his* sources and incorporate them into the information system.

Some features of the Strategy Room will naturally be unique to the needs of each organization. One special feature is a section devoted to the report of the day. Here is an opportunity for operating people to acquaint top management with every type of information flow available, from factory job card to financial statement. Surprisingly, many executives find use for information they did not realize existed. After a time report redundancy will also identify information pollution. Yet the presentation of one report or form each day, taking no more than 5 minutes, will often arouse the interest of top management in many long-neglected areas and provide insight into them. Most organizations will be able to run the new reports section for 2 to 3 years without any repetition.

The "alternatives board" is normally a blank section of the wall or room consisting of cork board and chalk board. It is the section which recognizes the chief executive's responsibility to integrate known situations and problems and to develop opportunities based on the combination of his personal horizons and the limited focus of the Strategy Room. Here is the place for the manager and management scientist to work together on cost/benefit analysis, model building, project monitoring, and contingency planning. The charts, statistics, maps, list of expenses, and the like, are a represenation of the real world. The trained analysts and management scientists can provide immediate data or methods for alternatives. Furthermore, this is the point where more comprehensive plans can be made. All, however, must be done within the real-time operating world of the chief executive. In this room the management scientist can appreciate the immediacy of a strike, the failure to deliver key supplies, a disastrous accident, a proposed new acquisition, or a government decision which cannot wait for elegant evaluations, sophisticated mathematics, and time-consuming techniques.

The Strategy Room offers benefits to all active participants. The staff learns of the immediacy of top management decision making. Top management sources of informal information are illuminated. The CEO can briefly employ his own time plus staff aid as his inducement to participate in the Strategy Room. He is able to present the analytical staff with a problem in a short period of time. By the next day or the next week its members should be able to present, by bringing to bear their technical talents, pressure reducing estimates of possible solutions considered logical, rather than complete but useless studies presented 6 months too late.

"I WONDER . . .?"

The Strategy Room may or may not be the place to have a computer terminal. Very few systems have inquiry design equal in both detail and summary capability to the demands of top management. What does management want to know? Possibly anything and everything, and usually with comparisons or selections that have not been programmed.

If you can select on every variation of every field in some major files, if you can sort the file, and if you can summarize on every numeric field, you might consider placing such a device in the Strategy Room. If the machine is there, it must be prepared to react to the chief executive's question: "I wonder if . . .?" We will discuss this type of approach further under "Probes."

MEMORY DUMP

The unique organizational data base in the mind of the chief executive officer is of vital importance to his staff. If the CEO is away on a trip, is sick or is on vacation, then so is his data base. Some of the information in the leader's brain is needed for the decision making process conducted by various subordinates. But because the sources are his alone, the CEO's directives are sometimes considered arbitrary and mysterious. When he is busy or away, no one can make an evaluation because possible key strategy information is missing. If the boss is a theory X man (i.e., an authoritarian manager), no one dares make a decision.

When the chief executive is made aware of this problem, the corrective action is quite simple. A weekly meeting with his subordinates (and not just "key" subordinates) where the CEO makes the entire presentation—where he dumps memory—is invaluable to his staff. Now its members can appreciate the necessity and reasons for some of the actions, and can begin to understand how the chief executive's mind works. Interrelationships and mutual understanding are improved. The chief executive need not tell all from his data bank—from his natural memory. But he should make a determined effort to share what he has acquired from his oral sources and transfer it through a weekly debriefing session to his subordinates.

SUMMARY

The chief executive officer is a special person. The characteristics of verbal information collection through brief encounters develop an individual who responds primarily to today's pressure, utilizing his personal data base.

Subordinates and management scientists will improve their effectiveness by understanding the CEO's characteristics and providing more immediate responses appropriate to the understanding and terminology of his information collection system. Attempts to develop fixed sets of data for the chief executive based on data processing or management science views of the problems should be discontinued.

Evaluations by Systems of the manager's sources of information and the establishment of a Strategy Room should improve the interaction with the chief executive. The optimum device is a weekly meeting where the manager disseminates value statements, gossip, and other information into overall organizational guidelines.

Think twice before you prepare to second-guess your CEO and present to him plans and information you think he needs. Wise men don't need such advice, and foolish men won't heed it.

CHAPTER 10

Professor Peasecod

"Good morning, gentlemen . . . mm . . . mm . . . ladies. This begins part four of the Summer University Management Executive Refresher and Development Course.

"I am Professor Peasecod. Like most of your other instructors in SUMERD, I am from the Graduate School of Business. Since each company group in the class has representatives from a wide variety of disciplines, yet almost everyone of you makes use of the computer utility, the faculty has included this hour to review standard systems development processes. We are going to discuss . . . ."

"Chief," Hugo whispered, "Professor Peasecod doesn't look older than twenty-two or twenty-three."

"I know," the Chief mumbled back sarcastically. Although he hadn't said anything yet, the Chief was quite disturbed about the whole program. Imagine spending $1150 a person for five people to come to this *thing!* Four mornings and two evenings of work, then golf and swimming every afternoon, picnics, and entertainment for the families. Really it was just like a paid vacation. As for what they had got so far on Monday and Tuesday . . . well, the golf was the best of the lot.

"Let us then," the Chief tuned back in on Professor Peasecod, who was staring at him, "let us then begin by examining the many steps that some of you or your systems analysts need to exercise in order to completely, accurately, and successfully define and implement information systems. On other days, the lecturers defined for you such management processes as the decision making cycle and the administrative cycle. This morning we are going to define the systems development cycle."

The Chief noted that most of the others in the class were eagerly taking notes. In fact, Hugo's notebook was half full. He sighed. Maybe he was just getting too old.

Professor Peasecod continued. "I have identified some fifteen segments in the development of the systems cycle. Before we begin, however, let's name the various systems tools that might be used to analyze and solve problems. Then, as we discuss the segments of the systems cycle, some of you will be interested in determining which tools might be appropriate. Why don't you begin to suggest some of the systems tools to me? I will write each one on the board."

The slender girl from Tribophysics, Inc., had her hand in the air first.

"Yes?" asked Professor Peasecod.
"Flowcharts," she offered.
"Certainly," the professor replied as he wrote the word on the board. "Next . . . in fact, just call them out as quickly as I can write them down."
"Writing procedures," said a man in the back.
"Forms design," offered Hugo.
"Forms control."
"Records management."
"PERT, CPM, linear programming," added Hugo, using terms whose complete meaning he did not clearly understand.
"Work simplification and work measurement," suggested the Chief, getting caught up in the enthusiasm of the group.
"Decision tables."
"Documentation."
"Fact gathering."
"Ideas."
"Numbering systems."
"Gantt charts."
"Equipment selections," from the Chief again.
"The ideal concept," from a tall man in the front.

"Interviews."

"File organization."

"Analysis," said the slender girl from Tribophysics.

"Synthesis," chimed in the Chief.

"Comparison," shouted Hugo.

"Slow down," yelled Professor Peasecod. I've got to switch to the next blackboard. You are really a fine group. I think that Professor Icarus' session on creativity has stimulated this class."

"Creativity," suggested a bald man with a red mustache.

"Brainstorming."

"The Delphi technique."

"File design and data base," again from the slender girl.

"Modeling simulation and Gantt charts," added Hugo, not to be outdone by anyone.

"I think we've had Gantt charts already, Mr. Knott," said Professor Peasecod.

"Measurements," continued a gray-haired man.

"Evaluations."

"Maintenance."

"Validations."

"I think we should include some of the major machine tools of information processing, such as computers, OCR, MICR, CRTs, collators, sorters, copy machines, and word processors," stated Mr. Streeter, whose personality, handsome features, graying hair, and deep voice had made him the informally accepted class leader. The group generally murmured agreement as the professor wrote furiously.

"Any more?" Peasecod inquired.

"Office layout."

"Questionnaires," from the front row, as the answers seemed to suddenly slow down.

"Sampling techniques."

"Simulation."

"We had that one!" five or six people yelled at the same time. There was a long pause. Clarence King was about to raise his hand, but Peasecod was already continuing.

"Well, that is really fine. I think you've provided a larger list of systems tools than any previous class. Our basic objective this morning, however, is to examine the segments of the system cycle. Keep these tools in mind. Some are a bit redundant. Some overlap. At one time or another in the systems development process you may have use for a number of these tools.

"It is important to recognize, as you did, that a wide variety of such tools exist. Not all are used in equal portions, or at all, in some steps of the systems development process."

Analysis	Interviews
Brainstorming	Linear programming
Collators	Maintenance
Comparison	Measurements
CPM	MICR
Creativity	Modeling
CRTs	Number systems
Data base	OCR
Decision tables	Office layout
Delphi technique	PERT
Documentation	Procedures
Equipment selection	Questionnaires
Evaluations	Records management
Fact gathering	Sampling techniques
File design	Sorters
File organization	Synthesis
Forms design	Validations
Gantt charts	Word processing
Ideas	Work simplification
Ideals concept	Work measurement

Figure 11   **Systems Tools Described in Peasecod's Class.**

Peasecod erased the boards. "Now, if there are no questions, let's look at a series of flip charts that I have here and review the segments of the systems development process."

THE SYSTEMS DEVELOPMENT PROCESS

Segment One—Problem Definition

The *purpose* of this first segment is to define as completely as we possibly can the specific problems that the system will attempt to solve.

The *probable steps* necessary to fully exercise this segment might be:

○ Define the reasons for investigating and developing the specified problem.

○ Prepare a list of all possibly affected persons and departments, and possibly interested groups, in this area.

○ Summarize the design objectives of the proposed system, possibly in priority sequence or time development sequence.

THE SYSTEMS DEVELOPMENT PROCESS

Segment Two—Existing System Documentation

The *purpose* of the second segment is to guarantee all participants, especially the analyst, complete understanding of the present operation.

The *probable steps* necessary to complete this segment might include:

○ Collect flowcharts, procedures, forms, and job descriptions related to the present system.
○ Determine approximate volumes of transactions and file sizes.
○ Determine processing times of the transactions, including minimum desirable response times.
○ Collect costs of all labor, materials, and equipment. Include an appropriate application of overhead. These costs will aid in the determination of whether or not any new proposed system can be cost justified.

"Now the third segment is . . . yes, Mr. Horner, you have a question?"

"Yes. Perhaps you intend to include this in the next segment, Professor Peasecod, but I believe that another type of cost should be included."

"All right, Mr. Horner, what is it?"

"Well," Horner replied, "it seems to me that any existing system might have costs associated with its inability to perform certain functions. Perhaps the lack of statistics or some vital information could lead management into a bad decision."

"That could be true," Peasecod smiled, "but we shouldn't use non-quantifiable costs. We have far too many new systems cost justified by the opportunity for so-called better decision making."

Mr. Streeter raised his hand, and Peasecod nodded to him.

"Perhaps that is true, but I think that Mr. Horner has a point. If, for example," Streeter continued, "you have discounts not taken by the Accounts Payable Department or inventory purchased when a sufficient supply is already on hand, you have incurred costs because of the dynamics of the existing system."

The class murmured agreement. Peasecod brusquely added the following to his Segment Two flip chart:

○   Determine clearly definable costs avoidable with a new system.

He then hurried on to the next flip chart.

THE SYSTEMS DEVELOPMENT PROCESS

Segment Three—Initial Analysis

The *purpose* of the third segment is to provide a general overview of the proposed system with enough information so that the reviewing and approving authority can make a rational decision on continuation.

The *probable steps* necessary to complete this segment might include:

○   State the benefits which are achievable by the new system, either in narrative form or as a list.
○   Provide a general overview of the proposed system, including its limits.
○   Prepare a list of estimated equipment, space, manpower, computer capacity, and so on, needed to support the new system.
○   Estimate the operating costs of the new system.
○   List all possible alternatives with narrative, indicating the basis for each rejected alternative.
○   Prepare a summary of findings with estimates of project difficulty, time to completion, and costs, and a recommendation for further investigation or discontinuing the project.
○   Schedule and hold a review of the initial analysis with the approving authority.

"I believe we call this activity a feasibility study in our company," said the tall, slim girl near the front.

"Professor," Clarence King spoke for the first time in this session, "I would like to add that this segment requires an important dimension of responsibility."

"How do you mean, Mr. King?"

"Well, at this preliminary analysis stage, nothing has been approved—correct?"

"That's correct," Peasecod said as he sat down.

"Selling the new system is then important at this stage in the life of the project."

"True! That, Mr. King, is why I have placed "Benefits" on the flip chart as the very first item in Segment Three."

"That's not what I'm getting at," said King. "In my organization the analyst collects and organizes this material, but it is the requesting department that formally writes and even presents the proposal. We make sure that the man or department that asks for the new system is completely involved in the preparation and presentation of the formal request."

"I agree with Mr. King," said the Chief. "In our company the systems people write the proposals, but the requesting department is responsible for the content. We've had some bad experiences where the computer people tried to shove a project down our throats."

"That's right!" Hugo added unnecessarily.

"Any more comments before we go to Segment Four?" Peasecod asked as he rose. There were none.

THE SYSTEMS DEVELOPMENT PROCESS

Segment Four—Project Control Plan

The *purpose* of the fourth segment is to provide definitive plans of probable costs, project organization, and priority relative to existing approved projects. With approval of the initial analysis as outlined in Segment Three, this segment is the stepping stone to all following activity.

The *probable steps* necessary to complete this segment might include:

○   Divide the project into tractable units of work accomplishment, usually no more than 80 man-hours per unit.
○   Prepare a schedule, including checkpoints and completion dates.
○   Estimate the size of the project team, including time and people required from the functional area.
○   Schedule and hold a project plan review session with the approving authority. If a staff commitment has to made by both Data Processing and the functional user department, management of both areas must approve the plan, the priority, and the commitment of resources.

"It seems we have to waste an awful lot of time with reviews," blurted Gil Parvet. "When I develop a new system, it stands! I don't keep modifying and revising." Hugo noted that Gil's cheeks always became bright red when he spoke.

"That sounds like some of the people in my company," Mr. Streeter commented drily. The Chief noted the perturbed look on the faces of

THE SYSTEMS DEVELOPMENT PROCESS

Segment Five—Information Gathering and Analysis

The *purpose* of the fifth segment is, through a systems investigation, to collect necessary detailed information. This is a repetitive process which usually requires that the analyst return many times to his sources for additional data. If the problem is very small, much or all of the data can be collected during the initial analysis.

The *probable steps* necessary to complete this segment might include:

○ Hold detailed interviews with all participants in the present system.
○ Carry out work sampling to measure the time expended on each job step.
○ Prepare or review up-to-date organization charts and forms flowcharts.
○ Determine the point at which each decision is made, regardless of the formal lines of authority.
○ Review the proposed solution and possible alternatives in light of the new information.
○ With the entire project team, conduct a critique of the proposed system, taking into account the differences in perceptions, values, and experience, with particular emphasis on the comments of the user group.

---

the other two men from Streeter's firm. They obviously were the target of his remark.

Streeter continued, "So many of these people seem to build opulent systems that are far beyond ordinary needs."

"And perhaps the person or department who must use and live with the system is trying to steer a battleship when he needed a motorcycle," added Ed Lindquist.

"I think, Mr. Parvet," the professor said, "you are hearing some of the common complaints voiced by people outside of the data processing community. And that's very good! One of the major objectives of the Summer University Management Executive Refresher and Development course is to share experience and ideas. Well, let's go on."

"Whew, Chief, they sure gave Parvet a hard time."

"He deserved it," the Chief shot back. "He's one of those egotistical systems people."

As Hugo opened his mouth to say his usual, "Right, Chief," he remembered that he was the company systems analyst.

THE SYSTEMS DEVELOPMENT PROCESS

Segment Six—Systems Design

The *purpose* of the sixth segment is to accomplish the actual detailed systems design.

The *probable steps* necessary to complete this segment might include:

○   Prepare general graphic displays of the major elements of the system.
○   Prepare a second level display of the interactions of the subsystem.
○   Prepare a narrative description of the overall system operating in a mainstream logical sequence.
○   Prepare input specifications.
○   Prepare file specifications.
○   Prepare report layouts and specifications.
○   Prepare general interface specifications between the manual and automated operations.
○   Develop the necessary internal controls to ensure that accurate data will be processed through the system.
○   Produce an implementation schedule with cost revision if major variations occur from the project control plan.
○   Review the system as designed and all supporting documentation for validity and continuity.
○   Review the parts of the system relating to each primary contact for accuracy and completeness.

THE SYSTEMS DEVELOPMENT PROCESS

Segment Seven—Customer/User Review

The *purpose* of the seventh segment is to provide all interested parties with an opportunity to review the requirements, capabilities, and benefits of the new system. The individual average user is asked to approve the design. We thereby gain performance acceptance.

The *probable steps* necessary to complete this segment might include:

○   Arrange for a presentation by the project leader of the problem, proposed solution, and benefits.
○   Review, as necessary, the documentation.
○   Explain the cost and work requirements of the new system.
○   Discuss with the participants: concerns, questions, and the opportunity to develop a feeling of "sharing" in the new system.

"I don't think that last item will work!"

"Why not, Mr. Parvet?" Peasecod asked.

"Because in our operation everyone is so dead set against any new system, particularly a computer system, that they'd take this opportunity to chop the thing to pieces."

As Professor Peasecod discoursed on the necessity of selling systems and gaining user acceptance, Streeter was thinking, "I'll bet Parvet tries to jam his ideas down the user's throat." Hugo was thinking, "I need to be a little stronger in my presentations, like Parvet." And the Chief was thinking, "Hugo seems a bit like Parvet."

"Shall we go on?" asked Peasecod.

THE SYSTEMS DEVELOPMENT PROCESS

Segment Eight—Management Review and Approval

The *purpose* of the eighth segment is to allow the top reviewing authority to make a final decision on the desirability of the project. The effort to this point has been to collect well defined, well documented, and well accepted plans for a new system.

The *step* necessary to complete this segment will be:

○   Provide a summary presentation that enumerates the problem, the solution proposed, and the costs and benefits of the present and new systems.

"And do it with a bit of style," added Mr. Streeter.

"Certainly," concurred Peasecod.

THE SYSTEMS DEVELOPMENT PROCESS

Segment Nine—Detail System Design

The *purpose* of the ninth segment is to define the logical operations of each subsystem in detail.

The *probable steps* necessary to complete this segment might include:

○   Define all input, output, and storage files required for this operation. Write specifications.

○   Define the logical flow of data through the subsystem. Write specifications.

○   Review subsystem specifications, organization charts, and procedures.
○   Confirm that the timing of all subsystem operations will allow appropriate merger of inputs and outputs in the necessary sequence. All the parts must fit together.

"Could you give us an example of that last item, Professor Peasecod?" asked Lindquist.

Before he could reply, Horner interrupted. "I think I can supply an instance of that kind of coordination."

"Go ahead," said Peasecod.

"Well, we found in my company that factory production orders were issued to make parts on a schedule that couldn't be met. Even though we knew about the commonality of parts, we didn't examine the status of dies—not machine capacity, mind you—just the dies necessary for a particular production order. Many times the job could not be done on schedule simply because the die was not available, even when machines and manpower were idle."

"We've got a package to do all that," sniffed Parvet.

"Thank you, Mr. Horner. Does that answer your concern, Mr. Lindquist?" asked Peasecod.

"Not completely. I am in the banking business, and these manufacturing examples don't apply to me."

"I'll give him an example so we can move on," said Parvet, his cheeks a blazing red. "When you run a payroll, you have to have the gross pay *before* you calculate taxes. O.K.?"

Lindquist nodded agreement. Peasecod pursed his lips and moved on to the next flip chart.

THE SYSTEMS DEVELOPMENT PROCESS

Segment Ten—Computer Solution Design

The *purpose* of the tenth segment is to develop specific problem solutions using the computer utility. Prior emphasis has been oriented toward user problems and adequate solutions. It is critical, at this step in the process, to define and evaluate minute details.

The *probable steps* necessary to complete this segment might include:

○   Define exactly the computer processes to be used, including a general program flowchart.
○   Define each computer program and the reasons for its position within the general program flowchart. Include sorts, edits, and utilities.

○ Provide the explicit specifications which are the instructions for computer programming.

○ Provide data movement specifications in narrative and flowchart forms to verify the exact content of all fields and files at each step of the process.

○ Prepare any unique algorithms and manual references necessary for accurate descriptions of complex steps in any program.

○ Develop final form design, now taking into account detailed hardware considerations.

○ Review computer solution design for completeness, accuracy, open ended ability to handle new situations, and capability to deal with errors and exceptions.

THE SYSTEMS DEVELOPMENT PROCESS

Segment Eleven—Program Design and Coding

The *purpose* of the eleventh segment is to perform the necessary computer oriented activities. Here we produce sets of programs to accomplish the specifications previously developed.

The *probable steps* necessary to complete this segment might include:

○ Write program flowcharts. This step is especially important if the problems are complex.

○ Code the instructions that direct the computer to perform each specific operation.

○ Prepare test data to insure adequate execution of the program.

○ Prepare test data for control, limits, and error situations.

○ Develop necessary conversion programs to load new master files.

○ Prepare keypunch instructions.

○ Write instructions for computer operations to handle files, program input, and output.

○ Develop a user manual for the preparation of input, output, and exceptions to make processing as technically accurate as possible.

THE SYSTEMS DEVELOPMENT PROCESS

Segment Twelve—System Test and Installation

The *purpose* of the twelfth segment is to test the complete system, validate its performance, and determine the adequacy of the computer operation instructions and the user manual.

The *probable steps* necessary to complete this segment might include:

○   Administer a program test.
○   Administer a subsystem test.
○   Administer a total system test.
○   Review all tests, including the adequacy of instructions and documentation to meet each situation.
○   Execute the actual changeover to the new system.
○   Make a formal presentation of the new system to all interested parties. Many functions or departments not previously involved might be interested in making use of the system or planning similar adaptations.

"I believe we should mention here," Peasecod added, "that this segment of the systems development process is more time consuming than any other."

"More than programming?" Lindquist asked.

"Yes," replied the professor. "At this point the systems analyst owns the new system. He has been more intimately involved with the complete total process than any other person. When problems arise with any facet of the system—programs, input, you name it—it's up to the analyst to resolve the problems."

"And you know," commented Mr. Streeter, "if the problems are very severe, he literally takes over some departments or functions."

"That's right! I'm sure you've all seen situations where the analyst left his department permanently and took over a user group."

Several heads nodded in agreement.

THE SYSTEMS DEVELOPMENT PROCESS

Segment Thirteen—Final Documentation

The *purpose* of the thirteenth segment is to compile a final, complete set of documentation. The work of the many preceding phases is integrated into a permanent library for current and historical use.

The *probable steps* necessary to complete this segment might include:

○   Collect and condense the problem definition and initial analysis concepts.
○   Verify the project control plan.
○   Verify general systems description and systems design concepts.
○   Complete the design of flowcharts and documentation.
○   Prepare user guides and operation manuals.

THE SYSTEMS DEVELOPMENT PROCESS

Segment Fourteen—Conversion Evaluation

The *purpose* of the fourteenth segment is to evaluate the ability of the new system to meet the original design objectives. At the same time we have the opportunity to clean up any errors or omissions that are now evident.

The *probable steps* necessary to complete this segment might include:

○ Conduct a meeting of all users and data processing personnel and invite free flowing discussion of the system.

○ Write a report to the approving authority, discussing the ability of the system to meet its design objectives of time, costs, and benefits.

○ Ask an outside evaluator, preferably the internal auditor, to review the entire system and report his findings to the reviewing authority.

Parvet spoke up: "The auditors would never understand it."

THE SYSTEMS DEVELOPMENT PROCESS

Segment Fifteen—Maintenance

The *purpose* of the fifteenth segment is to provide necessary updating of the system to make its life as long as possible within a changing world. Maintenance changes arise primarily from two sources: error correction and necessary modifications.

The *probable steps* necessary to complete this segment might include:

○ A problem definition in writing from the user or Data Processing.

○ Review and approval of the change by an authority appropriate to the economic size of the change.

○ Systems investigation.

○ Development of coding or systems flow or manual changes.

○ Testing.

○ Installation of changes.

○ Final documentation and review.

○ Beginning a maintenance log.

PEASECOD'S PARAMETER

"Maintenance completes and starts again the life cycle of a system. There is a period of time over which a system will survive. It is a function of the adequacy of the first fourteen segments," Peasecod lectured. "While some theorists argue that a good deal of maintenance effort is necessary at the start of a system, I must disagree! If the fourteen building steps have been thoroughly completed, the new system will begin without—as many of you practitioners call it—"bugs."

"But this situation will not last forever," he shouted. "As time passes, the organization and the world it functions with change, even the computer utility changes. This constant change is disruptive to the system and the daily operations of the Computer Department. The last item of Segment Fifteen refers to the control tool you use to evaluate the life cycle of a system."

"He sure is pouring it on," Hugo whispered to the Chief.

"The control is what I call a maintenance log. It records each incident of maintenance and the amount of time spent working on it. Some of you in the room may be unaware of the fact that most systems and programming operations spend 60, 70, even 80% of their total work time on maintenance."

A few people looked surprised.

"That's not us, is it, Hugo?" the Chief asked quietly.

"Never measured it!" was the confident reply.

Peasecod continued. "We know that the programs and the entire system require more maintenance as they grow older. But how can you measure the point at which the systems cycle should be initiated once again and the system completely redone? For this objective of measurement of the system's useful life I have developed a theory which I call Peasecod's Parameter." He smiled broadly for the first time that day. "It goes like this:

PEASECOD'S PARAMETER

When the time recorded in the maintenance log approaches the original systems development time, the existing system is dying and the systems cycle should be repeated for a complete new development of the system.

"I'm writing a book on the subject. In fact, it was my doctoral thesis. I'm quite excited about it. Umm . . . any questions?"

A few in the class shrugged.

THE PROBLEMS

"Well, then, any questions or comments about any of the segments of the total systems cycle?"

"I have a comment," said the tall, slim girl who Hugo had decided was very cute.

"Yes, Iris?"

"I don't know how the others feel, but in considering experiences with my company—well, we don't go through so many steps in the systems development process, or do this just as you've outlined them. We are careful; we investigate, document, and review; but your program of fifteen segments seems to involve going back and back over the same material again."

Peasecod frowned slightly. "Most of the academic studies on the subject identify this many phases or steps. Many writers even elaborate to eighteen or twenty aspects of the cycle."

"I think they must be crazy." The speaker was Parvet. "I develop systems in no more than five of your segments."

"I bet you do," thought the Chief as he raised his hand and spoke. "I must agree with Iris. While everything that you've proposed is worthwhile in a theoretical sense, it just isn't practical in an actual problem situation."

"If we consumed all the steps outlined here to get a job done," Lindquist said, "we'd never be finished on any kind of schedule."

Looking for some support, Professor Peasecod turned to the reflective looking Clarence King. "Mr. King, would you care to comment?"

"My position," Mr. King said softly, "as treasurer/controller of Antrorse Industries is such that I am basically a user of systems, rather than part of the development process. I find little disagreement for myself in accepting fifteen, sixteen, or any other number of segments. You see . . . in my position I leave the technical aspects of systems design to others far more qualified than myself."

Peasecod smiled. Hugo noted the hushed atmosphere in the room. Although Mr. King did not command the authority of a Mr. Streeter, his eloquence, coupled with his low tones, made everyone listen intently.

"I must express, however, an element of difficulty with some of the early segments. The orientation of the problem development is far too one-sided." King glanced around the room and continued. "As chief financial officer it is my job to evaluate new projects, from any source, in terms of their worthwhileness. I do this by making sure that each new project bears an assessment, set in quantitative terms such as a rate of return or net present value."

Mr. Streeter raised his hand. "Certainly there is a great deal of merit in what Clarence says. And from his financial point of view every project must maximize the use of assets. But, having been president of a number of companies, I find I have a different point of view."

Several people were obviously startled to learn that Mr. Streeter was a company president. Iris thought, as she now placed the name, that it was no wonder the others in his group deferred to Mr. Streeter.

"The systems development problems that we tackle at Star Steel are often determined by the tastes and values of my managers."

"Probably," joined in Parvet, "they are also determined by the vigilance of the stockholders."

Streeter's face drained, and he turned almost completely around to stare at Parvet. Everyone now realized that this was *the* Mr. Streeter and recalled the problem he had had with the Securities and Exchange Commission. The silence was deafening! Before Streeter could reply, the professor had caught Ed Lindquist's eye, and with a silent nod pleaded for a comment.

Lindquist answered the call for help. He had intended to speak anyway.

"Professor," the sound of his voice made Iris jump, "I must agree with both Mr. King and Mr. Streeter. My job is marketing and advertising. We are forever trying to reach all different types of people. The points of view of a financial manager and a chief executive officer have been just expressed—and they are quite different. It is my personal belief that far too many firms have a myopic approach toward systems development."

"Could you elaborate?" sighed Peasecod, happy to avoid a scene.

"Well, I believe that frequently organizations will equate profit improvement with cost reduction. New systems then are based on a problem which is really a reaction to an adverse profit situation." Lindquist looked down at his hands and went on. "All too many times the system problem presented for definition, as in your Segment One, can be simply stated as a management plan to reduce costs and save money."

Lindquist noted several looks of agreement and warmed to his subject.

"Most of you can't remember the recession in 1957. It wasn't as bad as 1974–1975, but it was bad enough. In those years I worked for a manufacturer of washing machines. Business was off, so we went through a typical cycle of reducing costs to save money. Management cut back severely on research and development and on advertising. And the big systems projects were a new credit and collection system to get rid of the deadbeats, and a sales analysis system to strengthen our marketing."

"Did they help?" asked the Chief knowingly.

"Of course not! By late 1959, business had picked up again in the white goods market but not at our company. Then the old man initiated a new study—a major project—aimed at the compensation system for our salesmen and distributors. He proposed an elaborate new incentive system to get things moving. The data processing people went wild!" The memory made Lindquist chuckle. "At the same time my department initiated some market studies to find out where the business had gone."

"And?"

"We found a definite shift in customer preference to more efficient, feature oriented products which our competition had developed. While we had been working on projects to save money by cutting R & D, the competition had built a better mousetrap."

OPPORTUNITY

"Professor Peascod?" It was Jay Horner. "I think we are all basically having difficulty in various ways with your Segment One."

"Oh," said Peasecod, not sure that he or anyone else really had any problem at all.

"Yes! You see," Horner went on quickly, "the very name of the first segment is "Problem Definition," and it sets a mood for the rest of your systems development cycle."

"I don't believe I understand!"

"Well, professor, with your segments you assume at the beginning that every system must be developed in response to a problem. I don't believe that to be true."

"Go on."

"I think that most systems are developed along the line of the segments you've outlined. I'm a systems analyst, and I have actually performed many of those steps, although never as many as fifteen. But unfortunately," Horner gestured somewhat wildly, "most of our work is somewhat of the type Mr. Lindquist described."

"You mean it's initiated to save money?" asked Peasecod.

Horner frowned. He wasn't used to taking a position, and perhaps an unorthodox one at that, in front of such a large group.

"No, I don't mean to save money!" He heard himself talking too loudly. Taking a deep breath, he continued. "The problem with your systems development cycle, the problem with Mr. Lindquist's washing machine company, and the problem with most designed systems is that they are very short sighted and generally seek only to solve problems."

"That's why we have information systems departments," said Parvet.

"No! Mr. Streeter got nearer to the truth when he spoke of the tastes and values of his managers."

"You mean we should design for organization goals," offered Iris to be helpful.

"I think he means management by objectives," said Peasecod.

"No, I don't," Horner said again, too loudly. "Goals are more long-range affairs such as Mr. King was describing with his financial evaluations. And management by objectives means that first we set targets to describe what we will accomplish, and then performance is both the basis for stating the objectives and measuring movement towards the objectives."

"That's substantially MBO," said Peasecod, "although we also talk about quantitative and objective yardsticks as tools to measure how well a manager is doing."

"Don't get me off the track. I'm not talking about MBO." Horner was beginning to feel that his ears were warm. He wondered whether he looked as red in the face as Parvet.

"I'm trying to say that the framework, the attitude, of systems development is generally negative: it starts with a problem! But it doesn't always have to be problem oriented. Why can't the systems cycle start out with an *opportunity* to do something in a better way?" Horner's face now *was* red. He wondered if, perhaps, he'd said too much. But he had seen cases where the concept of opportunity systems had stretched the mental talents of an entire systems department.

"You know," he went on, "if we are not constantly bombarded with problems, you will find that systems people have much more potential than they are normally allowed to express. Problem statements limit their horizons by definition."

"I believe I understand your point," said Peasecod. "You might start Segment One by examining methods of improving inventory management, rather than reducing inventory costs?"

"Exactly!"

"Or perhaps generating as many high return opportunities as possible, rather than eliminating paperwork?" offered the quiet Mr. King.

Horner nodded his head in agreement. "I don't mean to really find fault with the systems development cycle that we've seen here this morning." He now felt more confident with his philosophy. "All I want to add is that every system should not be developed as a problem. The world is full of opportunities. Our systems would live longer and be more successful if we broadened our outlook beyond problem solution recommendations. We should begin by stating the opportunity, and then let the systems development cycle begin."

"A fine idea," said Professor Peasecod.

PART 3

Structured Systems

Is it possible to mold a massive information structure into a comprehensible and manageable entity? The answer is a resounding "Yes!" In the earlier chapters we examined problems, people, training requirements, communication requirements, and needs for general understanding.

In Part 3 specific, tested tools are offered for the improvement of any information processing scheme. Three plans are presented to promote organization, then control, and finally interdiscipline understanding.

The enemy of a computer information system is change. Few organizations adequately cope with this problem. The following chapters illustrate how systems and their documentation can be made to live and breathe.

Finally we will peer into the future, where we will find a very different world.

CHAPTER 11

The Job *Can* Be Finished

The general findings of studies related to the successful application of computers seem to indicate that "keys of achievement" can be expressed only in very general terms. Even the frequently quoted studies of McKinsey & Company, Inc., have found that it is seldom possible to identify the application of computer technology which now or in the future offers the most beneficial return to a company. Many times the results of the application do not justify the expense!

Today, technical hardware capability is far ahead of our ability to develop economic payoffs on many of the new applications. Profitable results are less evident, yet new applications continue to proliferate. Management is frequently dazzled by the science of information systems and operations research. Worse yet, management is goaded into using these tools by glib incompetents seeking self-aggrandizement.

Up to this point we have probed, tested, and criticized the people, machines, and systems involved in an on-going organization. We have offered specific and frequently short-term suggestions for improvements. We have presented generalized training programs for the systems analyst and the triumvirate of requestor/-

user/manager. Now we will begin to develop three specific and vital steps which, if taken, can lead toward a level of success not yet attainable by anyone, anywhere, who is responsible for information processing management. What is this level of success? We define it as follows:

> *The successful information system provides all routine and general exception requirements for operating personnel, based on normal organizational activity. New information requirements are always modifications to the existing information system and are fulfilled by a minimum caretaker staff without disruption to the existing informational and organizational structure or substantial additional resource allocations.*

Impossible! Well, perhaps. In certain circumstances the organization will never achieve the level of a successful information system, yet some others will be highly successful. In fact we like to think that there are three types of organizations where the mix of people, information science techniques, and even company philosophy can doom or nourish the information system.

The first type of organization we call . . .

THE N. CHAMBERLAIN ORGANIZATION (WHERE NOTHING WILL GO RIGHT)

In some companies the skill of the technicians, the quality of the hardware, or even the complete understanding by almost everyone of the needs for appropriate information will not serve to motivate the management. If any company is managed badly (and many are), a computer information system will only make things worse. Let us look at one such company.

One Friday evening Hugo and I were sitting around, having a few beers, when Hugo's brother Burt came in. From the look on his face, you could tell Burt was down—really down!

He came over, of course, when he saw us, and began telling us about the problems with his job. He'd been a systems analyst at the N. Chamberlain Company for almost 3 years, and the poor guy really had a story to tell.

Burt's Story

"That Chamberlain Company has to be the craziest place! You guys wouldn't believe the man I went to work for 3 years ago. He'd been a big deal in the conglomerate that bought Chamberlain. I don't know what happened, but he was sent down to us as controller. I think it must have been a demotion.

Naturally DP reported to him. And you know what? Here Chamberlain had a roomful of some of the fastest Monolithic Computer gear on the market, and this guy wouldn't allow any new applications! That's right, nothing new! I found out that I was hired for maintenance!

"It seems that the guy had had a fight with a Monolithic salesman years before—and he hated the company. In fact, it wasn't just Monolithic—he hated a lot of things. Everybody was scared to death of him. He'd fire people for almost no reason. You never knew what was right.

"I went in to see him one day after I'd been at Chamberlain a few weeks, and I proposed a new order entry system. The company had just scores of clerks copying and consolidating, and I had all that beautiful Monolithic equipment. Well, I just started to point out to him some of the opportunities available, and he began to chew me out. He gave me twenty reasons for not doing the system I hadn't even really proposed yet. He even told me to mind my own business! He'd scream at me, then he'd calm down, then he'd scream again.

"I was shaking all over when I came out of his office. One of the other guys laughed and told me he thought the man had megalomania. I've got to look that up some day."

Burt ordered another round of beers and continued.

"I would have quit, but later in the week he did the same thing to Mr. Basher. Now Mr. Basher was the division president and also came from the conglomerate home office. He wasn't afraid of the controller. So later that week we had a new controller, and DP was switched to report directly to Mr. Basher.

"My boss, Mulvey, was really elated about the change. Imagine the DP manager reporting directly to the president! But Mulvey found out pretty soon that it wasn't all that great. You see, Mr. Basher was trained at conglomerate headquarters too; in fact, he had to go back there once each month and report on his activity. That was really a grind. Every buck counted, and he demanded fantastic things from every department. Well, all the managers had to produce, and since the DP door had just been opened, everybody wanted to get in. Boy, did we work!"

"I remember," interrupted Hugo. "That was the year you worked Christmas Eve and Christmas Day and New Year's . . . ."

"And every Saturday and Sunday for months," finished Burt. "What a hassle! Poor Mulvey just about fell apart. He tried to please everybody. The cost of data processing went up about five times in one year. We automated Purchasing, and then lost all its vendor history records. The purchasing agents didn't know where they stood. We had all the order records in the machine. Then we got into Personnel, and the confidential officers' salary list got out. Wow!

"But what really did us in was the incentive system in the shop. Mulvey and I both worked on that. The factory manager made Mulvey start it up before we had all the bugs out. We paid some of those guys as much as $999.99 per hour. Then Mulvey couldn't fix things, and the pay was screwed up the second week. Mr. Basher fired him."

"And that's when you got promoted?" Hugo asked.

"Yeah, Mr. Basher gave me Mulvey's job, but with a new title. He made me director of data processing. Boy, am I thirsty," said Burt.

Since Hugo made no move to buy, I ordered another round. Burt thanked me for the beer and continued with his story.

"Being a director at Chamberlain is really something. You get an office with a door and a rug on the floor, and I could even eat in the executive dining room.

"What I had to do with DP, though, was to slow things down. We were trying to do too much, too fast. Those managers were just using DP to get Mr. Basher off their backs. So I established a budget and some long-range goals and had some meetings with the managers. We all agreed that there were some things that people could do better than the Monolithic equipment. Mr. Basher even attended the last meeting and expressed every confidence in my ability. Gee, I was surprised. After that, I didn't have any problems with my budgets and plans and with setting priorities. The one big thing I wanted to do was fix that order entry system I told you about. A great number of clerks were still there, and things were still moving slowly and costing Chamberlain a lot of money.

"It wasn't hard to get the sales manager and the marketing VP to agree to allow me to automate order entry. In fact they told me to do whatever I wanted and just keep them informed. What an opportunity!

"I pulled most of the DP staff off other jobs and started a crash program. We ordered our first CRTs, put all the inventory on disk and all the customers on tape, designed new forms, and were ready to go within my scheduled time of 7 months."

"Wow!" The word slipped out. I was impressed, and I told Bert so.

"I know," said Bert. "I did what everybody else tries to do. But Murphy's law really hit me. Mr. Basher was pushing those guys for better margins. So they let half the order entry people go the same day I had the system ready. I guess the other half that stayed weren't too happy with our new system. But those clerks would never even try to enter the orders the way they should. I never got 50% of the entry speed that Monolithic promised. And, of course, we never planned on the contention between programs in the CPU. That hurt too. But it was the price changes that really got me. Two days after we were up on the new system the marketing VP gave me a copy of a *confidential* new price sheet. It was a two-price system when we had always had only one price before. It was so confidential that he gave me the sheet the same day the new prices became effective.

"That was Monday. There was nothing I could do. It was impossible to change something so complex that rapidly. So this afternoon, I had to quit. But what gets me is that Basher has just made my assistant, a guy that I've barely got trained—Basher made him vice-president of data processing. Can you imagine that!"

Yes, it is hard to imagine, but many Chamberlain companies do exist. Regardless of the talent of the individual workers, the organization is shaped by and responds to the major executives. If through luck, longevity, relatives, friends, or the Peter Principle less than competent people have attained high positions, we cannot expect the organization to overcome the failings of its leaders.

Bert, too, can be counted among the less than capable people. He certainly made some glaring, yet common, errors. The schedule for development of a CRT order entry system within 7 months was far too optimistic. The system may have been too sophisticated and ambitious. It appeared that management abdicated to Bert the responsibility for systems design. In fact, would the new system support the user or simply delete people? Could the sales manager and marketing VP manage any better because of the new system?

In the N. Chamberlain Company nothing will ever go quite right. The problem is one which we are not prepared to address here. The problem is people. Fortunately it is not always this severe.

We have a second, less critical type of organization called . . .

THE C. BROWN COMPANY (WHERE THINGS CAN GO RIGHT)

Fortunately most companies are made up of intelligent, responsive people, aware of the organization, aware of the outside world, and even aware of each other. People in the C. Brown type of organization also want to make things right.

But the information analysts need every bit of help they can get. We have therefore suggested remedies and educational courses to transform good people into competent people. Applying some of the suggestions previously made to clean up the information environment may enable us to make things work better. While all the forces of human nature work against us, considering and implementing some of our remedies will, at least, prevent things from getting worse.

It is possible in the optimistic environment of a C. Brown Company to ask questions which might make a strong DP man blanch. Such questions might be:

- May I see the detailed project plans and your schedule?
- How do you plan to evaluate the system after it is installed?
- What are the standards for day-to-day operations?

The systems analyst who is a doctor of business will have the answers to these questions, for in the potentially successful C. Brown Company it is necessary to overcome the bland administrators, the zealous technicians, and the loquacious salesmen of COM, POS, more core, and other mechanical restoratives not necessarily appropriate to the organization's needs at the present moment.

This is a most difficult job! The good analyst and the good company can control, to some extent, the information explosion. Yet most managements have a difficult time just keeping up with disparate *internal* information. It frequently comes from different origins, and one item may at times be irreconcilable with another from a different source. Not only are there gaps in the system as it tries to meet the information needs of decision makers, but also the sum of the information parts is not equal to the whole organization. The good systems analyst, although an expert in jigsaw puzzles, finds that he still loses pieces, at least once in a while.

Three positive actions can be taken to make the sometimes insipid C. Brown type of company in a . . .

J. SEAGULL ORGANIZATION (WHERE THINGS ARE ALWAYS GOOD)

This is the inspired organization where the equipment, people, and objectives mesh well together. The Seagull Company recognizes that some change will always take place. And this change is treated as part of the ordinary challenges faced continually as the company reaches toward higher levels of success. Even with utterly unparalleled innovations in information processing, change can be controlled to appropriate levels and remain undisruptive to the organization. *The job can be finished!*

What changes and what does not change in information processing? It appears that three elements continually change.

- *The hardware changes.* If you want to use bigger, faster computers, then plan to modify almost everything to fully utilize the hardware. Don't put all the blame on the vendors. The users have had enough installations under the same roof, using cards with round holes on one side of the room and cards with rectangular holes on the other side of the room, to make us all ashamed. Tape versus disk, core size, minicomputers, CRTs, distributed processing, brand changes, terminals and so forth offer more continued change.

- *The languages change.* Take your pick: APL, PL/1, COBOL, ALGOL, FORTRAN, JOVIAL, or a thousand others. The information computer installation in your organization uses more than one language. It probably uses several. It may use more new languages in the future.
- *The software changes.* Dramatic changes take place in the ways in which data and programs are handled. These changes are usually more complex and more significant than hardware changes. Right now, your systems programmers are either starting or finishing the installation of a new software release.

These three elements of change consume major portions of data processing staff time and budget. You hear about these activities. You live with the conversion problems that they generate. You pay for them in terms of time and money. Yet it is difficult to correlate this expenditure to results in terms of sales and profits. The merry-go-round may go faster, and its tune may become prettier, but if you wait a bit the same horses will come around again. It is therefore vital to recognize what does not change.

What does not change is the organization, its elements, functions, and general purpose. The service or product you manufacture, distribute, or sell has not changed basically over the years. Similarly, the employees, customers, and markets have not changed appreciably. In some cases (women's fashions, home furnishings) we see the past simply evolving into the present. In other businesses (life insurance, refrigerators, book publishing) almost nothing has changed in a generation.

Sometimes, certainly, the organization modifies its objective in order to survive. Note the instances where medical science has completely eliminated certain dread diseases. The charitable organizations set up to combat these diseases and assist their victims did not go out of business. They simply adapted their operations to a new disease. The point is that they continue in much the same business, dealing in much the same way with the same clientele.

Let's look at the product or service you dispense and determine whether we are making a sweeping generalization or a factual statement.

If you are a manufacturer, wholesaler, distributor, or retailer, you have customers. If you operate a bank, finance company, insurance company, police department, church, university, or the like, you have accounts, loans, policies, prisoners, parishioners, students, and so on. The transactions between your organization and the appropriate second party are normally repetitive. The recorded data about this second party generally conforms to your requirements and your industry's common standards. Furthermore, all the data on employees, inventory, credit, purchases, advertising, market surveys, and so forth remains basically the same consistent, bare-bones facts over long periods of time.

For the purpose of argument, let's assume that you operate a fire department. Your organization has been in existence for a long time. The objective was and continues to be providing a service on demand. Your business started small, as all businesses do, with old equipment and limited territory.[1] As time went by, the territory expanded and the equipment greatly improved. You now have trucks, power ladders, water mains, an electronic alarm system, two-way radio communication, and new chemicals to fight fire. The equipment is constantly changing and improving. Employees have been born, worked, retired, and died, and the organization continues on, still working toward its same objective, still putting out fires.

The change which is important is the meaningful utilization (management) of the ever improving work tools available to assist you in meeting the objective of your organization. As we observe the fire department, we find it has many new tools. Yet the basic objective has not changed: a service is still available on demand. Equally important, we note that the basic transaction, consisting of a fireman with ladder, ax, and hose extinguishing a burning substance, is the same one that took place hundreds of years ago.

Although your organization is probably not a fire department, on the other hand it is unlikely that you are involved with something like the Polaroid camera. Here a completely innovative product challenged established industry markets and consumer habits.

The product you make or the service you dispense has not changed appreciably over the years. Oh, you've substituted plastic for many of the metal parts, you've streamlined the design, the advertising people have come up with a lot of razzle-dazzle about the NEW product—but it's still basically the same. Likewise, the customers are basically the same, and the *information* is basically the same.

Some organizations do succeed at the expense of their competitors. What does it? Advertising does it for some (Avis), marketing is the answer for others (IBM), product quality (Xerox) helps many. Beyond these types of examples we find few organizations which are dramatically successful because of the impact of production control, accounting, personnel, data processing, or administrative services.

---

[1] The first paid fire department in the United States was started in Boston, Massachusetts, in 1679.

Figure 12   **The customers don't change.**

Many organizations are secure financially, strong in the market-place, and continually successful only because their leadership has appropriately blended the minimum necessary support services, utilizing necessary basic information, with the transaction producing function. The realities of appropriate asset administration of people, things, and information structure have been recognized by the management.

In this J. Seagull type of organization we do not see management carrying out extensive programs of restructuring the company, only to retreat in the opposite direction a few years later. We do not see centralization followed by decentralization followed by centralization. We do not see salesmen paid commissions one year, no commissions the next, and then commissions again. We do not see salesmen replaced by representatives, followed again by representatives replaced by salesmen, again, and so on.

The management *does* strive continually to manage better. But it understands that something like an audio response system for a customer's bank balance is expensive and will not appreciably lure people away from the competition. The management understands that a skills inventory generally creates as many problems as it attempts to solve. It understands that if its inventory is not highly volatile (such as women's fashions), on-line, real-time inventory data through a POS system may be a most expensive and even destructive adventure into absurd information processing.

In the well managed J. Seagull Organization we find three information tools to maintain the consistency necessary to fulfill the long-term demands for meeting the second party in the transaction successfully. The three cornerstones necessary to relate good managers to the repetitive transactions in the marketplace are:

- A primary data base.
- A standard library of knowledge available from the information system.
- A consistent method of communication between the organization and the computer.

With these three tools we can diminish the impact of computer change. With these tools we can maintain a realistic outlook toward the marketplace and not be overwhelmed by electronic information processing glamour. With these tools a C. Brown Company can become a J. Seagull Organization. And, most importantly, the expense of conversion, disruption of information service, and the changes demanded by the requestor/user/manager can be controlled to the level where, in terms of systems development, *the job can be finished!*

Let's now begin to examine each of these vital tools.

THE PRIMARY DATA BASE

A certain limited number of record types are used by your organization to measure its activity. Most commonly you use information related to these areas:

1. Transactors—the customers, accounts, policyholders, patients you service, and so on.
2. A product or service bought or sold.
3. Employees.

For the sake of discussion let's talk about a transactor who is normally thought of as a customer. The customer's existence will require us to keep certain information about him within the company. We will need to know his name, address, purchases, accounts receivable data, salesmen, sales territory location, product purchase restrictions, advertising literature requirements, financial arrangements data, credit rating, credit limit, shipping arrangements, extra invoices required, freight costs, special pricing arrangements, and, finally, customer number.

It does not matter at this point how such records are kept. They can be on paper, microfilm, magnetic stripes on ledger cards, punched holes in cards, or inside a computer. What is vitally important is the necessity for RUM to recognize that the dozen or so items listed above are the limits of what may be available in terms of data. Your business may require a few different pieces of data from those listed. Seldom will anyone need more than twenty items of information about a customer.

The managers of marketing, advertising, order filling, shipping, and credit all make use of the same information. From this set of records they might ask:

- Where are our customers?
- Who are poor credit risks?
- Where are freight charges eating up the margin?
- Where are sales volume patterns changing?
- What did the customers buy?

There are other questions which we can ask if we connect the customer to the individual products. But in terms of the customer alone—the person who makes our organization exist—we soon reach a limit in the variations of information we can request. This is not to say that new vital customer measurement factors won't be developed. They will! But after we have sales analyses by territory, region, and area, by salesmen, by customer size, by general product groups, in dollar sequence, in item purchased sequence, and by a variety of assorted combinations of the above, where can we go?

The Primary Data Base has logical common sense limits. It consists of only a few types of records from which we draw most of the information for analysis and control. Although space is available to add new data (as new concepts develop), you will find that little space is necessary for this purpose. If the record developer had the necessary insight of a doctor of business, his systems experience has already captured most of the data appropriate to automate.

Some links to other records are necessary, and we will discuss the development of the Primary Data Base and refinements in the next chapter.

In any information situation the available data upon which any type of report is based is limited. The data is also generally the same in any industry. It is important to organize each *base* and record the few vital elements of data only *once*. Not only is this single recording, this nonredundant retention of limited vital data, the simple foundation for understanding and control of information, but also this most fundamental Primary Data Base will survive the frequent hardware and software modifications that seem to go on forever. Working with fewer sets of records simplifies the conversion tasks in data processing.

The Primary Data Base will not prevent proliferation of reports and pollution of the information system. At times, in fact, it becomes a simple source for unlimited rehashing of the same tired data. We therefore need a second tool to curb *management by minute variation.* We call this second device . . .

THE REPORTS BOOK

Mark Eting, the national soft line sales manager for Hunker Products, ran into the data processing manager's office. Mark Eting always ran!

"Wade, I've gotta have two reports right away!"
"O.K."
"I want a report by customer of everything they bought last year. I want it by product number, showing units purchased and sales dollars."
"But . . . ."
"The second report I need is sales and the open accounts receivable balance for each customer. I want a separate list for each salesman, and I want it in sequence by the largest customer to the smallest customer. Got it?"
"Yeah, Mark, but first I think. . . ."
"Wade boy, I gotta run. Get 'em quick, will ya? Our whole sales campaign will depend on how fast you come through."

Before Wade had a chance to say anything else, Mark Eting was out the door and running down the hall.

Wade was of course used to Mark by this time. He had the exuberance required of a man in his position as a national product manager. It was almost impossible—in fact, definitely impossible—to hold Mark still and get him to listen when he first came out with an idea. Wade waited until the next day and then called.

"Mark? This is Wade. Say, you know the two requests you gave me yesterday?

"Sure," replied Mark, who was now fidgeting because he was tied to his telephone cord.

"Well, that first report you asked for, which will list each product sale for each customer. . . ."

"Units and dollars!" interjected Mark.

"Yes, well, we have, as you know, over 3000 customers and more than 2000 active products."

"So I need it, Wade boy, just as soon as . . . ."

"Just a minute, Mark! That report will be over 50,000 pages long. It will be higher than the ceiling. Maybe something a bit shorter might be easier to work with."

"Umm . . . maybe you've got a point, Wade. Let me think about that one a bit. Bye!"

"Wait!" But Wade was too late. Mark had hung up and was already off down the hall again.

While Wade is dialing again, let's evaluate for a moment what happened. Both Mark Eting and Wade are dedicated and reasonable people. Wade just exercised some common systems sense and stopped the development of a large dose of pollution before it ever got started. This type of effort should be expected in a C. Brown organization.

"Mark, this is Wade again. I'm glad I caught you still in your office. Oh, you left and came back already! O.K. Look, Mark, I wanted to ask you about the other report. You know, where you need total sales and the accounts receivable balance by customer for each salesman. . . ."

"Sure, Wade boy, and don't forget the biggest customer to the smallest."

"Right, Mark. Well, I wanted to tell you that I took a look in my Reports Book—you know, where I keep a sample of every report we have the ability to produce—and I found that we already have just about what you want. We have it by territory number instead of salesman's name."

"Well, that's just about the same thing!"

"Right," continued Wade. "It's in customer name sequence, not dollar sequence, but most salesmen have only fifty to sixty customers."

"Well. . . ." Mark hesitated.

"Mark, the big difference is that you can have this report today, if you can use it, rather than wait 3 weeks for me to free up a programmer."

"Hey, Wade boy, why didn't you say so. Great, great! Send it up today. I need those 3 weeks to move my guys over the quota. I'll *make* it work. Bye!"

Wade was pleased. He had once again saved his group the effort of writing a program when something suitable already existed. Time and again Wade had found that good functional managers generally needed similar reports in order to accomplish their tasks. Promotions, retirements, and attrition brought forth a constant stream of requests from new managers for variations on the same theme.

Wade did not tell Mark Eting that the report he was accepting was designed by Mark's predecessor. Nor did he tell the production, warehousing, advertising, and purchasing people that some of what the current managers requested had been developed years before as their predecessors, and even the present incumbents, attempted to move from their present positions to points of possibly better control and then forgot about the reports.

Wade knew there was more than one way to skin a cat. His Reports Book frequently saved the expense of buying a new set of skinning instruments. This simple yet excellent tool is a pollution fighter. The Reports Book is a necessary requirement if the job is to be finished in a J. Seagull organization. With the help of the Reports Book *the job can be finished.*

We will have more later on this vital tool. Now, however, let's mention one final necessity to fight pollution and move data processing out of the whirling environment of constant change. We call this final contribution . . .

THE LOGIC PACKAGE

Almost everyone has heard about documentation. It comes in various sizes, shapes, and levels of complexity. It is almost never up to date. It is usually written by data processing people as a mandated requirement from DP management, in an effort to follow a computer solution. And sometimes no documentation exists in any form whatsoever.

Within the realm of information producing systems, the computer has become unquestionably the prime contributor of quantity and even quality data. Yet you may find that controlling a computer information system is much like owning a brand-new imported car. As long as the car runs well, you are complimented, admired, and even envied. When the car needs inevitable maintenance or repairs, however, mechanics shake their heads. They don't understand the car. They don't have the manuals, tools, parts, and savvy to easily repair it.

Unfortunately, the computer information system that you have today is much like a new type of foreign car. No one—we repeat, *no one*—understands what the machine does with all the problems presented to it. That is a bit frightening, but unfortunately it is the most common of circumstances. This situation has little to do with the complexity of the hardware or software. Nor does it represent a condemnation of the highly qualified technical programmers who make the machines produce.

Many organizations have made extensive efforts to discipline the sequence of events involved in using a computer to solve a business problem. In fact, in many situations literally millions of dollars have been spent in various methods of documentation.

Perhaps you use one of these:

- *Flowcharts done by the systems analyst.* This type of charting is frequently quite general and provides a loose framework for the programmer. Although the programmer complains of many loopholes, he enjoys the full scope of machine opportunities. If, however, the analyst has strong programmer training and interests, the programmer will find the flowcharts extremely detailed in terms of hardware options. He may be strongly incensed that his creativity has been inhibited.
- *Flowcharts done by the programmer.* This type of flowcharting is always necessary. The man who makes the machine perform for the business explains to himself and others, in some degree of detail, how he has done the job. Many programmers prefer to do their flowcharts *after* they have coded the job, especially when other documentation is available. Frequently the programmer's flowchart, or an automated printed version of it, is the only documentation that exists for a job.

    The programmer flowchart is a highly technical, usually strongly abbreviated and personalized document whereby one man explains to himself how he makes the machine function. It is very difficult to relate this type of documentation to the realities of the business problem involved and related ramifications.
- *Decision tables.* These have been rabidly supported by a minority of documenters. The decision table movement flourished in the sixties, waned, and now may again be gaining support. The physical construction of the decision table allows for the presentation of alternatives. It is less than an appropriate medium, however, when used to document the common, voluminous, sequential problem steps normally found in any program.
- *Narrative documentation.* This common method of documention consists of writing in paragraph form the outline or even the detailed steps required to solve a problem. The systems analyst has used the narrative with considerable success. Some organizations have gone so far as to hire English majors to write for the analysts in an attempt to purge any ambiguities from the text.

The flowchart and the narrative have been commonly accepted as methods of documentation in the data processing world. Unfortunately most documentation strategies are oriented toward capturing on paper *original problem* solutions. Generally we find imprecise methods of keeping documentation current. So, while we must avoid the technicalities of the decision table and the flowchart, as well as the obscure verboseness of the narrative, we continually fail with *any* method *to keep the documentation current.* When the time comes for change, for revision, or for conversion, we must all too often ignore the documentation and start from scratch. Why? Because the business process never stands still. The information system, within programs and between programs, has been changing, although often minutely, every day. The organization itself has been changing every day. But since documentation emphasis is placed on original creative work, maintenance and updating have fallen by the wayside. Here we pay the price in people and money and in the catastrophic failures recorded in the news media.

Because the documentation tells us only where we were and not where we are, it fails to accomplish its purpose: *to accurately reflect the current problem solution logic executing within the computer system.* You watch your dollars slide away as the programmer says quite truthfully, "I will have to rewrite the entire system. No one can figure out how it runs!"

We will tell you in Chapter 14 how to solve this problem with a method called the Logic Package.

The remedies are not difficult to take. Your organization can soar above the level of the C. Brown type of company up to the blissful blue skies of J. Seagull, where the information processing systems are appropriately relegated to the position of just one other support group necessary to make your organization succeed. Data Processing does not need to be the asset absorbing, time consuming, pollution proliferating department that it is today. Your objectives can be met, and change can be controlled.

Remember that three tools are needed: the Primary Data Base, the Reports Book, and the Logic Package.

CHAPTER 12

The Orchestra

The successful information system in a superior organization has been previously defined, in part, as one which "provides *all* routine and general exception requirements for operating personnel based on normal organizational activity." To put it quite simply, a superior organization doesn't become surprised by the normal, changing activities in the marketplace.

This successful information system is possible! Regardless of the service or product your organization provides, we find it self-evident that all of the functions within the organization can be reduced to three:

1. *Work flow* consisting of a network upon which a product is developed, manufactured, distributed, and sold or a service is dispensed and processed.
2. *Information systems* based on the internal and external transactions resulting from the work flow or necessary to support the work flow.
3. *Decision network* relating the work flow to the information system through organization structure. This decision network makes the immediate and long-term evaluations necessary to regulate the work flow or decisions based on the work flow.

Work flow networks and decision networks must be supported by an information system. It is the maximization of opportunity, through the evaluation of available information, that will provide the springboard for success. Comprehension of the importance of this interrelationship will seldom, by itself, generate success. Yet use of the information system is the necessary foundation for the control and creativity required to more successfully place your transactions in the marketplace.

We can't *make* a manager dynamic and creative. We can't *make* an organization successful. But we can provide the foundation upon which a good manager can plant his feet and make the organization grow. This foundation is not a series of reports. In fact, there is no vital report, fact, statistic, or ratio which is or can become the alchemy of organizational success. It is constant appraisal of the work flow network and imaginative use of the decision network that bring success. And the foundation upon which we can confidently rest our evaluation is called the Primary Data Base.

THE PRIMARY DATA BASE

A Primary Data Base is a logical structure of information. Seldom, except in television commercials, do we see people who are split right down the middle with one half going in each direction. Yet it is most common for an information system (even without a computer) to experience such a split personality. We don't call the parts (again as on TV) right side and left side. We call them (for example) Payroll Department and Personnel Department. Then you may have some considerable problems in attempting to put the halves together. Or consider the customer. Is he divided into pieces by lines of business? Is his credit data somewhere else? How about his accounts receivable and his sales history? How many ways is he split? Is this fragmentation of the logical information structure all we can offer a good manager as his foundation to make the decisions necessary to mold his good company into a most successful company? We think we can do better.

The Primary Data Base (PDB) is vital if the data processing group is going to finish the job. Within the computer system a PDB will facilitate retrieval of information and maintenance of records. Technically this is not the requestor/user/manager's concern. Retrieval of information to build reports is the province of the DP people. The same is true of the addition of information, the deletion of information, and the change of information (commonly called maintenance). Yet without the PDB structure, data processing spends large amounts of time combining different sets of records (payroll and personnel) to provide vital reports. Much more time may be spent in maintenance as the system tries to keep various sets of records coordinated and equally up to date. While time and money are spent to retrieve and combine and maintain various records in a non-PDB environment, the user languishes in a dark cave of inadequate knowledge. The problems encountered and the opportunities lost through mammoth gaps in appropriate communications are the subject of untold anguish by the RUM seeking to manage his environment appropriately. How can he put the puzzle together if he can't get all the pieces?

The Spring Joint

Back in the days before the National Computer Conference, we always found time for some great bull sessions concerning the industry.

I remember particularly one warm afternoon during an early spring joint. We all gathered in my room to rest our feet after looking at I don't know how many exhibits. Herb was there. So were Grace and Alan and several others. It was so warm Grace had taken off her hat!

We talked about COBOL, minis, the Australian Computer Society, and just about everything you could imagine. Perhaps because of the tech sessions we somehow got on to education and training.

During a millesecond lull in the conversation *(everybody in that group liked to talk)* Neal asked whether we'd like to see a historical gem in the process of systems development. Neal had his billfold out and was pulling a paper out of it before anyone had the opportunity to object. Grace looked the other way, expecting the worst. But Neal wasn't kidding! He had a report which his father had done in the late 1930s. It seems that his father was an efficiency expert who had attended a symphony in Boston. While technically oriented toward the subject, this man just didn't have much of an ear for music. But he certainly knew his job and was dedicated. When he came home from the concert he wrote a report. Neal read it to us, and it broke us all up. I'm sure he was putting us on, but it was funny. It went something like this, as nearly as I can remember.

The Report   "For considerable periods the four oboe players had nothing to do. The number should be reduced, and the work spread more evenly over the whole of the concert, thus eliminating peaks of activity.

"All the twelve violins were playing identical notes; this seems unnecessary duplication. The staff of this section should be drastically cut. If a larger volume of sound is required, it could be obtained by amplifying apparatus.

"Much effort was absorbed in the playing of demisemiquavers; this seems to be an unnecessary refinement. It is recommended that all notes be rounded up to the nearest semiquaver. If this was done, it would be possible to use trainees and lower grade operatives more extensively.

"There seems to be too much repetition of some musical passages. Scores should be drastically pruned. No useful purpose is served by repeating on the horns a passage which has already been handled by the strings. It is estimated that, if all redundant passages were eliminated, the whole concert time of 2 hours could be reduced to 20 minutes and there would be no need for an intermission.

"The conductor agreed generally with these recommendations, but expressed the opinion that there might be some falling off in box office receipts. In that unlikely event it should be possible to close sections of the auditorium entirely, with a consequential saving of overhead expenses, lighting, attendants, and so on. If the worse came to worst, the whole thing could be abandoned and the public could go to the movies."

While we all had a good laugh, Suki seemed particularly to enjoy the report.

"You Westerners," he said, "you haven't yet begun to appreciate the integrity of the whole being. I look at the electronic marvels you develop, and the sophisticated software, and wonder why you spend so little time relating it to the company that pays the bills for renting it. Everyone talks as if the company is there for the computer installation, rather than the other way around. That story about the orchestra wasn't so funny when you look at the way one part of the business is automated first, and then later some other part is tackled. I think the industry has spent most of its time since the mid-1950s eliminating oboe players."

"And I suppose it's different in Japan?" asked Alan.

"Yes, drastically so," replied Suki. "In my country we never stop learning. People join an organization and expect to stay for life. Unlike you job-hoppers, our people retire from the company they start to work for. The employee becomes totally dedicated to his company, since he knows it is a lifetime job. He is therefore expected to work toward the organization's development as a total entity, and not just functional or short-term goals. The company in turn may provide housing, vacation trips, baby-sitters, and things like that in addition to a guaranteed job."

"Paternalistic," muttered Herb.

"Well, maybe it is," continued Suki.

"But what I am trying to tell you about is our method of combined self-improvement and a broader outlook, all of which is helping us build some dynamic organizations."

"How does it work?" asked Grace.

"It starts as soon as a man leaves school and joins an organization. He is assigned to an older worker who watches out for him—sort of a godfather. This man is not his boss, but just helps him along and keeps an eye on him."

"You mean this 'godfather' makes sure that the new man does things right so he will get a raise and get promoted?" questioned Pearl.

Suki replied, "Not really. In our system the worker gets a raise even if he does not do well. It's a matter of seniority."

Several people shook their heads, but Suki continued.

"Then not only the new employee, but everybody in the company, goes to school. You would have to be acquainted with Zen Buddhism to understand why. But basically everyone continues on a program of self-improvement. The whole idea is to enable a man to do his present job with continually widening vision, continually increasing competence, and continually rising demands on himself.

"When he learns about other people's jobs, he understands why it is necessary for him to perform his own tasks carefully. In our Japanese factories our engineers and methods people design jobs *with* the work crew, not *for* the work crew as you do."

"And this expensive training, promoting incompetents, and paternalism is a better way?" snorted Herb.

"Aahh, you Americans! You think only your way is best. We have some problems, just as you do . But let me tell you this: our education for the complete organization is beginning to pay off. Our total knowledge and sharing of functional requirements and problems is eliminating bottlenecks you haven't solved yet. Your organizations spend half their time just trying to get departments and divisions to work together. Just wait. You think all we Japanese can do is make radios with cheap labor. You Americans think you can travel around the world, buy up land and companies, and make anything. By the 1970s you'll see Japan buying *your* companies!"

Although I haven't seen Suki in years, his message has stayed with me. In his own way he had explained that a more comprehensive understanding of the entire organization resulted in a better mousetrap. A simple but complete organization of information into a comprehensible structure *can* make an organization more successful. And since I listen to music on a Japanese hi-fi and my TV set is Japanese and my car is Japanese, I must say, "I believe!"

Why Bother?

Compiling the Primary Data Base is unquestionably thought to be a complex and costly chore. But it is vital for you, as the *conductor* of all or part of an organization, to utilize this cornerstone of management control through information provided by a PDB. It is possible for a few exceptional managers to lead well by instinct. A few others may also do well with complete knowledge of a few business functions, especially the discipline in which the manager trained. But for most of us it is necessary to draw all the functions together, blend, refine, and modulate them, and then *lead* the organization to success. As in an orchestra, each part must start as directed, do the appropriate job capably, and finish as directed. To accomplish this task all the parts must be led by a man who *knows the score.*

The Primary Data Base is the tool that allows the manager to orchestrate his environment. Most importantly, the PDB provides *simplified understanding* of a very complex organism, which is the business itself. Business and technical functions tend to obliterate simple, necessary tasks. There is a "prima donna" complex in all of us which, over time, refines the work to absurd levels of detail. As an organization ages, it becomes a labyrinth of minute detail, reports, and forms.

If the PDB were an orchestra, the music it would play is "We Shall Overcome!" The PDB is the information pollution fighting enemy of management by variation of data. It forces standardization upon the organization. Input of information must meet standard requirements. Just as a member of the orchestra must be an accomplished musician, so the data entered must meet certain admission requirements. For example, a new charge account may require a credit validation and rating before shipment of the order. The standard input requirement into the data base, in this situation, becomes the control for three functions (sales, credit, and shipping) to coordinate their efforts.

Beyond input standardization, the PDB influences the development of single-entry input. By its construction the date base fosters the logical collection of input information at one time and in one place. Not only are data processing costs reduced by simplified handling, but also an orderly yet demanding process of input actions must be maintained.

An equally important benefit of the PDB is that it minimizes redundancy of files and file content. Remember the skills inventory that Hugo was trying to develop? Miss Miller and Hugo found the same data recorded over and over again. This repetition does not occur only on paper. It occurs all too frequently within the computer system as well. It is a most natural outgrowth of the automation of pieces of the business, and pieces of the information system, at different times. The expense of this natural system is more than input costs, maintenance costs, or continual program modifications to combine various files. The *real* cost is management's inability to understand the organization, its interrelationships, and its position in the marketplace.

If the conductor fails to call upon his percussion section, the concert will be flawed. If he continues the trend, soon no one will be attending his concerts.

The Concept

The Primary Data Base concept is really quite simple.

1. *Identify* the basic transactions which are the foundation of the organization. There are only a few. You purchase items. You

employ workers. You sell an item or a service. Perhaps you manufacture a product. Beyond these basic transactions, how vital is the rest of the information flow to your organization's success? Oh, without question, you must file quarterly 941a forms, listing earnings for Social Security purposes. But this type of report and data *is not* vital to you or your business. *It is,* however, necessary for the controller and his function. Therefore, if you can identify "employees" as basic, rather than "Accounting Department" or "Payroll" as basic, you have defined one of the primary pools of information for yourself and almost all business requirements relating, in this instance, to people.

2. Through the data processing group, *organize* the information about the basic transactions into a few sets of records (files). The physical construction of such data base files is not significant to our discussion. The concepts and ability of your DP people and the physical constraints imposed upon them by the hardware will force them to develop their own approach to data base development. It is absolutely necessary, however, to repudiate the mistakes and apparent necessities of the past.

Information (data) must be recorded only once in its complete transaction form. It may update various parts of the same record, but for different purposes. For example, an employee's paycheck should be captured in total with a historical record of all deductions and withholdings. This *picture* of the paycheck and stub is not a PDB record. It is a historical record retained in an electronic medium (perhaps magnetic tape) for low, but required, future demand.

Nevertheless there is a PDB employee record which consists of vital personnel and payroll events. Except for pieceworkers, this record is the source of pay rates, the source of authorization to pay (payment is automatic unless stopped by an override entry), and the source of various necessary financial accumulations. Balances, such as those resulting after FICA and savings bond deductions, and commission payments, are recorded here. These balances will be needed and used again the next pay period. It is important to recognize that the necessary PDB record is "employee" and not paycheck or payroll.

One more example may be helpful. Let us examine that most vital transaction, the sale. What is involved? A sale involves movement in an inventory record. Balances of the item must change. A sale involves a customer. Amounts in dollars and perhaps an accounts receivable balance must change. But the sale itself is a historical record, like the paycheck. It must be captured and retained, but it is not a PDB record. The data base records are "customer" and "inventory," and the transaction record (a sale) updates both of them and becomes a historical record.

Without question a considerable degree of data processing effort, information dissemination, and management analysis revolves around the sale record. In certain cases this transaction record will be a PDB record. In far, far too many cases the information about a sale is captured, reviewed, analyzed, and resummarized in unnecessary and meaningless reports. We find in too many situations sales records by item within customer, or even by product line, far too voluminous to generate meaningful management action. Such detail can usually serve to prove any side to any question. The customer and inventory PDB records already contain meaningful data which is seldom used. Few companies will examine the sales history within the inventory record and prune the products that consist of 80% of the line but only 20% of the sales. In many cases we find one-third or more of the line generating far less than 1% of the sales. Yet each item in the line incurs the same expense within the catalog, the information system, and to some extent the physical storage system. But it is the transaction record (the sale) which is continually analyzed, while the vital inventory movement data is ignored.

The Primary Data Base record is not the transaction. It is rather a few different basic records around which most transactions revolve. In a manufacturing organization we might find that only a few such records are needed. They might be:

EMPLOYEE
INVENTORY
CUSTOMER
PURCHASE ORDER
ACCOUNTS RECEIVABLE
BUDGET RECORD
SALE
PRODUCTION ORDER

Ideally these few PDB records serve as the single entry accumulation points for most of your organization transactions. These few records become the foundation for success. They are limited in scope to the most vital data. They are consistent in terms of forcing transactions to meet standards. They provide a simple link between the user, the manager, and the organization. It is this link, based on commonly accepted and understood data, that allows the operating manager and the chief executive officer to manage by innovation and to master the marketplace. It is hard to go somewhere else if you don't know where you are. The PDB gives you your bearings.

THE KEY

The well read manager is familiar with the many classical and current theories of the management process. While a current favorite happens to be management by objectives (MBO), we cannot ignore some of the other valid, although sometimes conflicting, hypotheses. In addition to MBO we have management by communication, management by results, management by exception, management by participation, management by motivation, and so on.

One of the most intriguing theories (and perhaps the most valid of all) is management by CSROEPM.[1] The author's abbreviated title stands for "Management by Communication, System, Results, Objectives, Exception, Participation, and Motivation, and he argues, quite validly, that no single technique is itself sufficient for good management. It is the combination of various management theories, personal style, and information which makes the successful manager and the successful company. But any style manages *with information,* and the key to the information pool is the simplicity with which it is organized.

Only two steps have been identified for the conceptual development of a data base. These tasks are, again, as follows: first, identify the basic transactions, and, second, organize the transactions into a few files. We now must add a third task: *beware of the complicators*.

Into the information arena stride the technicians, the salesmen, and the "make mountains out of molehills" gang who want to compete for your attention and consume the budget. A few words of warning about each of them.

The Technicians

Talk of a data base will bring out the very finest jargonese among your DP people. They will speak at length of organization structures, indexing techniques, randomizing techniques, access methods, backup,

[1] William H. Bayliss, "Management by CSROEPM," *Harvard Business Review,* March–April 1969.

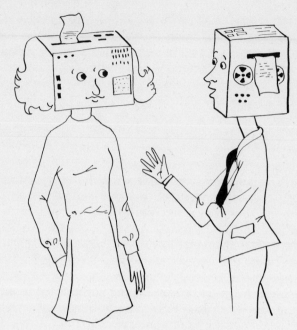

Figure 13   **The technicians.**

restart and recovery techniques, file reorganization, and many other technical matters. DON'T EVER BECOME INVOLVED IN THIS KIND OF CONVERSATION! Don't even listen! When it starts, stand up and leave, or tell the DP people to handle their technical problems in their own department. Insist on *recording only basic transactions and developing just a few files.* The DP people can do these things if they understand that you really intend to maintain simplicity. Technical considerations have scuttled far too many systems. Don't participate—demand a simple system, and data processing will deliver it.

The Salesmen

Talk of a data base will very shortly bring salesmen. They will present to you a variety of products. Some of the names you may hear are IMS II, System 2000, TOTAL, GIM, GIS, Disc Forte, ADABAS, IDS, and Mark IV. What are these products? Well, with marked degrees of capability, each of these can be classified as a data base management system—DBMS for short. These packages are designed primarily to link data, maintain the connections, establish new records, delete old ones, and finally provide a reporting system capable of cross referencing, sorting, calculating, and extracting information. There may be some disagreement over the details of a *generalized* system, but a DBMS has to support a wide variety of data representations and a broad range of operational capabilities.

There are strong arguments favoring a DBMS. A vendor supplied and documented system will be more easily maintainable and better supported than a product designed by your own DP personnel. Furthermore a generalized system may be more adaptable to data management requirements accompanying institutional changes.

But, if we turn over the coin, we find that almost any DBMS is an intricate bit of software. It is probably second only to operating systems in its complexity, overhead requirements, and maintenance problems. Furthermore both data processing hardware and business organizations are complex and diversified in structure. Thus a DBMS must be very general and very large to handle the diverse data and functional requirements existing within all types of potential customer organizations. Upon installation of a DBMS, the computer operations manager will repeat loudly the first two DP words he ever learned: "More core!"

While there is an appealing argument from the salesman to simply rent his DBMS package and thereby avoid an impossible task, a do-it-yourself approach has some merit. If your programmers are technically competent (and most are), you should consider the advantages of a DBMS written in house. A tailored system will be considerably more efficient with little loss in flexibility. Your primary data base can be designed to your own needs and specifications. Remember that a DMBS package accommodates the files and data already there and produces the same existing reports, as well as new ones. It perpetuates what you have. You may need something better. Before you buy, ask yourself this question: "If I am going to buy a generalized DBMS to handle all of my information systems, why didn't I purchase a general accounting system or budgeting system or asset depreciation system years ago?"

The answer to this question is a function of both time and money. Consider the cost of a DMBS projected against the value and time of an in-house development. If you are willing to accept the previously suggested concept of a Primary Data Base and the fact that every organization contains major pools of data, unrelated to other pools of data, you are at the threshold of a major challenge. It is now possible to consider that you *can* write your own DBMS. Pick an obviously definable collection of data. For example, try "employees," "customers," or "inventory."

Take a creative systems analyst and a hot-shot programmer or two, and turn them loose to build a DBMS.

Many times the effort produces delightfully rewarding results. Several small "home grown" packages may in total be much cheaper and certainly more efficient than a major generalized package. Although we are at the forefront of internal change with our DP tools, many professionals shy away from internal software development. "Why reinvent the wheel?" they ask. Yet this truly exciting experiment of building a partial DBMS is probably within the cost and technical limits of your staff. A sincere effort may prove highly rewarding.

The "Mountains out of Molehills" Gang

The final *complicator* in a data base development scheme is a group we call the "mountains out of molehills" gang.

A Primary Data Base is a shortcut to management control. Any shortcut—in fact, any change in present routine—is normally regarded as a threat by most human beings. If data from transaction A was accumulated on report B and made a part of report C, then moving the transaction directly into the PDB will cause a tremendous stir. Unique, once-a-year, specially handled transactions will now become vitally important. Short-term, short-sighted objectives may impede a PDB construction. Don't let the EDP technicians frighten the users with technical jargon. And don't let the users distort the systems design with every aberration of data that pops into their heads. Both groups can be members of the same "gang." Keep the miniminds at bay by taking the full-blown committee designed PDB recommendations and time schedule into consideration. Then demand that the schedule be cut by one-third or one-half only by reducing the size and complexity of the data base. If you are tough enough to enforce such a plan, you will find the DP people can get it on the air, the user group can function satisfactorily with the results, and the whole organization will operate a bit better and a bit cheaper.

The Three-Dimensional Data Base

We have defined the Primary Data Base as consisting of vital sets of transaction records written into a few simply structured major files of information. The PDB reflects *now* status within the organization. Most business and management decisions are based on just such now information. When times are good, the PDB is projected into the future and management talks about forecasts. When times are less than good, the PDB of past times is reviewed and refined (employee head counts suddenly become important), and management talks about budgets.

Our most important version of the data base is the *now* information set which we call the PDB. It reflects the position of the organization today. The PDB removes the chains of obscurity imposed by the accounting cycle. Sales, amounts payable, amounts receivable, even payroll and depreciation can be calculated each week, each day, perhaps each transaction, depending on your needs, for the PDB is the reflection of the business *now!*

A secondary data base is compiled by capturing relevant points of time and storing them for normally low activity, archival, and historical use. The SDB can be dumped and saved on a cheap medium such as tape. Then it becomes possible to compare past points in time, combine them, project them, and develop forecasts from this secondary data base structure.

The Mutated Data Base

For all of its advantages a data base has a great danger built into it. The simplistic design of the information structure develops a finer level of understanding at the requestor/user/manager level. Not only can RUM see daylight; he also can frequently see opportunity for improvement with management information tools. This is as it should be. But there is a great danger of information pollution. Too many reports may be developed with minimal justification. At the conscious level this pollution can be controlled, and the next chapter will offer specific remedies for too much paper. Frequently, however, we find a lack of perception on the part of all concerned as a data base is used by RUM and time passes. It is a fact that *data bases breed!*

Data bases breed by comparison and by calculation. A comparison occurs when two or more sets of data are put together in a form not commonly available, or a set of data is sorted into a new sequence. Then the new sequence is saved. It may be added to and acted upon. The same situation occurs when a set of data has a factor or factors applied against it. Again it is saved, added to, and acted upon. In other words something as simple as sorting the inventory into sequence by annual sales dollars, developing one new piece of data, and saving it creates a mutated data base.

Because the information in the PDB has been altered and the new data has been saved, we now have a new data base. We can expect management to call upon the revised data base structure, in addition to the PDB, for new reports and evaluations. The new structure may

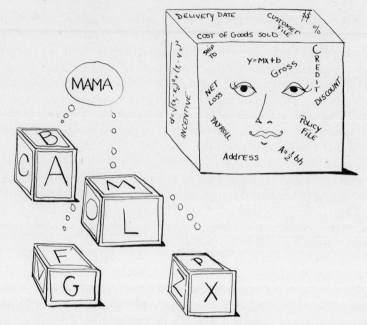

Figure 14   **Data bases breed.**

itself be modified to still something else—a third-generation data base.

Over time these mutations will bring back the clouds of confusion that generally obscure profitable data processing applications today. If the combination or the sequence or the factoring is of sufficient importance to be retained, add it to the PDB. Don't build expensive iterations of similar data, slightly modified for slightly improved computer or human operation. Previously we have argued that the computer must never run more efficiently at the expense of any human need or organizational goal. By the same token we must never build new data bases for slightly improved organizational results. The expense is far too great. If the objective is not dramatically demonstrable, it is not worth the effort and the consumption of resources incurred by creating another version of the data.

Management control must be exercised, or, like rabbits, the PDB will breed.

CONCLUSION

If you are processing information on a functional basis, plan to develop a Primary Data Base. If you think that you already have a data base, review its structure. Does it collect your few major transactions into just a minimum number of files which become the source for your major decision networks? Probably not, because the computer information system was put together over many years with little recognition of appropriate basic interrelationships of functional information points.

If, hopefully, you intend to build a superior information system, begin today to develop a PDB. Don't let the software and hardware salesmen tell you what you need. Don't let them make modifications which slightly improve a less than ideal basic information structure. *And don't get a larger computer!*

Do identify the few transactions and files that are the basis for most of your management decisions. Make a plan and start slowly. Save what you can of the existing information structure. But use a doctor of business systems analyst to organize the project and to develop a realistic schedule, measureable goals, and a satisfactory staff. Finally, supply management support to get the job done.

The key to management control through the use of information systems is a Primary Data Base. As the conductor, as the leader of many professional talented experts, it is *you* who blends their many different sounds into an orchestrated piece. The musicians, within the limits of the capabilities of their instruments, the score you've arranged, and their technical ability, play *your* music. They do not create their own tunes.

The Primary Data Base is your musical theme. An outstanding performance requires the application of your leadership.

CHAPTER 13

The Reports Book

Mr. Dillon's eyelids fluttered a bit. He was drowsy after a heavy lunch. The buzz of his intercom abruptly cleared his head.

"Yes, Mrs. Forish?"

"Mr. Dillon, the Reverend Mr. Phoenix is here to see you."

"Send him right in, Mrs. Forish."

"Mr. Phoenix, I am so glad you could find time to come today. Since you've agreed to become a member of Dillon's board of directors, I felt it would be most appropriate to give you some insights into our operations, as well as a tour of our facilities, before your first board meeting."

"Thank you, Mr. Dillon. As a man of the cloth, this is a new experience for me. I really know nothing of the leasing and franchising business."

Mr. Dillon soon discovered that the Reverend Mr. Phoenix was completely truthful. For over 2 hours he explained in the most rudimentary terms the nature of the leasing industry and the Dillon Company's business. But then he also had no complaints. He had selected the clergyman to join his board of directors basically to establish and maintain the standards of integrity and credibility so often lacking in the business world.

Finally Mr. Dillon suggested a tour of the offices. He was more accustomed to asking questions than answering them and explaining so much detail gave him a headache. Yet, he had to admit, the Reverend Mr. Phoenix was learning quickly.

Today, as always, the outstanding feature of Mr. Dillon's tour was the final stop in the computer room. From the *Harvard Business Review,* vendor courses, and his own people, Mr. Dillon had some understanding of what the Monolithic computer system did for his company. He was particularly proud that, years ago, Dillon's had been a beta test site. The computer room itself was impressive! Locked doors required a passkey, and the noise, operator chatter, and flashing lights made quite a show.

Drinking all of it in, the Reverend Mr. Phoenix finally turned to Mr. Dillon and asked, "What is all of this equipment doing?"

"Well," replied Dillon quickly, noting that nothing was coming off the printer, "it must be updating some records."

"How can you tell?"

Slightly exasperated, Dillon answered, "For all the rent I pay on this equipment it better be doing something!"

The Tip of the Iceberg

It doesn't matter exactly what the Monolithic computer was doing at the time Mr. Dillon and the Reverend Mr. Phoenix were watching it. At the time it was being observed, it was not producing any reports, messages, or directives for the human beings working with it. A computer, in fact , must often run in this mode. Our point is this: a computer information system will generally not benefit any decision making process until it produces some results in a form understandable by human beings. Furthermore, any report, information, or prepared data put together by a computer or by clerks or by managers must serve a useful purpose. Unfortunately, much of the information which is produced, from any source, serves no purpose at all!

Our objective in this chapter is to clear away the shrouds of fog surrounding the information part of the iceberg, which is generally visible and its dimensions definable. But remember that every organization must pay for the entire iceberg (invisible preparation costs, as well as somewhat visible results). We find that even the portion above the surface is usually not well recognized, completely understood, or, for that matter, even stable.

Since reports are the visible, usable output of the information system, we will offer a device to control and illuminate these expensive products. We call this tool the *Reports Book*. It is by far the least expensive control, and the one easiest to install, suggested for your use. It will in turn provide for you the highest level of control for the expense and effort required. Additionally, the Reports Book will provide a threshhold for improved performance and possibly some data processing cost reductions. But first let's look at. . . .

THREE HISTORICAL APPROACHES TO INFORMATION CONTROL.

Information production has long been recognized as containing volatility demanding control. The sheer number of repetitious information documents produced by accounting, data processing, personnel, and the various production aspects of the business simply cries out for some form of control.

First Approach: Report Numbering

Usually the amount of regulation in regard to standard information production is minimal. Beyond the commonly accepted requirement of a title (which is often ignored), the most frequently used control is a report number. In fact, if a report number (i.e., A, B, C, D, etc., or 1, 2, 3, 4, etc.) exists it often becomes the internal organizational identifier for the document. The monthly budget statement, for example, may become commonly known as the "B-1."

Such structuring is a first positive control approach. The report number allows two individuals or two departments to talk about the same information. It positively identifies the container of data (the report) with the shorthand exactness necessary in an organization filled with "sales reports," "margin reports," "budget statements," "production reports," and the like.

Second Approach: A Paperwork Controller

In a world long cluttered with the ever increasing results of faster information production devices, and a more complex marketplace with strangling regulations, each organization has reacted. Whether your facility is 1 year or 100 years old, it is continually making new responses to the current situations it encounters. Seldom, however, does it take the opportunity to discontinue information flows previously generated to meet demands that are now no longer vital.

Such proliferation was recognized by the management of larger organizations long before the commercial development of the computer. A human being has become the second classical control, filling the gap developed by functional lines and busy daily routines. Then and now it is not unusual to find a company official with the title of "forms controller" or "data controller" or "reports controller." The goals of such a position are classifically legitimate:

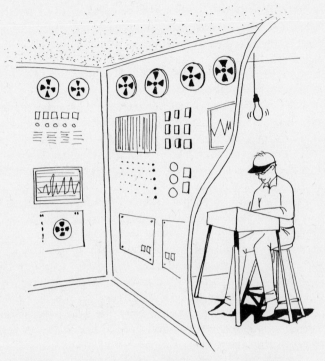

Figure 15   **Faster results with the same old methods.**

- Develop and maintain a minimum level of standards.
- Appropriately design reports for both human and machine use.
- Assign control numbers to each report.
- Prevent redundancy.
- Assist report developers with the construction of information in accordance with their needs.
- Weed out and discontinue unnecessary reports.

The goals are rarely achieved!

Unfortunately, the function is often placed with the Purchasing Department. Because forms and paper are expensive and come from outside the company, it has been frequently argued, quite successfully, that the control of forms should be delegated to a purchasing agent (PA). In these instances control numbers are rigorously assigned and "best buys" are made, but little else is achieved in the way of control. The vastly more expensive aspects of pollution are ignored as the daily ongoing demands of purchasing are satisfied.

More often the "reports controller" resides in the Data Processing Department. This individual has the opportunity and the background necessary to provide a wider range of appropriate controls. All too frequently, however, he loses his credibility as he delves into the technical aspects of information production. His horizons, like those of the PA, are frequently limited.

The PA sees and evaluates to some extent all special forms. But the massive bulk produced by the computer is beyond the demands of his function, since he buys only the stock paper without the ability to evaluate its use. In turn the position, when in the Data Processing Department again faces severe constraints. Here the reports controller can often make many valid contributions to machine generated reports. But the preprinted forms associated with non-DP information generation are all too frequently routed around him or simply purchased directly.

Neither position deals adequately with the mountainous financial information flow generated and supervised by the sometimes cantakerous financial controller. As guardian of the assets, he may exempt his own function from report controls, while at the same time fulfilling the position of top management for data processing.

In instances where the function is successful within the goals outlined, we often find an extremely powerful executive holding or controlling the position. Success is often related to the personality of the incumbent.

Third Approach: A Reports Inventory

The third common approach to report control is called reports inventory. As the name implies, a physical inventory is taken. Each report is identified, its content determined, and its distribution documented. The reports inventory affords an excellent opportunity to illuminate redundant and irrelevent reports. It highlights improper distribution whereby detail reports flow above the levels of management needed to act on them. The inventory exposes pockets of unnecessary data flow where certain executives are on far too many distribution lists.

The reports inventory is a favorite tool of the outside consultant. It is simple to perform. It produces immediate savings. It justifies the consultant's work. The same technique can be used effectively for internal cost reduction programs. The inventory is worthwhile as a housecleaning device. But just as the speeding motorist slows down when he spots a policeman, and speeds up again when the latter is out of sight, so too with the reports inventory program. It will clean up bad

situations, and it will reduce costs. But it leaves nothing to prevent
the same situation from recurring again and again.

WHY ARE WE HERE?

More than anything else, information processing staffs are seeking
to provide a product of *quality* information. No matter whether a computer or a human being produces the information, resources are consumed to produce it, transport it, evaluate it, and file it. Worst of all,
"it" may not be at all what is wanted, what is vital, what is correct, or
what is capable of being produced.

The historical controls already mentioned generally fail to fulfill
the vital goals of making the information system more meaningful.
Report numbering is good control, but that's all it is. A reports inventory only looks backward. And very few "report controllers" ever find
time to make things better, since much of their work revolves around
the technical aspects of their prime job functions.

Just the other day I was having lunch in the company cafeteria with Pearl,
our agronomist, when Norm and "Mo" came over to join us. These two fellows
are both entomologists (i.e., they studied bugs) and were so wrapped up in their
work that they never did anything but talk shop.

The last time we had met, they had talked all through lunch about
Chionaspis furfura. Pearl told me later that they had been discussing the life
cycle of mealybugs.

Today, however, seemed a little better. Mo was from the Mideast and was
describing some of the wildly different and funny species from his part of the
world. I was fascinated, in fact, as Mo described a member of the Tineidae.

It seems that Mo had been born and raised in the city of Tabrig, in north-
western Iran. After studying entomology in the United States, he returned
home for further research. Less than 50 miles from his birthplace, Mo found in
the swamps of Lake Urmia one of the strangest insects in the world, called
Lysimachia nummularia or processionary caterpillars.

These inch-long insects feed upon pine needles. As Mo described them, they
move through the trees in a long procession, one leading and the other
following—each with his eyes half closed, and his head fitting snugly against
the rear extremity of his predecessor.

Mo was delighted to find such rare specimens and attempted an experiment. Finding a group on a large pine tree, he directed them patiently around
the trunk. After many tries he succeeded in getting the first one connected up
to the last one, thus forming a complete circle which started moving around in
a procession that had neither beginning nor end.

He expected that after a while they would catch onto his joke, get tired of
their useless march, and start in some new direction.

Figure 16   **The processionary caterpillar.**

But not so. Through sheer force of habit, the living, creeping circle kept moving around the pine tree, around and around until the insects dropped from sheer exhaustion and ultimate starvation.

Additionally, as a scientist, Mo had observed that an ample food supply of pine needles, plainly visible, was near at hand. It was outside the range of the circle, however, so the insects continued along the beaten path.

While Mo indicated that the caterpillars were following an instinct, it occurred to me that many of my colleagues performed their functions out of habit, custom, tradition, precedent, past experience, "standard practice," or whatever term you may use, but they were following it blindly.

They mistook activity for accomplishment.

They meant well, but they got no place.

Unfortunately many of the reports used by RUM seem to tumble blindly out of the clerical or computer system. These reports, in themselves, have type characteristics as strange as those of the processionary caterpillar.

TYPES OF REPORTS

Transactions.   Information is processed because some activity took place. Sales have been made, checks have been processed, labor has been expended in the factory, shipments have been sent, and so on. Transaction type data reports may be generated basically for three reasons:

1. To record the activity of the transaction.
2. To record secondary effects from the transaction.
3. To report information status as a result of the transactions, with summaries.

Time.   Information is processed because a period of time has elapsed. The most common time transaction is the monthly financial statement. Each common period of measured time (i.e., day, week, month, quarter, and year) brings with the turn of the calendar a slew of reports. Time type data reports are produced with three possible different sets of data circumstances:

1. Activity took place during the period and is duly reported.
2. No activity took place during the period, but a report is still generated.
3. Real-time (NOW) activity is the period of time, and you have a current exact status, such as a radar screen, an electrocardiogram, or an airline reservation system.

Exceptions.   Information is processed because a set of circumstances has been determined which might require action. Some sophistication begins to appear, since a deviation from an established norm or a particular set of sought-for conditions is reported. Exception type reports generally fall into the following categories:

1. Exceptions outside of preestablished limits, which are reported on a scheduled basis—for example, all checks over $10,000 cashed today. To some extent this is also a time report, since even if no checks of this limit were cashed, the information system would work to make this determination and then report the absence of the exception.
2. Exceptions from the existing file data, prepared as a nonrecur-

ring report and usually applied against some form of data base with a report generator—for example, all items for sale with inventory on hand greater than last year's sales of the item. This type of report is far from new. It has been hard coded or clerically prepared ever since records came into existence. The two criteria of data base and report generator make the exception report a feasible management tool.

Probes.   Information is processed with intense, detailed inquiry for a period of time. The probe data so developed did not previously exist in its present form, and its production is not intended to become a part of the normal flow of information. Usually a probe results from a special management program or the interest of a key executive in a particular subject. The detail and complexity of the information place the project beyond the capabilities of the report generator and/or the file organization. Probes generally exist in three forms:

1.   The quick and dirty (Q & D) probe is the familiar request from the front office for special information *now:* The Q & D probe is usually directed at the Accounting Department for financial facts. It results in a flurry of fuzzy figures, with much anguish and allocation by the controller. If directed toward the Data Processing Department, the oldest programmer is pressed into service to work all night to code up something in a simple but antiquated language everyone else forgot.
2.   Calculated probes are well thought out, extensive inquiries which may change management policy by providing insights into alternative courses of action. For example, a study of freight rates by rail, truck, and seasonal product movement by territory might not be possible through the exception reporting system and might require a special probe.
3.   Future probes are simulations and forecasts which examine some history and some imputed market trends to provide keys to the future.

BLOOD TYPE S (SURVIVAL)

Sometimes earlier we noted that information is the life blood of any organization. Type of business, size, and objectives do not matter. Unless you know where you are, you will never be able to move anywhere else or to know if you get there. Yet misuse of information and lack of information (intended fraud or the charismatic manager not considered) will stifle progress and occasionally cause failure.

A not so obvious handicap to a manager's ability to manage involve trying to match real-world conditions with information. Why, so often, do we have a mismatch? Some of the reasons are as follows.

Excessive Volume.   The high speed printer may some day be classified as an enemy of society. Its ability to produce 1000, 2000, 3000, or more lines per minute has not yet been matched by human ability to read and digest at these increased rates. Obviously there should be a balance between the rate the machine is able to produce and the user to meaningfully consume. And the balance is continually upset by the DP manager seeking the most desirable cost/performance ratio from the printer, the user who says, "I might as well have all the records—it costs the same," and the programmer who says, "Why not add these two columns of data—its free!" Few meaningful decisions are ever made from sheer volume of reports.

Excessive frequency.   Much information simply does not take into account the appropriate decision making cycle of the recipient. Because reports are issued too frequently, many have no effect on a manager's performance and produce no benefits for the organization. All too many companies have daily sales, daily production, and daily inventory status reports. Yet in many cases it is totally impractical to think about daily production schedules or daily sales campaigns.

Too frequent reporting cycles can hinder management performance and reduce profitability. First, if the data show wide fluctuations of values in a short period of time, the manager may react to a false signal and take action when none is appropriate. Second, a too frequent reporting cycle causes the same problem as too much volume. If new information is supplied before the manager has had an opportunity to fully evaluate the current data, he may postpone any decision until the new data is evaluated. This continual reappraisal is characteristic of managers who never make any decisions.

Lack of understanding.   Each and every decision process has associated with it a period of time before a decision can be made, which can be called analytical lead time. This lead time is violated by too many and too frequent reports. But equally important is the situation where the manager makes a decision based on instable data or false assumptions. What happens if the manager fails to grasp the correct content of the report?

F036:   10/10/76   9/30/76   PAGE 10

AREA 57		WEEK	MTD	PTD	YTD
062	BROBDINGNAGIAN FARMS		131	131	306
064	SUNE CARLSON INC.		10	10	13
083	RISBURG & SLYVAN		51	51	51
091	TECHNOLOGY-EARTH		44	44	298
146	GERALD S. MORTIMER		108	108	248
148	LINCOLN DAVIES CO. INC.		173	173	394
174	REES SISTERS INC.		410	410	740
181	DENNIS PHELPS				1-1
252	D. L. GRIFFITHS & CO.		61	61	141
273	MITCHELL ENGINEERING INC.		15	15	276
297	BROWNELL INC.		20	20	220
309	ABOTT-WIGTON		10	10	50
313	ROBERT SHAW		98	98	333
330	SAMUEL W. CALDWELL		72	72	126
360	HENRY B. HOOVER INC.		28	28	53
371	DAYLSTROM DYNAMICS				42
540	ENO & BETSINGER		75	75	75
761	S. C. COOPER & SON INC.		40	40	96
	AREA 57 TOTAL		1,346	1,346	3,563

Figure 17

Figure 17 illustrate a technically bad report. It has no title. What are the values—dollars? What is the period of time which encompasses this activity? Figure 17 is an example of poor communication! The user *did not know* what the numbers meant. His interpretation was incorrect.

Misinterpretation by RUM at any level occurs continually even with the most commonly used reports. Usually, the capsule of information presented by the report is technically accurate. Most preparation provides for a standard level of accuracy via some checking device. But technical accuracy is not the problem; the difficulty lies in understanding and interpreting the data.

Anyone ever responsible for a budget has met with the Accounting Department on numerous occasions seeking interpretations of monthly charges or variances from budget. Fortunately not all data reports are subject to such financial ambiguities (the accountants prefer to call them "allocations").

Yet some, in fact probably all, of the following situations do occur from time to time in your organization. Each has the potential of producing serious consequences.

1. *The extra copy.* A report is issued on multiple-copy computer paper or is reproduced. Each recipient must read it and—act? The dissemination of some reports provides the proper situational perspective needed by a few key individuals to project future guidelines. But a good many "extra copies" elicit unnecessary questions at lower levels or, in some cases, cause action where none is required.

2. *The predecessor copy.* One of the most dangerous information situations occurs when an employee in a new position receives a report designed for and used by the previous incumbent. Why did the predecessor get it? What did he do with it? Dare the new man cancel it? Almost never! In fact, in many instances it will be explained by some lower level clerk whose enigmatic interpretation is accepted as gospel and a new cycle of confusion beings.

3. *Metamorphosis.* Like the processionary caterpillar, which turns into a beautiful winged insect, the message within a report can also change. Any report is a collection of facts translated into human messages from preestablished agreement. Computer reports are particularly vulnerable since they develop from a program with finite limits which are no longer controlled by human activity. Many reports of specialized activity (a certain product line, tool and die use for a particular machine, etc.) will probably record activity within a certain range of numbers. When, therefore, this product line expands to the point of using some numbers beyond the range previously planned, the corresponding activity is automatically excluded from the reports. Why? Because the computer still collects data in the range determined years ago by programmers and RUM's long moved to other positions. Why don't we catch the incomplete report? Because the report is of limited scope (by definition), and the messages developed through this reporting system cannot be verified. The data then sent to RUM is not representative of the events being observed.

4. *Summarizationitis.* This is a most common disease of information. It involves combining, at all levels, transaction data regardless of

individual magnitude, special business programs, or unusual circumstances. Information summarized often becomes distorted in the communication process. Sophisticated and vital intelligence is oversimplified as it is boiled down for easy reading by top executives. Although managers frequently confine themselves to reviewing short reports which reduce voluminous data to a few lines, the simplifications are so great that they cannot possibly develop a grasp of the questions they are expected to decide.

Hampered by misinformation, many segments of RUM will use Q & D probes to illuminate the confusion, conflicts, and potentially terrible errors.

5. *Fog.* Many reports contain mysterious, sometimes ambiguous codes which are nowhere explained in the report. See Figure 18. This facsimile of an actual report contains, like so many others, symbols, abbreviations, and in many instances even blank spaces, all of which are important and indicative of certain conditions. What great divining authority can explain to RUM the necessary meanings? How often, in fact, does RUM ask?

Failure reinforcement.   The last major problem condition which results from misunderstanding the nature of information revolves around the failure syndrome. Although exception reporting is well recognized as an appropriate management tool, all too often the exception is defined in such a way as to illustrate only unfavorable variances. The salesman or production worker who is striving for high goals and high efficiency can become quite disturbed because *management by exception* only highlights his mistakes. We all recognize the problem with units of government which must spend the funds budgeted to them in the current year or face reductions next year.

The general emphasis is on punishment rather than a combination of reward and punishment.

AN INEXPENSIVE SOLUTION

The consequences brought about by a lack of appropriate information are obvious to all of us. In the real world of an ongoing organization we find that activity results from a system of interrelated decisions whereby decision output often becomes the input for another decision. Would the government, management, and auditors have acted as they did with the Gulf of Tonkin, Penn Central, and the Franklin Bank if better information had been available?

It has been our objective to indicate in this chapter that the com-

```
                    CUSTOMER FILE DETAIL REGISTER        004-094      PROCESSED 05/06/75                          PAGE  1

*CUST NO.   ST.NO.  CUSTOMER NAME   FIRST LINE ADDRESS   2ND LINE ADDRESS   3RD LINE ADDRESS   ZIPCD   ALPHA   ZONE*
44964-000   D  000  BRAKER MFG CO.  1301 SOUTH ST.       BROCKWAY PENNA                        15824   BROCK   000
SN TC SC STC  CCD  BP NO.  AG LOC  SSN OR EID  NYD RN  PN  IF SINVC LE VAL  ICLE  CT  CRL  $  PDUE  A/R  BAL DTE
00 95 37      065  834017                      **      24  2                        T

PROD TD TANKSIZE EST-GAL  STX STTE PTTE  PCD  PDIF  TVA MXPR FRPR  SVCR  DISC ADC DPB  PSP  PSFR SSP SSFR HAC PDT DTE LB DSL BLND
010 1                     137  E    T    483  0315-              0025                584                            03041
010                       137  E    T    483  0315-              0025                584                            12300
020 2                     137  E    T    483  0345-              0025                584
020 1                     137  E    E    483  0345-              0025                584                            12310
130 1                     137  E    E    747  0050- 30-          0025           1    667
130 1                     137  E    E    747  0050- 30-          0025           1    667                            12310
142 1                     137  E    E    747  0050- 30-          0025           1    667
142 2                     137  E         747  0050- 30-          0025           1                                   12310


*CUST NO.   ST.NO.  CUSTOMER NAME    FIRST LINE ADDRESS   2ND LINE ADDRESS   3RD LINE ADDRESS   ZIPCD   ALPHA   ZONE*
23900-010   D  070  ERIE LACKAWANNA RR  SECTION TOOLHOUSE  BROOMFIELD PA                        15824   ERIEL   000
                    ERIE LACK RR        BROOMFIELD PA
SN TC SC ST C  CCD  BP NO.  AG LOC  SSN OR EID  NYD RN  PN  IF SINVC LE VAL  ICLE  CT  CRL  $  PDUE  A/R  BAL DTE
04 40 37       065  834465                      **      24  3   5                    Y

PRD T CNTR-FRTO TANKSIZE EST-GAL  SB  PSP-PFT SSP-SFR  SBPNO  STX STN PTN TP PCD PDIF  TVA MXPR FRPR SVCR DC AC PP DTE L B DSL BLND
010 2 0171-1271 124       500     PO #191-5310-1-270   834465 137  E   F  2  484 0250-                      0180 3
210 2 0171-1271                                        834465 137  E   F  4  000
900 2 0170-1270                                        834465 137  E      4  000

RECORDS WRITTEN     2
```

Figure 18

187

plex information structure is large and expensive. Reports are the tip of the iceberg. The usable, visible portion of the reporting system is supported by expensive machines, DP professionals, and innumerable clerical people in many operating functions. Their costs and the cost of the product they produce are staggering! Furthermore their positions must be justified and enlarged through continual modifications and so-called improvements to the reporting system.

Next we considered the common types of reports: transactions, time, exceptions, and probes. All are at some point necessary. All exist. The variety and different characteristics of the reports, however, tend to complicate the decision making systems dealt with by RUM.

Finally, complications were explored as we examined the wide variety of difficulties that beset any reporting structure.

The information system is the very life blood of the organization, and it flows to all the extremities of the company. Can this monstrous information structure be organized? Can it be controlled? Can it be managed?

The answer is an emphatic "yes"! The information system can be improved simply, cheaply, and within the level of organization *you* control. The monolithic information structure can be modified by *you,* as the recipient, whether the source is data processing, accounting, or any other function.

The method is quite simple. It consists of only one new tool, called THE REPORTS BOOK.

Rule 1.   The Reports Book is simply a single-page copy of every different report that comes into or goes out of your function. To this report, you do one thing. With a red felt tip pen (the writing stands out) write on the copy the following information:

1.   The sources of information.
2.   Limits to the information if any.
3.   Identifications of all codes.
4.   Options available.
5.   Frequency of distribution.
6.   List of recipients within your own function.

Figure 19 illustrates a sample marked page from a Reports Book. Five of the six suggested pieces of information are noted. Imagine the difficulty of interpretation for a new or inexperienced employee within the positive identification of numerous pieces of data as provided by the written notes.

NON PAYMENT CANCELLATION 045-929 7/12/75 Page 8.

ID NUMBER	SQ GRP TRX	BATCH DATE	NAME & ADDR	CANCEL EFFECTIVE DATE	MONTH PREM	P L N	F / S	U N S	M O D	E / T	ADJ	NET DUE
0 169-28-9494	900 28	07/12	TYLER PAUL 222 SOUTH RIVERSIDE STONY BROOK, NY 11790	07/01/75	6.50	S	2	1	9	0		6.50
0 179-36-4934	900 29	07/12	JACKSON GERALD E 1111 ASHWORTH RD. FT. WORTH, TX 76101	07/01/75	3.50	S	1	1	9	0		7.00
0 206-09-8698	900 28	07/12	WORLEY ANITA MOREND RD. LOUISVILLE, KY 40201	07/01/75	13.00	S	2	2	9	0	5.00	21.00
0 725-07-1070	900 28	07/12	DODD JAMES 15 EAST 5TH STREET MIAMISBURG, OH 45342	07/01/75	6.50	S	2	1	9	0		13.00
9 000-10-0029	700 28	07/12	CANGDAN FRANK 325 DELAWARE AVE. CLEVELAND, OH 44144	07/01/75	13.00	S	2	2	9	0		6.50

Codes

SQ = SEQUENCE
GRP = GROUP
TRX = TRANSACTION CODE
PLN = PLAN: A = FULL HEALTH
B = EXTENDED HEALTH
S = NORMAL HEALTH
F/S = FAMILY STATUS: 1 = SINGLE
2 = COUPLE
3 = PARENT & CHILD
4 = FAMILY
UNS = UNITS 1 THRU 0
MOD = BILLING MODE: 1 = ANNUAL
4 = QUARTERLY
9 = MONTHLY
E/T = ENROLLMENT TYPE: 0 = PURCHASED COMPANY RECORD
1 = CONVERTED FROM "M" PLAN
2 = CONVERTED FROM "P" PLAN
3 = COMPANY
4 = GROUP
5 = FIELD

Source = Open Policy File
Limits = Health "A" only
Frequency = daily
Distribution = ① code clerk
② agent control

Figure 19

It may take as long as 1 year, because of annual reports, to collect a one-page sample of every report. Ideally such a project might be assigned to an information custodian in the Auditing or Data Processing Department to perform the task for the entire organization. Such an assignment would enlighten everyone and identify more fully conflicting responsibilities and redundancy. The custodian, in turn, is just what the name implies. He or she makes no decisions but simply collects the reports.

Besides marking the already noted information on the face of the report, two additional rules must be enforced by the reports custodian:

Rule 2. No change of any kind can be made to the report until the custodian is informed.   Our assumption here is that the information you receive is your property. You are expected to exercise the decision making and administrative processes, based to a great extent on the reports you receive. This rule does not give you the authority to make changes or prevent them if they are not your delegated responsibility. It does say that, *if* you are to use the information tools provided, you must be made aware of modifications which, in turn, may cause changes in your decision assumptions. The alterations may render the information useless for your management requirements, but at least you will not use faulty reports.

Rule 3. No employee in a new position within your function receives any reports until he has reviewed the Reports Book.   This harsh rule can be easily enforced by the Reports Book custodian. Any employee leaving a position is removed from all distribution lists. His successor is *not* placed on any distribution lists. He or she must visit with the Reports Book custodian, survey the range of information, and select the reports necessary to perform the function. Since most new people never receive any training, the visit to the Reports Book becomes an eye opening opportunity to evaluate the decision making resources of the organization. Such a visit will curb redundant requests for information, allow employees to use modifications of existing reports rather than starting from scratch, provide old and new employees with the opportunity to manage with information, disperse some of the technocrats' coded terminology fog, and even hopefully eliminate the infamous "predecessor copy."

If you choose to expand the Reports Book custodian function to somewhat improve the quality of messages your organization produces, consider also some of the following rules for DP *and* accounting and other information producing centers:

Additional Suggested Rules
- Every report has a title.
- Every report has a unique number.
- A summary page or change in format is a new report requiring a new number and place in the Reports Book even if produced by the same program.
- All report codes are identified by a footnote or code sheet printed with the report.
- All abbreviations (when they must be used) are identified by a footnote or on the code sheet.
- Every page is numbered.

- Every page is dated with the period of time covered and the date the report was produced.

There are then only three requirements for successful implementation of the Reports Book:

- *Rule 1.* A single-page copy of every report is collected in one place in the Reports Book, and certain information is noted on the face of the page.
- *Rule 2.* No change of any kind can be made to the report until the Reports Book custodian is informed.
- *Rule 3.* No employee in a new position within your function receives any reports until he has reviewed the Reports Book.

Change is the enemy of understanding. The inability of the report user to adequately comprehend report content because of the many reasons already cited can now be overcome. Maintenance of any control over a period of time is difficult. But the establishment of our third rule forces a desired dissemination of knowledge. This meeting of the user with the information library promotes a vital exchange of understanding.

For all the complexities of your information systems, the three rules governing the Reports Book are simple and easy to follow. The problem of understanding information has long been realized. Until now the problem has been answered by the physical organization of the material (report numbering) and by structuring the entire function (forms control). Yet both of these solutions treat the symptoms of the information iceberg and not the problem. Our information user not only needs organization and formal structuring, but also needs to know what is available within the entire spectrum of prepared reports.

The Reports Book is both an organized and a structured method of controlling information. But it is also much more. It provides the information user with insights into all facets of the organization's information utility. What does the organization know? What does the organization *like* to know? Of this tremendous collection of data, what will help him to do a better job? The Reports Book provides the answers.

CONCLUSION

If we can agree that information is the very life blood of any organization, then without question such a vital resource must be not only controlled but also managed. Yet today much of management pours this life stream of operational messages on the ground, and continues to make decisions intuitively! Why? Certainly not for lack of authority or resources, but rather for lack of a controllable vehicle to organize and focus the available information resources and then manage intelligently. The Reports Book is the vehicle. It is the second of three suggested methods (data base building was the first suggestion) to make your organization superior.

CHAPTER 14

How to Talk to Programmers

THE SOURCE

We have discussed a variety of sources for the proliferation of information pollution. Without question the computer, because of its speed and programmed intelligence, is our prime source of voluminous data and even, sometimes, information. While the quantity of reports is always a problem, our quest must be for quality.

For nearly four generations (of computers) we have waited for the computer information systems to rise to the oft promised Elysian heights as a top management participating assistant. We still wait! And another generation or two won't improve the situation. Mechanically and electronically we have more capability than can be used with general business information processing requirements. Then, why . . . add a code, add a card, add a peripheral, make a minor modification to a program, and the whole system may come tumbling down. Worse yet, sometimes do nothing, and the good and faithful system will still collapse. Finally, the most frightening and discouraging situation of all involves the long trusted computer reporting system which has provided timely and faithful information benefits and now, suddenly, is identified as always having contained a significant error.

There are two problems with computer information systems. The first problem relates to the business itself.

The business situations which the computer system deals with are only hazy reflections of true business realities. Neither the requestor/user/manager nor the programmer fully understand the impact of each other's work. For his part, RUM assumes that the myriad of problem variations and obstruent data situations are understood by the DP staff. In turn, the programmers obliquely assume that the problem stated is the problem evaluated, and therefore immediately begin computer solution programming. Neither is correct. *The first major difficulty with the computer solutions is that the general problem is quite often never fully understood by anyone!*

"Documentation is the castor oil of programming—managers think it is good for programmers, and programmers hate it! In fact, managers know it must be good because programmers hate it so much. . . ."[1] Professor Weinburg goes on to argue, quite validly, that there is no way to force programmers to produce good documentation. Yet these same programmers will often find it difficult to follow what their own programs are doing because of the many problem dimensions, loops, branches, and undefined complications. Good documentation is unquestionably desirable and even necessary for a successful information system. Yet how many times have you been told, "We must rewrite the programs" or, even worse, "We must rewrite the entire system," because no one knows how it works! It seems that no matter how much effort and money are poured into the documentation stream, we keep coming up dry.

The second problem, then, revolves around documentation. Almost all systems of documentation never accomplish their appropriate purposes because they fail to accurately reflect the *current* problem solution logic executing within the computer system. Most documentation systems explain how a problem situation was solved with a computer when the program was originally designed. Surprisingly, a good deal of our documentation is written *after* programs are completed and accepted. Documentation emphasis is placed on the original creative work. But the organization is changing, however slightly, every day. Occasionally it follows that the computer information system must be modified. And modified and maintained it is, but documented it is not. Seldom is the impact of a maintenance change ever considered in relationship to the total system.

The second major problem we then face with computer systems is

[1]Gerald M. Weinburg, "The Psychology of Computer Programming," Van Nostrand Reinhold, New York, 1971, p. 262.

that most documentation does not explain the current dimensions of the situations in question. Our concern is not so much how the program works within the computer, that is, individual program instructions. That problem can be improved by continual monitoring of the necessary programmer documentation. Rather, our concern is: *what is the situation being processed now for the business by the machine?* If we don't know where we are or how we got there, it is difficult, even procedurally dangerous, to modify in the hope of making improvements.

THE ARGOSY HARDWARE CASE

After World War II we saw the rapid expansion of Argosy Hardware franchises into nineteen states. Exploding population, new products, and an aggressive sales force led by Nahum Weinwurm made Argosy Hardware stores a strong regional competitor. Lines expanded from traditional hardware to include housewares, decorative items, lawn and garden supplies, small appliances, and occasionally some specialized soft goods. Early on, Sid Litt, the controller, recognized the necessity for product control programs to support a huge financial operation, which eventually grew to a 60,000-item inventory and over 1000 retail stores. Argosy had been somewhat of a leader in the development of wholesale computer systems for picking, packing, shipping, invoicing, and inventory control. A product numbering system was vital to the success of almost any of these programs, and eventually six-digit unique numbers were assigned to most of the products in most of the lines. By the time Mr. Weinwurm died in 1968, he and Argosy Hardware had enjoyed 20 years of spectacular growth. Old Nahum's son, Bobby, then moved up, from vice-president for marketing, to the president's chair.

His training at the Wharton School and the opportunity to try his own hand led Bobby to some new approaches. Jerry Fawnline was hired to modernize the computer system. Norm Scheckel came on as controller, and an ex-marine major, John T. Farnsworth, was hired to stop the excessive pilferage and inefficiency in the multilevel, sprawling old buildings which made up the warehouse. It was only Bobby's intense desire to prove himself that kept him going and on top of the many facets of the business.

Soon Bobby was deeply involved with the forced retirement of Sid Litt and the near unionization that developed from some of Major Farnsworth's new policies. Both had a negative impact on the company. So, when Jerry Fawnline proposed an inventory stratification program in the March 1972 staff meeting, Bobby immediately supported this very positive program. Eight major product lines with almost ninety product groups made merchandising extremely difficult, and equal warehousing and control treatment for each of 60,000 products ridiculous.

Major Farnsworth and Norm Scheckel were eager for better internal controls. Bobby, on the other hand, recognized from his marketing experiences that the Argosy stores also faced a goodly number of problems. He knew that not a single store was anywhere large enough to stock all of the 60,000 items. Furthermore the store people did not know what to reorder, how much to reorder, or when to reorder.

By August of 1972 Jerry reported back to the staff meeting with the following two proposals:

1. "Build an inventory stratification report by product group. List all items in sequence by sales dollars within each of the ninety or so groups." All of the largest sales dollar items would be classified as A items until 60% of the total dollars for the group was reached. The next 30% of the sales dollar items would be classified as B items, and the remaining 10% as C items. It would then be possible with this report to prune the line. Bobby argued some C items would be necessary for a complete line but went along with the proposal. Stocking objectives and ordering procedures would be modified with this report. The advantages were obvious.

2. "Build a report of each Argosy store's purchases, indicating the purchase history activity and the stratification code." Bobby looked forward to building a more consistent Argosy image of product and a more profitable consumer acceptance. At the present time each store stocked pretty much what the owner "felt" would sell well. If Bobby could identify the profitable items to his stores, he could begin to depend on more patterned ordering, less inventory, and a somewhat better level of wholesale management.

In June of 1973 Jerry delivered the stratification report. It was a shocker! Less than 8000 of the 60,000 items were A items generating 60% of the sales dollars. Over 30,000 of the items were in the C category, producing only 10% of the sales. Within the next year approximately 18,000 items were discontinued. None had annual sales of over $50.00. The sales force argued that the product line was being excessively pruned, but Bobby prevailed, telling the sales people that if they couldn't move $50.00 worth in the entire 1000-store system, the item couldn't be very important.

The project allowed Farnsworth to rearrange his warehouses more appropriately because of less stock. The buyers were happier because they could concentrate on the profitable items, and Norm was pleased with the improved turnover of inventory.

The store report part of the project was not so successful—in fact, it failed! Because the store personnel were accustomed to dealing with product lines such as "hardware" and items within the line such as "hammers" and "saws," the retail store owners never used the Argosy product numbering system very much in the store's daily operations. They ordered by product number, true enough, by turning to the Argosy catalog page labeled "hammers." They checked their receiving documents against actual shipments using both the Argosy number and the limited computer description. Within the restricted size of any Argosy delivery to any store, two, three, or even five different saws could be readily identified. But a list of annual purchases from Argosy with A items identified proved impossible; the list was hundreds of pages long for almost every store. Since the retail store people had no way of relating an Argosy number to a store filled with thousands of different items of merchandise, it was evident that no practical method could be used to match A item purchases to actual inventory.

The store lists were almost completely ignored!

Missed Opportunities

Argosy Hardware's achievements were considerable. Inventory position, cash flow, and internal controls were all strengthened and improved. The results of the systems were far superior to those of most new computer adventures. The lack of success with the store report and ordering system appeared to be readily explainable. The stores were not owned by Argosy, and the level of cooperation obviously required was therefore not available.

Unbelievable as it would have seemed to Bobby Weinwurm, the true reason for the failure of the store reports was his management staff's lack of understanding of actual detailed store operations. Many of the staff, and especially Bobby, had spent a great deal of time in retail stores, but as wholesale representatives. Jerry Fawnline's system was good, and his programming almost flawless. But the idea had been developed and was approved by a management group with multiple responsibilities, while the design was completed by a dedicated computer technician. As happens so frequently, it was a fine idea adroitly designed and programmed, yet it failed. The missing element of success was the systems analyst, the doctor of business who would, as his prime job function, have included in *his* development an awareness of appropriate and possible execution steps to make it work!

Moreover, the successful part of the system, the inventory stratification, was by no means as successful as it might have been. Jerry Fawnline performed a methodical stratification of some 90 product groups. Each group, whether it be lawn and garden tractors or furnace filters, was treated by the same computer logic. Because of the high dollar value of each lawn mower, some items that sold over $20,000.00 annually were classified as C items when stratified within their lawn mower group. At the same time, because of the low dollar values, some plumbing fixtures selling $350.00 annually were classified as A items within their group. Some entire groups, such as V-belts, actually sold very little and should have been discontinued. Generally, because of the computer logic, heavy volume piece movement of low dollar "traffic" items was ignored. What had been accomplished was good. With a creative systems analyst examining alternatives, however, it *might* have been possible to produce far better solutions.

Disaster

In early 1974 disaster struck! Sid Litt, who had been forced to retire by Bobby, led a proxy fight in which he gained control of Argosy Hardware. Sid's first order of business was to send Bobby packing. Then, as the rapidly moving economy placed more cash demands on the company, Sid decided to modify the historical cash discount rate structure based on store take and classification. Sid called in Jerry Fawnline and told him to make the necessary change in the billing system within 60 days—an announcement would be mailed to all customers at that time!

Fawnline got right on it. Nobody, they had learned, fooled around when Sid Litt gave an order. But much to Jerry's dismay, Sid's request baffled the Programming Department. Its members had changed prices and credit codes and maintained customer records every day, but *never* had the method of calculation of discount rates for stores changed. Available documentation for the billing system was basically for an older generation of computers of a different brand with reference to some off-line processes. The programmers did find a cryptic reference to a "discount rate structure table" entered into the documenta-

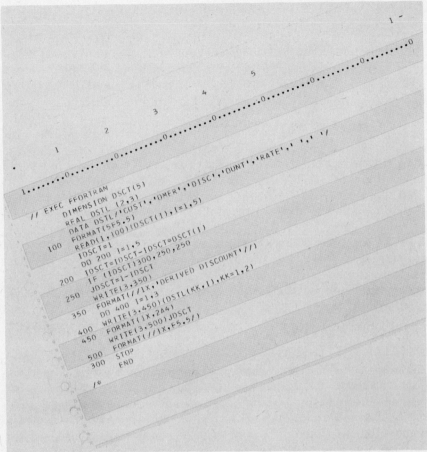

Figure 20   **Scrap of paper found in the math major's desk.**

tion in 1971 by a math major who had worked only 4 months, written in FORTRAN, and left one morning in a huff!

The programming people were at a loss. The routine could not be found to be changed. They even tried to override it with new routines, but then the whole system bombed.

Sid found he could exercise only one course of action. The entire billing system had to be rewritten at a cost of 7 man-years of effort. It was not ready until April of 1975, exactly 13 months after Sid had announced the change to the field and 12 months after Jerry Fawnline had left Argosy Hardware.

Will Good Program Documentation Help Us?

If we agree that finding out *how* the computer solves our problems is not only important but sometimes even vital, we have to ask, "Why can't anyone, including the programmers, easily understand how the jobs work? Is it this lack of understanding which makes change so difficult? Is the highly paid, pampered programmer inadequate to the task?"

The programmer is most often blamed for problems which arise from inadequate documentation. Programming is, to a great extent, a form of writing, and therefore can't we expect the program itself and supporting written documents to be clear and understandable?

The answer is "no!" The programmer is a middleman. He usually stands between a directed problem solution and a very complex machine. By interest, training, and experience he is most comfortable with the machine. But what a monster to be friendly with! The programmer lives with his machine in a world of frustrating constraints. The construction of the machine (no matter what brand) and the size and quantity of the configured boxes of electronic gear make each computer an almost unique set of opportunities and corresponding limitations. There are, for example, boundaries which the programmer must find because of the timing characteristics of the machine, as well as more serious boundaries because main and peripheral storage *is* circumscribed. Then, too, every programmer has more than one language ability in his head—and there are limits to each of the languages. The vagueness of the latest edition of the operating system, limited test time, a short deadline, and a knowledge of his own inadequacy all tend to make programming a demanding and sometimes emotionally draining profession.

The difficulties encountered in having a computer solve a problem are so great as to require the utmost dedication, concentration, and aptitude. And even this aptitude for crisp computer solution is unfortunately counterproductive to the organization's longer range goals. Business is change, within its very structed limits. But programs are written to utilize the optimum values possible with the existing computer configuration limitations. In many instances programs are purposely contrived to thwart change, especially when the programmer has found a "best way." Often, tight, efficient coding can't readily be modified. Thus computer efficiency and business adaptability become somewhat contradictory goals in business programming.

So here we have a group of people matching wits with a machine. And we say to them, "DOCUMENT!" But what shall they write down?

They will write their tricky techniques, and they will write their successes. They will write down their understanding of the problem in the minimum structure (hopefully without programming terminology) necessary to justify their course of action in combat with the computer.

The programmer thinks, and quite logically from his or her point of view, that only a small amount of "other" documentation is necessary. After all, the written code tells everything. Furthermore many installations require programmer flowcharts or have the purchased software ability to flowchart from the program itself. Besides, the programmer knows that the whole thing will probably be changed next week anyway.

The business environment is much like a hungry diner who wants to read the menu and make his meal choices; the programmer is an excellent chef but prepares only special dishes, not menus.

If programmer documentation is your only business standard, then programmers are solving your problems with their prime interests in mind (i.e., machine efficiency, no options not directly called for, and no future flexibility). The choice of programmers as documenters molds business solutions into unyielding logic structures unsuitable to accommodate business change.

Will Good Problem Documentation Help Us?

If programmers should not do the documentation, what, then, is the solution to our problem? First let's change the terminology. Documentation explains actions which are taking place or have taken place. All too frequently, documentation of a computer program is developed after the program is written. It is a representation of a solution evolved as the programmer confronted the computer.

A much more ideal product is called a specification. A specification consists of a problem definition, a method of solution, and the results expected. The specification is an attempt, when using computers to solve a business problem, to discipline a sequence of events *before* an attempt is made to utilize the machine as the appropriate tool to solve that problem. Earlier we examined various common forms of documentation or specifications (depending on how they are used), such as flowcharts, decision tables, and narrative.

Who should write specifications? Certainly not the programmer! The man we need is our systems analyst, the man of alternatives. Problem definition and problem solution logic must be developed through the application of the systems analyst's understanding of the complete needs and goals of the business. *Yet the systems analyst is not enough!* Not all systems analysts are good writers, just as good writers are not necessarily good analysts. Often the size of the problem, the complexity of the alternatives, and/or the loquacity of the intelligent, creative analyst produce a specification of uncomprehendible size and questionable objectivity. Note Figure 21; not only is some of the writing obscure, but also it is typewritten page 51 of 63!

A good deal of narrative specification work is marred by redundancy, confusion, and overburdening verbiage. Size (the number of pages) in itself frequently obscures the problem and the many possible

---

SPECIFICATIONS	PROGRAM NAME Edit & Maintain Heavy Gear Cost File HG-16
	DATE 6-4-74
	PREPARED BY English PAGE 51 OF 63

4.1   <u>Card Code K (change existing records)</u> - (continued)

4.14   For every Budget $ YTD and Estimated Cost YTD field in the card that is entirely blank, do not change the corresponding field in the tape record.

4.15   For every Budget $ YTD and Estimated Cost YTD field in the card that is numeric (can have leading zeros suppressed, but is not entirely blank), move the field to the corresponding tape record field.

4.16   For every Budget $ YTD and Estimated Cost YTD field in the card that has an asterisk in the left most column, move <u>packed zeros</u> to the corresponding tape record field.

4.17   A record code "T" cost record may, but not necessarily, contain a quantity control * (record positions 034-042), a unit price, discount percent, & freight allowance rate control * (record positions 043-051), a monetary amount control *(record positions 052-060), and a product code **(record positions 061-069).

     *Valid controls are to consist of signed numerics 000000001 thru 999999999

      **Valid Product codes are to consist of three 3-digit sub-fields, each reflecting unsigned numerics 000 thru 999. Full gear table in appendix 3.

4.2   <u>On the change in card combination with no errors in the previous combination:</u>

4.20   If the previous combination is a card code "A", add 1 to record count accumulator. Also, add the corresponding tape record fields to the gear accumulators and the total net change and addition accumulators.

4.21   If the previous combination is a card code "C", add the difference between the fields in the original (stored) record and the changed record to the total net change and addition accumulators. Add the fields in the changed record to the gear accumulators.

4.22   Move the corresponding tape record fields from the new or changed record and the card code to the detail lines 1 thru 4 and print.

     Write the new or changed tape record.

Figure 21

alternatives to both analyst and programmer. Furthermore, it is difficult to relate the programmer's efforts to the analyst's narrative. Never mind the countless programs which bomb out for misinterpretation of one word. All too often the programmer can (and sometimes must), use the nebulous narrative only as a raw framework of understanding basic to writing the program. Besides, who will ever know? Only the programmer of record can say to what extent he or she has translated the narrative logic into a computer solution.

Figure 22 is narrative written by a programmer. Technical terminology, acronyms, and very limited and structured diction, obscure

SPECIFICATIONS	PROGRAM NAME Create Employee
	File PM-7
	DATE 2-12-72
	PREPARED BY Auburn PAGE 9 OF 19

OPTION C -

    UPSI Bit B is ON
    'PC' input card has a 'C' in cc 48
    Master File - input and output
    Work File - Output
    Report - Layouts PL-PM-5 and PL-PM-6
    The purpose of Option C is to create the Work File
    and list all people whose leave of absence has expired.

OPTION D -

    UPSI Bit B is ON
    'PC' card has a 'D' in cc 48
    'RC' cards present - maximum of 35
    Master file - input & output
    Personnel Table Data Directory - input
    Personnel Table Data File - input
    Report - layouts PL-PM-7 and PL-PM-6
    The purpose of Option D is to update the Master File
    with the latest general benefit change.

OPTION E,F,G,H & J -

    UPSI Bit B is ON
    'PC' input card has 'E', 'F', 'G', 'H', or J in cc 48
    Master File - input & output
    Report - layout PL-PM-6
    The purpose of these options is to turn on specific print
    switches in the Master File (output) for specified records.

OPTION K -

    UPSI Bit B is OFF NO card input
    Master File - input & output
    Edit Detail Tape File - input
    Report - layouts PL-PM-8 and PL-PM-6
    The purpose of Option K is to add the retirees to the
    PER Master File.

Figure 22

the business problem. While doing his very best, the programmer is writing as if his reader will be the machine.

Documentation versus Change

Change makes program documentation and specification updating all the more difficult. The total business changes very little, but RUM is continually restless, dissatisfied, and probing. Modifications attempting to move today's reality into today's information structure are constantly made. But revision is the nemesis of documentation. Figure 23 illustrates a somewhat ambiguous piece of logic. You must relate it to the main stream of reasoning. But it is revision 19! How does it mesh with the preceding eighteen changes? Obviously this common method of recording change represents a cost savings. It is cheaper than rewriting the specification nineteen times. But can you figure out readily (if at all) what the computer is doing to you, when you have nineteen modifications to the main logic stream?

Other common forms of documentation/specification also offer problems. The highly condensed and abstract decision table is a superlative tool for technical situations, consisting of strings of decisions. Most nonscientific programming, however, is dominated by many ac-

SPECIFICATIONS	PROGRAM
	MONTHLY SALES ANALYSIS M-107
	REV. 19 / DATE 5/16/75
	PREPARED BY EVANS / PAGE 1 OF 1

Accumulate Current and YTD Net Sales per formula
number III for each item that has a 0 (zero) in
byte 63. Zero in byte 63 means this is an own
make product.

Print these accumulations at the end of processing
on the Grand Total Page per line 14 of print
layout PL-M-107.

Figure 23   **The nineteenth revision.**

tions interspersed with decisions. The decisions table does not adapt well to these situations.

Flowcharts offer a middle ground alternative between narrative and decision tables. Although the use of therbligs is far from standard, we normally find that every organization establishes norms for its flowchart symbols. The logic *can* be crisp and solutions comprehensible ... if the method is not captured by the technicians. If this technical transition takes place, however, the written words become programming terms, the logic becomes more puzzling, and the specification turns into mere documentation. Even a beginner in the business will utilize the full range of therbligs in his template. Even experienced analysts seldom note the obvious inconsistency of mixing the card

or tape   symbol with other symbols which are purely logical. Yet flowcharting is nearly always such a composite—
—direction combined with tools—medium mixed with message. Such interweaving of machines and logic does not commonly occur with the other methods of specification. It is, however, the threshold step to technical dominance of the flowchart tool. In Figure 24 we see a flowchart dominated by programmer methodology.

All too often the systems analyst retreats to narrative because it still appropriately separates him from computerized writing. So here we are with a real-world dilemma! The best method of logically expressing a problem situation and solution (the flowchart) frequently either bogs down into an inextricable quagmire or is simply abandoned for the artless but tractable narrative.

Every common method described can be and has been used with a great deal of success by someone. Unfortunately, the classic success stories involving any method of specification/documentation writing all too often revolve on the personality of the resident analyst or programmer.

THE LOGIC PACKAGE

Although each method of specification writing *can* adequately define a problem and present a solution, the situation is most often one of winning a battle and losing the war! No method of specification writing addresses itself to the common problems of a computer environment.

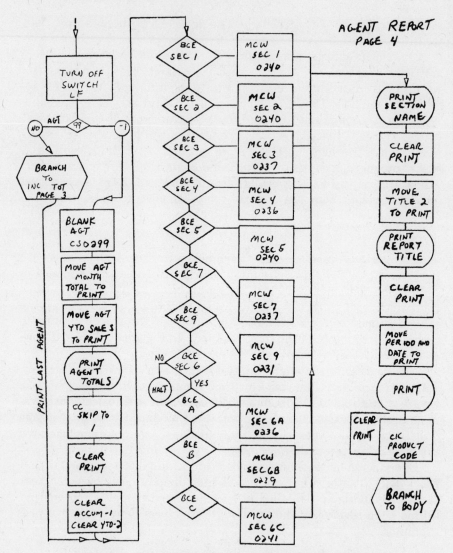

Figure 24   **Flowcharting in the hands of the programmer.**

The difficulties arise not from the lack of technical completeness or accuracy of the specifications themselves, but in their application to programming and the business. These situations can be alleviated to a great extent, by the application of very simple measures as we write our specs. There are four common problems which we must realistically face:

- Specification/documentation is almost impossible to change because the original solution logic is frozen into a typed or written medium. Therefore it can't be changed, or (almost as bad), the change is tagged on as an addendum.
- Possible and potential options are not included in the program. No one anticipates anything as the system is developed.
- Testing is difficult to impossible. The programmer has no way of knowing whether his program is correct until he places it on the machine *with* test data. *Then* he goes back to his *desk* and adjusts his program to reality.
- The requestor/user/manager must reject the early computer solutions because they do not portray what it was hoped to achieve. Revisions must be made because of misunderstandings between the systems analyst, RUM, and the programmers.

How to Talk to Programmers

A simple and enduring method of writing problem solution logic is called the LOGIC PACKAGE. While demanding the same modest discipline required of any method of specification writing, the Logic Package generally solves the four common problems of computer documentation. It consists of the same three basic requirements of any computer specification scheme, with some modification. These three parts of the Logic Package are:

1. Problem solution logic.
2. Files used, both input and output.
3. Results for human beings—the printed report.

Problem solution is developed in a simplistic form called the LOGIC CHART. This is a flowchart consisting of only three symbols, as illustrated in Figure 25. The rectangular symbol represent an action step; the diamond, a decision; and the circle, a connector. The use of only three symbols immediately eliminates any possible confusion relating to the dozen or more therbligs available in any template. Furthermore, it is impossible for the technocrats to adulterate this flowchart, since by definition and imposed standard it may contain only these three symbols.

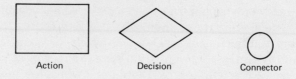

Action   Decision   Connector

Figure 25   **The three logic chart symbols.**

Although quite simple in form, the Logic Chart method of flow-chart presentation demands that a few standards be followed:

1. Everyone in the organization uses the same size paper and the same size therbligs.
    REASONING: With only two programmable symbols you can measure the relative size of the computer problem by counting pages of logic. Human differences of both the designer and the programmer will always be present, but with some records of each person's previous activity surprisingly close estimates of programming time can be made from a page count.
2. Symbols and the mainstream of logic go from the top to the bottom of the page and on the left side of the paper. Decision diamonds allow use of space to the right. If a piece of logic emanating from a decision diamond is too complex to fit on the same page with the mainstream, a connector must be used, taking the logic routine to a separate page.
    REASONING: Same as in item 1 above. Subroutines of any size are forced onto a separate page. This provides a more accurate method of sizing the program. It also distinctly outlines problem solution patterns of considerable size which may not be directly in the mainstream of logic.
3. A program identification block appears on every page.
    REASONING: Obvious.
4. The first page only of the Logic Chart contains a basic three-part identification section to provide an appropriate frame of reference and scope for the problem and the basic information ingredients used as tools of processing. The three sections are:

    • Purpose.
    • Input and output identification.
    • Notes.

"Purpose" and "input and output identification" are self-explanatory. Notes, however, may be used on any page where the business reasons or the systems analyst's reasons for the step in question will illuminate the course of action for either the programmer or RUM, now or in the future. Notes must also be used to explain options, choices of codes, methods of computation, rounding, government reference manuals prescribing the use of certain rates or routines, warnings in the form of enumerated other programs which must be changed if a change is made here (e.g., FICA rates and amounts), and so on.

The notes placed next to the flowchart symbols of logic provide all the detail that is necessary to support a simple logic stream but that would require *pages* of typewritten narrative if that form of specification were to be used. The simple notes, *together* with the Logic Chart, make the simplest and most complete problem explanation available to individuals with varied backgrounds.

REASONING: RUM will not particularly like this format, since even the use of two symbols may be a bit complex. Programmers will detest the Logic Chart, since they think it robs them of their much sought for "creativity"—they forget the many machine problems they face at this point. But the systems analyst, the key between the organization and the programmers, will find that this is the tool which allows him to pass back and forth, *with understanding,* between a loosely structured business environment and the fast but absolute world of the computer.

A sample of a Logic Chart is illustrated in Figure 26. Even without seeing the input files or the report the program produces, RUM can generally follow the limits which make items appear on the report. When the problem is more complex, the systems analyst, even one completely unfamiliar with the program, can understand and explain what is happening.

The Logic Chart is the appropriate conversational medium between analyst and programmer. It is the superior way of talking to programmers! As long as the programmer follows the logic stream, the problem will be solved for the business and not for the machine. Control of the sequence of events of problem solution logic is the business of the systems analyst. Machine logic is a different world. The Logic Chart will not generate a crisp program. But at least it will force the programmer to solve a problem which has been defined with established, anticipated results. Weird options, confusing constraints, and

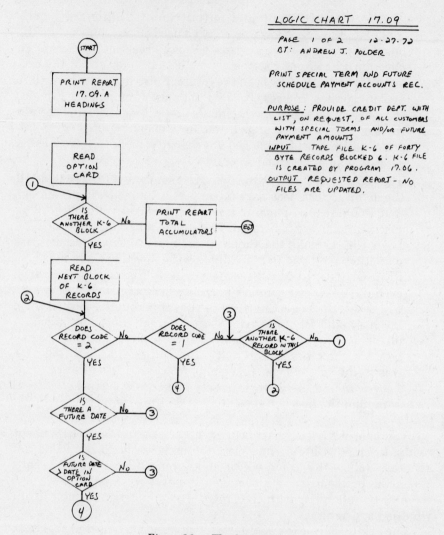

PAGE 1 OF 2   12-27-72
BT: ANDREW J. POLDER

PRINT SPECIAL TERM AND FUTURE
SCHEDULE PAYMENT ACCOUNTS REC.

PURPOSE : PROVIDE CREDIT DEPT. WITH
LIST, ON REQUEST, OF ALL CUSTOMERS
WITH SPECIAL TERMS AND/OR FUTURE
PAYMENT AMOUNTS
INPUT   TAPE FILE K-6 OF FORTY
BYTE RECORDS BLOCKED 6. K-6 FILE
IS CREATED BY PROGRAM 17.06.
OUTPUT   REQUESTED REPORT - NO
FILES ARE UPDATED.

Figure 26   **The logic chart.**

illogical logic will generally be filtered out as the programmer responds to the flowchart definition. Opportunity is at hand for better programming, since what we need from the programmer is a computer solution. He does not also have to develop or interpret a problem solution from what he believes many pages of foggy paragraphs to mean.

The second part of the Logic Package consists of attached copies of

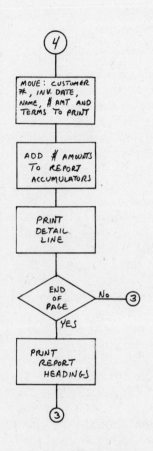

NOTES

ITEMS IN K-6 FILE WITH FUTURE
DATE > THAN STATEMENT DATE DO
NOT APPEAR ON THE CURRENT
CUSTOMER STATEMENT.

K-6 CUSTOMER A/R RECORD CODES:

   0 = NO CHARGE
   1 = SPECIAL TERM TOTAL BALANCE
   2 = SPECIAL TERM INCREMENT BAL.
   3 = CREDIT
   4 = REGULAR BILLING
   5 = OVERPAYMENT
   8 = SHORT PAYMENT

Figure 26   (Continued)

input and output files. All too often in any documentation scheme we find that file layouts are separated from the specification. Just as bad is the situation where an original file layout *is* attached to the specification.

Original file layouts in any organization should be treated with the same care and respect as 5-pound bars of gold. The problem is not so much losing the layout. Misusing it is the problem. The file layouts represent the life blood of basic information of your organization. Programs create files, add to files, and delete or change data in files. When a copy of the file layout is excluded from the documentation, interpretation is rendered far more difficult. A far greater problem occurs when the original is placed with the program that creates the file or one that uses the file. Soon we don't know where to look to find the original file layout. When changes are made or fields of data are added to the file on a copy, they may at times destroy or overlap other fields previously noted on the original.

The original file layout should be numbered, cataloged, and preserved in a library type environment. All additions, deletions, or other changes to this file must be dated and made only on the original. All codes and meanings of codes must be noted on the original. Every program using this file must be noted on the original document with the first date of its use. Every time a change of any sort is made to the original, copies should be produced and attached to the Logic Package of each using program.

The collection of all originals into one location will stop the production of redundant files. If codes are explained, this will stop the creation of redundant fields. Noting the programs using these files will prevent many of the frantic, confidence destroying "bomb outs" caused by a field change in a file when no one knew which programs used the record. And occasionally a file and its associated stored machine records can be eliminated when we discover *no one* uses this file any longer.

The final part of the Logic Package consists of results for human beings. Although the result may be a card or a format on a screen, it is most often a printed report or a printed form. The objective of most programs or strings of programs is to place in RUM's hands printed documents which express facts and occasionally interpretations for his use in the progress and development of the business. That is why the computer is here. If it did not produce information, statistics, reports, forms, projections, and the like, we wouldn't need the contrary beast. The output is the objective! A substantive report is what RUM and the systems analyst work so hard to develop. Certainly enormous amounts of meaningful calculation, accumulation, and extrapolation go on the machine before a report is produced. Although some of the output serves as a check that correct work is being done in the machine, most reports are actually used by RUM as a basis for additional activity.

With output reports occupying such an important position in the scheme of information processing, it is strange, but all too universal, that the planned development document looks like Figure 27. This ubiquitous method of designing the output report fails to represent in any sort of reasonable fashion the nature of the final product. Although title and headings will remain as shown, the obscure strings of X's fail to convey an adequate image of the end product.

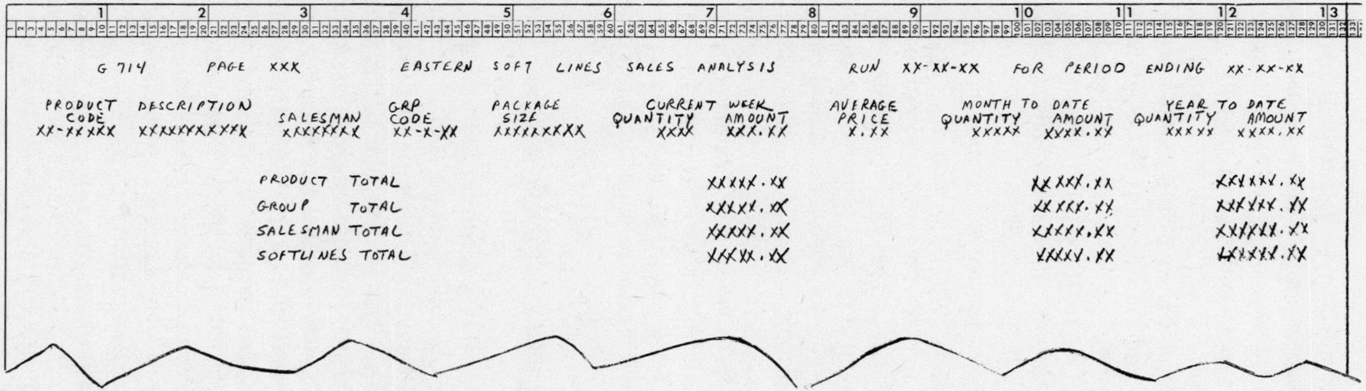

Figure 27 **Handwritten report layout.**

Frequently RUM never sees this X'ed layout or anything like it. All too often the systems analyst (even a good one) communicates by word of mouth with RUM about the problem and the system. Only a small part of the conversation is devoted to the product RUM will use as a result of system and programming efforts. Everyone assumes that his or her mental image of the result is everyone else's image. Then the report is produced, and the sky falls! Time and again analysts are called upon to redesign the system, followed by the Programming Department's being required to reprogram, because of a misunderstanding of the nature of the final product. This dilemma can be avoided.

The Logic Package must contain a *typed* output layout with at least three lines of simulated data (no X's) and all appropriate totals. Then RUM can and should review the proposed output and either sign it as acceptable or ask for changes. This typed layout is not difficult to prepare. It may take a half-day or longer to do a good job. In turn, months of rework may be avoided, since RUM can review some actual data, get a feeling for options, and, most importantly, note what he forgot about and have the system revised to include this omission *before* the Logic Chart is written and before programming.

The typed, signed, and approved report layout is simply another document included in the Logic Package. But its creation and use will add considerable productivity to your DP organization.

LOGIC PACKAGE EXTRAS—CHANGE

As previously described and illustrated, the Logic Package is composed of three parts: the problem solution logic flowchart, attached copies of files, and a typed report layout with data. Clear, simple presentation of a business problem in a consistent form is highly beneficial to any organization. In spite of this, the whirling swiftness of computer methodology development, coupled with managed and directed levels of business change, necessitates frequent program modifications. If the program changes, the documentation must normally also change. But that seldom happens! Some situations, such as hardware changes or operating systems changes, *may not* require documentation changes. But if you change *any* decision logic rules for any program, the specifications must change!

Narrative, flowchart, and decision table methods all fail here at the point of modification. The necessities of the business organization, the high cost of DP staff, and the enormity of rewriting or redrawing the specifications place accurate, *up-to-date* specifications beyond the realm of practicality. However, if you use the Logic Package, you have a way to keep up with change.

The unique structure of the Logic Chart accommodates change. By the combination of flowchart symbols on the left side of the page and a minimum number of necessary notes on the right, we have joined the best of two media. Additionally the composition of the two forms, flowchart and narrative, with everything handwritten in ink, provides the open space necessary to record change. Here is the method to make computer program documentation live and breathe:

1. Write your original logic in ink. It is permanent! If written in pencil, its life is in jeopardy from the nearest eraser. If typewritten, it is too expensive.
2. When a change is required, draw the modification flowchart blocks and notes in the open spaces on the face of the Logic Chart in red felt tip pen. Date the change. The red pen stands out. You can see how the problem solution logic changed. Figure 28 illustrates the changing of program logic; the "red" areas are shown in gray in the figure.

This method of changing specifications will not please aesthetically inclined analysts or programmers. It will never win any prize for beauty—but few have ever been awarded for "good looking" specifications. As long as the analyst is neat, the red pen will do the job. Best of all, it costs nothing! We *must* understand what the logic is calling on the computer to do before we can change the specifications. We must therefore read the specifications and find where our methods can be changed. As these change points are found, the modifications are marked with the red pen. If today you don't expend at least this much effort, perhaps we should wonder how you do get accurate and appropriate changes made.

When the change is somewhat extensive, use a new connector, such as ㉒ in Figure 28, which takes you to a new page. On the infrequent occasions when there are so many changes to the same page as to make the result confusing, rewrite the Logic Chart page. Even a few rewrites will generally indicate the inability of the analysts to find an appropriate solution or the business organization to find a stable course of action. Either situation requires measures beyond the scope of any method of specification system.

At last computer information processing history is before your eyes. It is possible for you to see, understand, and explain not only how

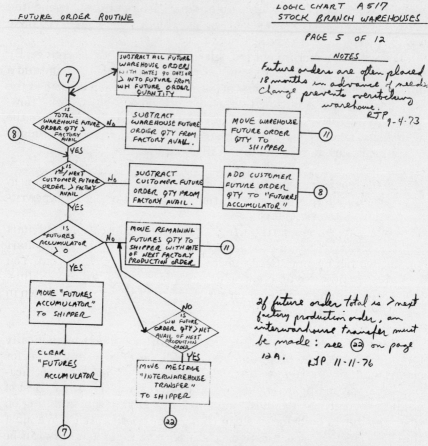

Figure 28   **Living logic—today's solution to a continuing problem.**

a program works but generally how it worked last year. You can explain how the information reports have changed. Sometimes it is even evident that RUM wants to go from where he is to where he's been, as you note that the latest change takes you back to previous logic.

Most vital of all to your business, the systems analyst, the programmer, and RUM will find that each of them can trust the Logic Chart to express the present parameters of individual business system programs. It is not necessary to unravel that labyrinth of technical deduction called the computer program. Such examination is expensive, time consuming, and often incomplete.

The Logic Chart represents the business. It tells us, quite easily, how our business information is generated. With the help of the systems analyst it is RUM's key to information reality.

LOGIC PACKAGE EXTRAS—AWARENESS OF ALTERNATIVES

The hallmark of computer processing is inflexibility! Options and alternatives never seem to be considered when programs are written. Requestor/user/manager's frustrations can be reduced if the doctor of business, the systems analyst, designs the solution, rather than the technician/programmer. Still, even a good systems analyst needs all the assistance he or she can get. The Logic Chart can help. This medium accentuates possible variations which *may* occur!

Times uncounted, expensive reprogramming has been done because a key code situation exhausted all the possibilities between 0 and 9; or no one *ever* thought that the sales price of any of the products would be greater than $99.99, or that anyone in the organization might earn more than $99,999.00 a year, or that. . . .

The open, uncluttered presentation of a problem in Logic Chart form can illuminate many of the probable ranges of activity. Business alternatives involving extensive change still can't be anticipated; who would expect a baby food company to sell insurance? But the Logic Chart offers insights into the more mundane potential business growth plans. And it is as good as the perception of the analyst using the method.

Figure 29 illustrates a small part of a problem which, through change and expansion, could cause considerable antagonizing maintenance. It is not difficult in many instances to build the opportunity for change into a program. Because change generally occurs within predictable limits, programs can be written which will accommodate many obvious alternatives. Opportunities with code structures are obvious. You simply make the fields big enough and avoid excessive program tests for validity—which are all too common in programs designed and coded by programmers.

In the factory labor situations in Figure 29 we find that alternatives of method of pay and computation of pay can be predicted. In addition to new departments, locations to insert new logic paths for the latest incentive systems or classifications of novel types of indirect labor can be appended to the logic.

But now a real benefit of the Logic Chart comes into play. As the systems analyst sits in communion with his developing plan, he *may* note a potential situation which has never occurred in the organization. Figure 29 illustrates a typical factory labor situation where hours of work generate pay. This traditional plan also uses work hours to calculate vacation and holiday pay. As the very first diamond decision indicates, if there are no hours in the input document this is an error and an error routine is involked.

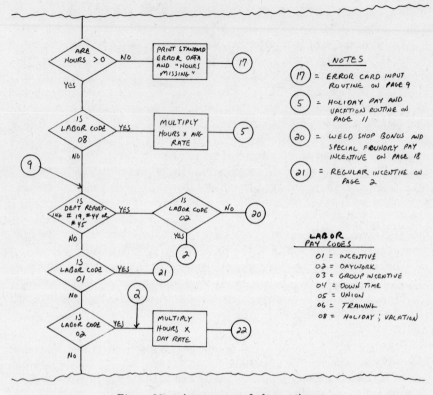

Figure 29   **Awareness of alternatives.**

Could it be otherwise? Could factory people with hourly rates ever be paid without any hours to multiply times their rate in one of the pay routines? *Perhaps,* and the alert analyst might note the omission. What if the founding father of the company died, and a special 4-hour paid shutdown took place? It couldn't be processed through holiday routine, since this routine deducts the hours paid from each employee's authorized pool of available time off. Or what if a cost of living lump sum payment was made, or the foundry bonus system had a calculation error for the last 6 months? In each unusual and unanticipated special pay situation hours would not or could not be used. A regular pay routine therefore could not suffice in these instances. No one ever would expect any of these situations to occur.

Fact tells the good programmer to test its limits for validity. *Tradition* tells the analyst to test its limits for validity. But the method of Logic Chart preparation offers two decision situations. When the decision test involves a range of activity (illustrated by labor codes), provision can be made to accommodate a potential range of change. The second decision situation is an absolute condition which either must be met or an error is declared (illustrated by the need for hours greater than zero). The Logic Chart defines clearly both types of decisions. The analyst's awareness of alternatives can expand beyond the limits of custom and common usage. The decision diamond clearly defines the rule which would be lost or obscured by narrative. By evaluating the possibility of rule change, the analyst can forecast system and program modification opportunities and build potential variations into the system. But the rules must first be visible. The Logic Chart puts them in view. Change can be forecast beyond tradition.

LOGIC PACKAGE EXTRAS—TESTING

Surprisingly, the Logic Chart is also of considerable benefit as we test the validity of a system. Rather than waiting for those nervous final deadline days, hoping the program will run, we can cut short the anxiety of the professionals and RUM's hostility by a three-step process of testing, using the Logic Chart.

Penetrating systems logic is not at all simple to develop. The broad spectrum of opportunity must now be segmented into specific and minute activities and decisions. Where does the analyst start? What steps come first? Narrative is the easy way out, since it is not as demanding as the sequential flowchart. Furthermore, ambiguity can be buried in a flow of words.

The clear, open development of problem solution logic with a Logic Chart offers three major (and necessary) test checkpoints for every system and its supporting program(s). These tests are:

1. The systems analyst test.
2. The RUM test.
3. The programmer test.

The Systems Analyst Test. This test comes upon completion of the Logic Chart flow. Normally this flow must be drawn twice. The first time, the analyst puts his thoughts on paper, recording specific action steps. This first attempt is always a hodgepodge because the main objective must be preceded by setup activities, validity tests, and minor but necessary exception routines. Here the problem solution is first developed in terms possible for a computer to process. The second writing of the Logic Chart results in the formal and final product. Then comes the systems analyst's test. Using cards or papers representing all valid and some invalid transactions, the analyst "walks through" the system. It can be done quietly as he sits alone at his desk.

The analyst may discover errors that pass his tests, assuming he is alert enough to plan for even the most improbable error conditions. Good transactions may not get processed. Some parts of the system may *never be used!* The prime results of the systems analyst's test are quite positive. We are now secure in the fact that the system works. We haven't foolishly waited for the computer to discover our logic errors. We cleanse the logic before we program.

Secure in the knowledge that the problem solution has now been translated into a correct computer solution, the analyst conducts the second test, *RUM's test.*

Rum's test. If the communication process has proceeded normally as the system developed, RUM and the analyst now have considerable understanding of each other's work. In this test, however, some actual transaction papers are used. The analyst walks through the logic with the requestor/user/manager. Major decisions are highlighted. Data processing housekeeping routines are ignored, as are error conditions that the system must prepare for. But RUM is expected to be alert for the proper sequence of events (when will the reorder point be tested?), special minor exceptions (an unusual pay rate for that one handicapped worker), and the like. Considerable conflict and hostility emanating from RUM and programmers can be avoided with this test *before* programming.

Moreover, RUM's test provides one final important piece of understanding. Assumptions are frequently made on both sides of the problem about who will do the work. For his part RUM assumes the system will take what he does today and accomplish results. Frequently, however, the analyst assumes a new piece of data, a new form, a new technique, or in general new work that RUM had not planned on providing. When the new work is outside the system, a good meeting with RUM to test the logic is necessary to highlight the requirements of the solution, beyond the computer. It is not at all unusual to find that work done at several clerical stations must now be collected into one point for the new system. The problem didn't change. The solution didn't change. But RUM's work routine and effort must be reorganized. Failure to recognize this reality has caused the delay of many a good system (and the failure of a few others) as RUM scrambles to utilize a system just turned on.

The RUM's test works two ways. Logic problems of the real world may be discovered for the analyst. And the analyst exposes work requirements that RUM must plan to accommodate.

The Programmer Test.   This is the final testing extra that the Logic Chart provides. Programming is a tricky and individualistic profession. No two programmers will ever write exactly the same code for the same problem. The clear flow of the Logic Package is translated into computer terms with varying levels of competence and understanding—and always with some earmarks of the personality of the programmer.

Even acknowledging these differences, it is the Logic Chart which solved the problem. Therefore programming *must* conform to the official logic flow. A programmer test is a two-way street. The analyst again moves through his logic, this time with the programmer and his code or his programmer flowchart. One objective is to ensure that the Logic Chart has been observed. The other is to determine, as the analyst did alone with his systems analyst test, that the error conditions are met and valid transactions processed.

When problems are complex, even the clearest logic and the crispest programming will demand a labyrinth of coding paths. The programmer test is the necessary meeting ground to insure that the code conforms to the problem solution flow stated in the Logic Chart.

This test is a vital part of the system/programming interrelationship of . . . learning how to talk to programmers.

LOGIC PACKAGE EXTRAS—MINIMIZATION OF REJECTED RESULTS

The combination of the RUM's test suggested above and the typed report form which is an integral part of the Logic Package deliberately draws strong ties of understanding between the user and data processing.

Requestor/user/manager must see a typed example of what he expects before programming starts and he must sign the document. This is not a chicken and egg situation. The output may be the end result that RUM expects, but it is the beginning of the systems development process. Although understanding and communication may be excellent, the cold, impersonal, typed report layout which is proposed changes abstract ideas into reality.

CONCLUSIONS

The Logic Package has synergistic impact on any organization. It is the tie that binds the three elements of information development——RUM, the systems analyst, and the programmer.

Information systems must be documented if we are to move forward. Change cannot be made from an unknown starting point. The Logic Package contains the simple, necessary elements of the information system. It is not complex, and it is easy to modify as day-to-day maintenance situations occur. Proper use offers the opportunity for generally error-free implementations. Moreover, RUM has the chance to evaluate methods, new requirements, and results before they are frozen into an expensive and sometimes inappropriate system. Programmers will initially express a dislike for the Logic Chart, since there is an implication that their creativity may be restricted. But the far less ambiguous specifications and fewer system errors and revisions that result will eventually gain their support.

The Logic package is the medium whose message becomes the vital common ground of understanding during the information development process. It is the third and final method suggested to make your organization superior.

CHAPTER 15

The End Is
Just Beginning

The meeting had not been going well. What had been a restless antagonism was now turning into open defiance. Some in the group were even muttering revolt. Many wanted to go back to the old ways of doing things.

The leader of the organization was tired. It seemed that this sort of thing had been happening for almost as long as he could remember. No one ever seemed to appreciate the problems he had faced. He brought himself mentally back to the meeting just as the speaker finished his remarks to cheers and jeers from the crowd.

"Anyone else?" he asked wearily.

"Just tell us when we can expect to get there," cried Baalem. The crowd shouted approval of the question, and Baalem grinned.

Before he could reply, Zohar was on his feet.

"You don't know, do you? You don't know if we'll ever get there! All we do is wander around through this wilderness. It's been like 30 years, Mo."

Now Moses was angry. "You all complain too much! Sure, this is not the greatest, but everybody forgets how it was back in the old days. Remember all that meaningless work you did. Remember when. . . ."

Nephag interrupted. "Mo, we all know that this is much different from before (Moses noted he didn't say 'better'). But for years you've been telling us about the great things coming. This idea of a Promised Land is fine if it's really there. Most of us have invested a lot in this trip, and all we have are assurances that things are going to get better. When will that be?"

Nephag's comments started everyone talking and shouting again. Moses saw the worried look on Aaron's face. Once again he sent his mind over the well worn path of reality and logic that had led him to this day. He knew that the past was far from ideal. With Aaron's help and some PRIME support they had traveled well and traveled far. Who else could get water from a rock? The land of milk and honey was just over the horizon. Moses knew it was there. The oft Promised Land was just around the corner. The only problem was to figure out how to get there. Something had to be done. Again the shouts of the crowd interrupted his thoughts. It was going to be another bad day.

TODAY

Except in a very small organization which is just receiving its first computer, the wild-catting for wells of clerical cost reduction with a computer are over. Few new computer systems can be located where the present methods can be economically improved by installing a computer system because none existed before.

Gone too, thankfully, are the glamourous days of the glass walled computer room and the CRT on the president's desk. The "show-off" complex was exhibited by far too many chief executives as they *personally* demonstrated their computer systems. It was not the hard realities of the economic situation that changed their attitude. Rather, it was the realization that computer systems generally dealt best with past factual situations and summarizations, while the desk top CRT offered an even more limited range of statistical evaluation at management levels.

Computer tools and computer applications were often motivated not by need, but rather by fascination. Like the company jet, they were more toy than tool. But today higher level management, in particular, has come to appreciate the reality of present computer information capability. These boxes of programmed intelligence basically process present or past activity, segregated by business function into the units of time and the organizations most suitable to the financial system. The output is, then, past facts. But the chief executive seldom makes decisions based on past facts—or, at times, any facts at all. His intuition, his business sense, his feeling for the marketplace carry the organization into the future. The information system has seldom supplied much help.

Improvements are slow, and unfortunately, even in the third decade of business computer use, we are still trying to extricate ourselves from the common situation of allowing the tool to manage us. Data inputs are continually restrained by the limitations of the programs. Flexibility is inhibited by monolithic hardware and software capability. Science fiction programs and stories are rampant with future computer monsters which "control us." Yet, in truth, we have yet to control them! These unfeeling beasts of the information burden already dictate many a human action or response. Today who *really* works for whom? Does the machine work for us, or do we work for the machine?

TOMORROW

Just as man learned to master his mechanical tools, so too we will conquer our marvelous electronic helpmate. The chief executive once managed his entire operation as a unit without a great deal of detailed information. The computer changed his organizational viewpoint because it quickly provided vast amounts of historical functional detail. Many an executive has been overwhelmed by such detail. More commonly, functions (particularly finance, which is always automated first) made a disproportionate impact on management thinking in relationship to their possible contributions to organizational success. Management's thinking was split into functional concepts.

Generally, up to this point, systems, have been designed with a specific functional objective appropriate to the requestor/ user/manager's sometimes limited goals. Some of these applications have been fascinating in addition to practical, such as real-time airline reservation and real-time bank balance systems. Others have been purely promotional, such as a voice response system. Throughout this period of bizarre growth, a practical foundation of good business reporting has generally been developed along functional lines. But a computer information system can be more. Decision making management and even some functional RUMs recognize that limited information horizons can, at times, be restrictive to profitable decisions. Many success opportunities lie with projections of the future, using evaluations of present and past. This is not modeling! The modeling tool attempts to forecast the results of policy decisions based on limited key operational and market inputs. But the next opportunity for progress lies with major business information combinations called operating systems applications. Here the various existing major elements of the company are tied together. We have yet to unify such entities as marketing, manufacturing, and finance into a homogeneous information system which will easily and appropriately respond with top management decisions. But that day is coming. Soon we will begin to commonly find the necessary business tools to unite the two existing extremes of functional systems and modeling. Operating application systems are on their way. And to change the face of the information processing functions and the DP Departments we can anticipate other changes that will take place in the not too distant future.

The Future with People

The role of the data processing expert in business society has always been troubling. His or her necessary technical expertise has made this individual stand alone and above many others in terms of pay and personal prestige. A caste system has developed, led by the Brahmin systems analyst and followed by systems programmers, analyst/programmers, programmers, computer operators, and finally the almost untouchable EAM (electronic accounting machine) operators. As in any closed society, measurements of accomplishment have been set internally by the group. The automatic exclusion of RUM from this group of DP experts has often meant that the requests and needs of the business organization receive priority equal only to that given the group's own internal computer system improvement tasks. It is true that many time and resource consuming internal DP projects eventually provide *some* organizational benefit. More often than we dare admit, however, these projects have been done to satisfy the ego and interests of analysts and systems programmers. Furthermore, the technical background of the DP group and the lack of measurement standards of good performance direct the attention of the group to this type of millisecond manipulation. Often, too, internal DP improvements have been the department's security blanket. It understands itself, the machines, and the operating system much better than it understands the business environment it was created to support.

With new hardware and software development future applications of business systems need not be linked so closely with a particular brand of computer or generation of operating system. Then we can expect a change in the physical location and status of data processing personnel. Model number of the computer, core capacity, and speeds will disappear as hallmarks of a company's progressive stance and the DP employee's capability.

The systems analyst's function will emerge from the DP Department as he or she becomes a member of a functional RUM group or of top-level decision making management. In turn, RUM and all management levels will train themselves in systems development requirements. Just as today most executives can define their own budgets, financial needs, and capital requirements, we can expect this same group to ally itself more closely to the information systems of the future. The parochial DP viewpoints and the limited functional horizons of RUM will break down as this group manages *for* the organization *with* information and the necessary, but limited, technical knowledge.

When the systems analyst becomes a member of the user group and functions truly as a doctor of business, a diagnostician of business ills, the caste system will break down and we can anticipate changes in traditional roles. Administrators will begin to replace technicians as the directors of computer operations. We can expect that, as DP operations continue to become routine, they will be run more like a factory—on a cost center basis, like other functions. Banks, manufacturing organizations, and even service bureaus are starting to place experienced liberal arts graduates and known administrators into management roles. Demonstrable skills of scheduling, resource allocation, personnel development, and organization planning far outweigh the merits of a technology background for a good DP administrator. Long ago it was found that the best surgeon did not make the best hospital administrator, nor did a good engineer always make a good engineering manager. Now it is data processing's turn to become professionally administered.

Systems analysts, because they will become members of RUM's organization, will experience improved relations between themselves and RUM—and the systems will benefit! It has not been at all unusual to consider many analysts as speed freaks. Their sudden appearance, quick questions, and rapid departure have been resented intrusions on normal organizational routine. And then . . . to show up one day with a completely defined system offended the sensitivities of almost everyone.

As more analysts spend training time to develop a human relations background, in addition to system training, we will expect our future analyst to slow his or her pace and consider the viewpoints and thoughts of all concerned with the new system. Although errors will always be made in applied information technology, placement of the analyst with RUM will provide more appropriate problem insights. Furthermore data processing will find a far more agreeable customer as aloof professional poise is discarded in favor of a partnership of problem identification and solution development with RUM as a fully accepted *equal* problem solver.

For programmers the future holds both good and bad developments. Good programmers can anticipate improved salary scales more adequately commensurate with their contributions to the organization. Good people are always in demand, and wage rates will rise to a level where capable programmers will be paid on a scale equal to that for good systems analysts.

The other side of the coin is not as bright. Programming is under attack from two sides since the obviously easy entry to the field and high pay stand out in today's marketplace.

Educational institutions have developed abundant course concentrations in data processing. Normally they are centered on the definable and teachable programming, usually with emphasis on the more technical aspects of the process. As more graduates are released to the marketplace, we are on the verge of a massive oversupply of programmers. Only a few of the most brilliant are needed to write software and new compilers. The rest. . . .? With something like only 200,000 conventional computers in the world they face an employment problem. Most older programmers are not even close to retirement!

Software houses and the computer industry itself are also attacking the programming profession. Since a great deal of file updating, editing, and file maintenance is similar in any computer situation, it is possible to write in house, or to buy, common routines and packages which can eliminate the necessity of individualistic hard coding. Computer manufacturers also promote such "turnkey" systems as a feature of their newer hardware products. Previously we noted that most businesses operate within definable limits of information modified by management variation. This "data base" environment lends itself to a programmerless output from a report generator package—that is, no programmer required!

Where openings are available, the profession will pay well, but many new programmers should, at best, anticipate careers as the entire DP staff of a minicomputer installation.

The Future with Systems

Although the concepts suggested in preceding chapters will improve any organization's systems, it is possible to envision much more drastic changes that will be coming in the future. Many of the new business systems will not really be systems at all! More information customers every day recognize that decision and action for the organization take place within loosely structured but nevertheless limited boundaries. Data base oriented processing is becoming more common.

Each day a stronger interaction between functions is being recognized. Transactions in the future will be processed to completion *at the time of initiation* because all necessary editing, record creation, file updating, and computation can be performed at one time. When a sale is made, inventory can be updated, plus new production orders started, plus sales analysis updated, plus accounts receivable updated, plus a cash forecast update, plus. ... We might begin to think in terms of depreciating our assets every day, of determining tool and die usage every run or every day (whichever is shorter), perhaps of doing an accounting closing and income statement every day! Management, of course, doesn't need an income statement every day, but then why should management have to wait until the end of each fiscal period? How much, after all, of the entire information process has been a fictitious collection of facts to match a period of time best suitable to the mechanics of the system?

Reporting systems will change. The information will flow as the business flows. Information systems will be melded into an organization process which collects and administers facts and reports. Managerial reliance on subjective judgments based on experience will be greatly reduced, although never eliminated. We will, however, see increasing reliance on *now* information available from the information system and developed, not from functions, but from the entire organization process.

The new future systems structure might be termed a *knowledge system*. Not only will it encompass the accumulated facts and information of the organization and be able to maintain a real-time reporting system, but also, most importantly, the knowledge system will provide a total perception of changing values and their impact. New combinations and interrelationships will be exposed. We can expect the knowledge system to identify and solve problems currently constraining profits from the business. New opportunities for more economical operations, improved margins, better markets, or invigorating new services will be semiautomatically developed. The machine will be able to support human management by total organization comprehensibility.

There is no implication here that machines will replace the management process. Rather, the knowledge system, with its interconnected files and data bases, will provide extensively broader foundations for meaningful, sensitive action. Today RUM may call up, on his CRT, a product record relating to his function. If he is a marketing manager, he may interrogate the product Z sales analysis history with variations by customer, sales territory, or salesman. If he is an order entry or sales force person, he will interrogate product Z inventory records, back order records, branch warehouse stocks, and so on. If RUM is a production manager, he will interrogate product Z's work-in-process record, bill of material, tooling availability, scheduling record, and the like.

Tomorrow, as the multiple strands of activity associated with product Z become bound together in a knowledge system, we will observe a progressive decision process. The marketing manager may still review basically the same facts, but any decision will be reinforced by other newly available data. There will be an opportunity to make any decision action with more beneficial results for the total organization. For example, a special sales campaign will be made *only* if enough inventory, plant capacity, and tooling capacity are available to meet anticipated needs. Or a decision to discontinue product Z may not be made when a large production order is on the verge of completion. Or, if a decision is made to discontinue product Z, that decision will *today* stop the toolroom foreman from replating the basic die at a cost of $4000. *Today,* also, the Accounting Department can stop depreciating this same die, scrap it, and write it off.

These types of responses are almost unheard of today. Statistical, financial, and operational facts of any management flow from function to function long after they can be optimumly exploited. Today RUM manages yesterday. In the future he may be in a position to manage today.

Policy making executives and RUM can anticipate the development of two excellent information tools. Both are available today in primitive form.

The first tool is an organization-wide report generator based on a knowledge system structure and available, with only minor constraints, to all members of the organization. Countless books have been written on the management process, dissecting it, structuring it, and formalizing it. Yet regardless of all theory, the manager, with a unique background of training and human experience, is forced to make determinations based on a firmly structured information system, littered with obsolete facts, obscure values, and limitations of scope, applied against his own individualistic human values.

The report generator is the key which can unlock whatever potential RUM may have to manage *with* information. The report generator of the future needs the unstructured, interrelated base of information provided by the knowledge system. As this base comes into being, RUM may exercise all of his ingenuity making independent analyses based on his selected criteria. The report generator will, furthermore, free RUM from the time consuming and frustrating delays necessitated by even the best programming function.

The information system then becomes an open book; all the decision makers must do is find the right page. The policy making group particularly can have a total *present* status oriented toward each member's needs and areas of interest. Management will have better information whereby to determine what to do. Its decisions can precede its actions by searching for opportunities to do things differently, based on today's realities.

Decision making in the future will escalate to a higher plane basically for two reasons. Decisions will be made on current, interrelated information bases which picture the total organization in its present condition. More importantly, the very few real decision makers will have the ability to construct their own information base for any determination. This ability will provide a sobering element to any decision maker's actions. Such "personal" construction will certainly cause much disagreement about the actual facts in any situation, but the ensuing dialogue will only promote more knowledgeable understanding. With these more appropriate observations, decision making will become better than we know it today.

The second information tool to undergo development will be interactive terminals available to RUM for his personal use. Since no two individuals manage any function in exactly the same way, it is appropriate to assume that many people use personalized information developed as an appendage to existing information structures. Everyone at one time or another has elected to keep certain percentages, personal graphs, or desired statistics based on reported operating data. Many managers of the future will exploit the use of a terminal to develop private information systems of their own. Most will be based on small files of particular data which each manager has found uniquely useful to his needs. Hardware/software improvements will allow updates to these personal files from the main knowledge system. At his discretion RUM can review his file status and modify or discontinue it at any time. It will even be possible to instruct the computer to alert the manager of threshold decision levels (previously established by the manager for his own evaluation) as each level is reached.

The main knowledge system and its report generator will provide a timely basis to allow RUM and policy makers to examine the relative advantages and risks in choosing new and different directions. With such a tool at their fingertips it is difficult to imagine that boards of directors will follow some of the disastrous paths which have led to bankruptcy. Then, too, many of the wildly inappropriate operating schemes of management can be better curtailed by a chief executive with available operating knowledge.

The individual, personalized data bases that interactive terminals can provide offer executives a unique opportunity. The chance to make independent analyses, even to the point of simulating the authority and responsibility of other executives, will allow managers who have an idea to develop it to the point of decision. All this has not been possible with rigid framework information systems. It might be assumed that management decisions will even become easier if all staff members have complete and identical information. Even if decision making is not made simpler, it will at least become more sensitive.

The Future with the Data Processing Department

With maturity will come standardization. As each function begins to take control of its own information inputs and outputs, the role of the Data Processing Department will drastically change. We can expect that DP will act as custodian of the major organization files, much as a financial controller is custodian of assets records, but not custodian of the assets themselves. Within the department, the operations section will become the prime element as it runs the hardware and regulates the files of data. Systems will generally migrate (as we previously noted) to the various functional groups and top level management. Programming will simply decline.

One position, that of data controller, will grow. This position within data processing is a necessary and vital key to a successful knowledge system. The data controller will provide the necessary structure of massive nonredundant records. He will develop appropriate organization-wide coding structures and resolve disputes relating to file organization. The enlargement of the data controller position will allow the orderly transition of the systems analyst from the "machine" organization to the more appropriate "user" group.

Just as a product designer does not run a factory, the data controller will neither manage the computer function nor become a systems "czar." It will be his job to contribute his special skills of organization and arbitration, allowing the systems analysts freedom of development. This will be a most difficult and challenging position, requiring huge doses of tact and job interest. The wrong person in the position will stifle the creativity of the analysts if he becomes dedicated to information structures rather than information uses. If the data controller is a hardware oriented person, he will inhibit appropriate systems developments for the sake of machine run time. But if we can fill the job with a person who has an adequate perception of the organization and the place of the information system within that organization, we will then have the vital link in the DP chain to carry us into the future.

Software packages consisting of standard application routines such as payroll or production control have been available for a number of years. Most frequently the salesmen for these products enter your organization through the doors of data processing. At times, however, the sales pitch (especially for the more expensive packages) is made directly to the treasurer, production manager, or key functional executive closest to this type of system. Beware! When you buy these packages, you are selling your future.

Every software package offered for sale has been a remarkable success somewhere. The reason it has been so successful is that the features of the organization using it match the features of the package. The situation should be just the opposite.

Packages do offer an inexpensive method of stepping into the near future. The overhead of extra machine time for the package, along with the restrictions of highly generalized methods of processing and reporting information, is easily offset by the obviously higher cost if you tried writing such a thing yourself. But what about your long-range future? Over the very few years of life of the package in your organization you have simply postponed the absolutely necessary step of constructing your own systems to meet your own needs. Your own programs can be open ended to begin linking themselves to the eventual knowledge system. A package is functionally limiting and must finally be discarded. Today is the time to build for the future. Make use of the available supply of programmers in the marketplace, and build your information system of common data files which will take full advantage of emerging hardware and software developments. Big organization systems, with their multifaceted compositions and unique management personalities, require equally individualistic information systems. Building such a system for the future requires that you build your own.

Smaller systems using minicomputers will of course enjoy the economical use of standard packages and turnkey systems. Here the package makes sense. It is used in a limited scope of standard routines when the organization is small enough to be managed by the personal observation of the chief executive. In fact, the minicomputer and the package, in a very small company, provide the base, the report generator, the flexibility, and the management understanding that we strive so hard to reach on a grander scale for the large organization.

Data processing hardware has always been faddish. The "My computer is bigger than your computer" days are generally gone—hopefully forever. We've played enough games keeping up with the generation of the Jones Company next door, supposedly to keep our programmers by always providing the most advanced and desirable tool. But programmers don't hop to the next job so frequently any more, and the new generalized business machine and operating system *may* be firming into less drastic business systems changes when generations evolve.

Fads are still with us, nevertheless. For the past 10 years we have read about the checkless society and electronic fund transfer (EFT) systems that are only 2 years away. They are still 2 years away! Computer on microfilm (COM) has equally been touted for years, but its cost still precludes common usuage. Word processing and point of sale (POS) are perhaps the hottest "new" ideas in the marketplace today. Yet neither (especially word processing) is at all new or different from the general hardware or processing concepts suggested for many years.

The common denominator of these "fad" systems is that they process only very limited segments of the total organization information stream. Word processing will type and edit repetitive forms, letters, and paragraphs. It has now, as it did 20 years ago, very specific and valuable uses—remember the Frieden Flexowriter! Computer on microfilm (COM) has value only if an organization, very large and produces widely distributed, voluminous reports—let's not ask now why it produces them! Both EFT and POS are a bit different. They are systems for the masses—if and when the general population agrees to losing the opportunity to use check float, to delay bill payments, or to hunt for an item not yet marked up on the grocery shelf. But regardless of the common use or consumer acceptance of these new systems, we must be concerned with their ultimate true values to the organization. Will we get more customers, more margin, less inventory with POS, considering its high cost and potential consumer hostility?

If it is accurately determined that a new system of hardware devices will allow the organization to manage better in the future, then proceed by all means. But try to wait until somebody else installs and tries it first. The real future with hardware is to spend more time making better use of what we already have.

The Future of You

Throughout this book we have continually referred to the bond of opportunity between the systems analyst and the professional manager. The tests of information pollution may have reflected the fact that this partnership had not yet functioned as well as it might. But with an analyst trained as a doctor of business and a requestor/user/manager with equally appropriate training we have the basic foundation of human talent to build a better system.

The future will be a long time coming. It will be "muggered up" by new generations of hardware and software and by fads like minis and POS. Yet the far more basic hurdle we must overcome is the monumental, ancient program library existing in everyone's computer shop today. Some installations are still writing in second-generation languages with all of their built-in software and hardware faults.

Almost no one has been yet able to take the time or spend the dollars necessary to convert old systems (even those of precomputer design) into systems of the 1970s. The languages may be "native," but the systems and computer logic routines are still primitive.

Three major tools have been offered to make the information system more receptive and responsive to your needs. First, the sometimes maligned Primary Data Base, which will eventually coalesce functions into the future knowledge system. The second tool is the simple, inexpensive Reports Book. Today, for all we read and experience with fantastically capable hardware, we are still not able to provide a credible, desirable product of information. It is time to begin to allow RUM to participation in the information development process. The Reports Book is the beginning of participatory systems. The third and final offering is the Logic Package. It is a combination of standard logic development and internal discipline. If rigorously applied, it will provide a bridge between user, analyst, and RUM which today does not exist. The Logic Package is a tool for the present if we are ever to reach the future.

Finally, some words of advice for the analyst and for the manager are in order. The end is just beginning. The wild and wooly frontiers of business data processing have been explored. But there is still more than a lifetime of work ahead of us as we attempt to develop the knowledge system. In the meantime:

To the analyst: "Design for RUM and the policy management of your organization. Do not design systems for the computer, and sometimes . . . build a system without the beast!"

To the manager: "Demand the future that you want from your systems analysts and data processing people. Only you can truly anticipate your business needs. Take an active part in the development of all systems. Most of all, demand more from your computer information system, and you'll get it."

The Dragsmar Evaluation [1]

In the preceding chapters we examined information, its development, and the organization which uses information. Then we related various test situations to a scoring system to obtain a rating of the information environment. But even within a small company the scope of the information system is very great. And the suggested tests are certainly only definitive enough to provide a modest degree of understanding of the size of the information pollution problem.

The DRAGSMAR EVALUATION is somewhat different. It is a previously tested assessment method for just one department—Data Processing. This department is the prime information source within the organization. Although you will recognize some of the test questions, the testing approach of the Dragsmar Evaluation is entirely different from the tests previously suggested. With the assistance of one or two key DP people and a few hours of time you may be able to answer a very

[1]Based on the article, "Evaluate Your Computer Installation," by William C. Ramsgard. Reprinted by permission of *Management Services,* January–February. Copyright © 1971 by the American Institute of Certified Public Accountants, Inc. This article was selected for the annual Lester Witte award as the outstanding article of the year.

vital question, "Is your computer installation really any good?"

Pick up any magazine or newspaper oriented toward business or a particular profession and read the ads. Big computers, minicomputers, terminals, languages, software packages, and consultants by the dozen offer the best of everything required to develop the ideal computer center. And, of course, you must have a magnetic schedule board, a tape reel truck, and a shredder to improve your operation.

Now, if you read the articles in that same magazine, you realize that something is wrong! Issue after issue contains bold documentation of a myriad of grand successes by others in information processing. But does your organization seem to measure up to these grand designs? Obviously something is wrong. Are your data processing personnel inept? Can your equipment be inadequate? With such a diverse selection of services and equipment, it just may be that the computer world is passing you by.

Wait a minute! A shredder or a software package won't make a computer operation run correctly. It takes good people, hard work, and a lot of time to develop a smoothly functioning organization.

It takes more than a product bright with Madison Avenue glamour to make everything run right.

What does it take? How does your group measure up? What you do need is a way to evaluate the existing data processing installation simply and effectively.

As you control an obviously expensive organizational resource, should you not be able to measure the quality of your computer products? There is, of course, no direct way to value the information product itself. One man's information is another man's myth! A computer resource evaluation must be made in the subjective terms of operation and information techniques and controls.

Following is the Dragsmar Evaluation, a rating system designed to guide the measurement of your computer operations. The Dragsmar Evaluation is best adapted to a business computer environment of no more than three separate (or combined) computer systems. There are seven major areas of evaluation:

1. Software.
2. Hardware.
3. Documentation and organization.
4. Planning.
5. Testing.
6. Personnel.
7. Protection.

The Dragsmar Evaluation allows both positive and negative values. Some common practices are clearly bad and are rated accordingly. Scores will range from −53 to +147 and may be judged as follows:

130–147	Superior
115–129	Satisfactory
90–114	Average
60–89	Poor
Below 60	Take immediate corrective action

A high evaluation indicates that the computer is well organized and managed. It fails to indicate whether the user is receiving the most appropriate quantity and quality of data to do his job, just as good accounting practices and financial reports do not mean a profitable operation. The computer output must be timely, meaningful, and properly used by the recipient.

A poor rating *does* indicate that the data processing function's planning and control are such that it *cannot* deliver a good product.

Following are a series of test questions which make up the Dragsmar Evaluation. You will need the assistance of the DP personnel to obtain some of the answers. Take the test. Following the test questions are comments and justifications for the question, the scoring, and the most appropriate replies. We recommend that you test and score first and read the comments later. Although some questions may not be completely appropriate for *your* organization, the range and variety are so great that there is little distortion in the final result.

Some DP professionals will be disturbed by several of these questions. Over almost 25 years of commercial computer history, very few report cards have been issued for our installations.

This testing scheme has been used by the U.S. Marine Corps, the U.S. Public Health Service, hospitals, universities, accounting firms, and other organizations in the United States and Canada.

DRAGSMAR EVALUATION

			Your
Software	Yes	No	Total

---

1. Count the active computer programs in the data processing library. If your organization is one of the Fortune 500, are there less than 1500 programs? If your organization is one of the Fortune Second 500, are there less than 1000 programs?

Software *(cont'd)*	Yes	No	Your Total
If your organization is smaller still, do you have less than 500 programs?	10	0	
2. Are sorts more than 10% of your computer programs?	5	0	
3. Are any programs run in simulation, emulation, or compatability modes?	0	5	
4. Are any major computer files organized randomly?	5	0	
5. Are most new programs written in COBOL or PL/1?	5	0	
6. Do outside software or consulting firms now write any of your production programs?	−5	0	

Hardware	Yes	No	Your Total
7. Does your company have gross sales of less than $20 million and two computers or gross sales of less than $100 million and three computers at a single site?	−5	0	
8. In the last 36 months have you made over five additions to core and/or more or faster peripherals?	−4	0	
9. Have you had more than three different models or brands of main frame (CPU) in the last 10 years?	−3	0	
10. Are productive meter-hours equal to or greater than 96% of total meter-hours?	5	0	
11. Excepting source data entry equipment, subtract one for each piece of unit record equipment now used (−10 maximum).	−10	0	

Documentation and Organization	Yes	No	Your Total
12. Review the program folder of some popular, frequently run program.			

Documentation and Organization (*cont'd*)	Yes	No	Your Total
A. Using some section of the material in this folder, can you follow *exactly* how *the problem* is solved, including how all calculations take place?	12	0	
B. If "No" to A above, can you generally understand how the problem is solved?	7	0	
C. If "No" to A and B above, can the DP manager explain *clearly* how the program works?	4	0	
D. If "No" to A, B, and C above, is there a program folder with something in it?	2	-10	
13. Can you normally locate master flowcharts indicating the total program series and requirements to accomplish this job?	3	0	
14. A. Is there a book, folder, file, etc., containing layouts showing the exact position and content of information within your tape or disk records?	7	0	
B. Is this set of records up to date?	4	0	
C. Is this set of records indexed?	1	0	
D. Are record layout copies kept in the program folder?	2	0	
15. A. Do you have a master Reports Book or file with one copy (or sample) of every computer report?	7	0	
B. If "No" to A above, is there a sample report in each program folder?	4	0	
16. Are most sample reports the latest reliable version?	4	0	
17. A. Is there a book, folder, file, etc., of card (or input document) layouts showing the exact position and content of information on each card?	6	0	
B. Is this set of records up to date?	4	0	

Planning	Yes	No	Your Total
18. Do you have an annual procedure that formally plans, evaluates and develops priorities for new automated applications in the coming year?	6	0	
19. Is there a formal system for evaluation and review of new requests for computer services?	4	0	
20. Is there a charge-back or memo billing system so that both the user and the chief executive can evaluate the worth of the output?	3	0	
21. Does Data Processing document for corrective action all reruns?	3	0	
22. Is Data Processing overtime proportionally equal to the overtime or less than the overtime generally worked in other departments?	0	−3	

Testing	Yes	No	Your Total
23. Is there a written procedure indicating either a plan or requirement to desk-check problem solution logic before programming?	5	0	
24. Is there a written procedure indicating either a plan or requirement to test a program?	5	0	
25. Are programs tested?	0	−5	
26. Are program test results examined most of the time by someone in Data Processing other than the programmer?	5	0	
27. Are programmers allowed to run their own tests on the computer system?	0	3	

Personnel	Yes	No	Your Total
28. Does the person who studies the problem (the analyst) also write the program?	0	10	
29. Does your organization have any type of planned training program for data processing personnel?	3	0	

Personnel (*cont'd*)	Yes	No	Your Total
30. Were more than one-third of the data processing personnel *originally* unit record or computer operators in your organization or elsewhere?	−4	0	
31. Were three-fourths or more of your analysts originally programmers?	−4	0	
32. Has at least 60% of your total DP staff been in this department 4 or more years?	5	0	

Protection	Yes	No	Your Total
33. Are computer room doors locked or otherwise access restricted?	2	0	
34. Does the Maintenance Department clean the room carefully so as not to raise dust?	2	0	
35. Are filters changed regularly?	1	0	
36. Are master tape and disk records made in duplicate and stored where fire, riot, or storm would not destroy both sets?	3	0	
37. Are the preprinted forms stored so that fire or a ruptured sprinkler head will not ruin all of them?	2	0	

Total Score ———————

COMMENTS OR EXPLANATIONS RELATED TO THE PREVIOUS QUESTIONS BY QUESTION NUMBER

Software

1. Well organized systems and programming will easily capture all systems appropriate to automate. Although each organizational environment is unique, the problems and solutions of businesses are generally quite similar. More than the suggested number of basic programs indicate poor systems planning, fragmented processing, and low grade solutions per program. An exception must be made for autonomous divisions using your central computer

system. Increase the base by 10% for each geographically separated, generally independent division.

Professionals will have the most trouble with question 1. The number of programs in the question must be an error? It is not! We ask for such a small number of active programs as a maximum in a well organized installation. Very few installations score positively on this question. Their programs have been written by technicians who did not have the opportunity to evaluate the business system.

In one recent actual case a firm replaced a machine installed in 1966 with a different manufacturer's computer. Not surprisingly the new machine brought about a 100% change in systems personnel. The 1966 machine had processed, as one program, factory labor input with eleven incentive systems, calculated gross to net pay, wrote checks, and set up all deduction registers. A new systems group with a 1976 machine and more core managed to do *exactly* the same job in twenty-nine programs.

2. Sorts indicate that data recorded and retained can be used over again for multi-information purposes. Lack of computer sorts indicates pre-first-generation off-line methods and/or poor information structure and retention. The minimum acceptable limit is one sort for each ten programs.

3. Only native language processing allows full hardware utilization.

4. Most computer manufacturers will advertise random processing, yet advocate that you practice various forms of sequential file organization processing. Although almost all business environment transactions take place in a random fashion, few computers are able to process data that way. Normally the master records in the computer conform to tape oriented, second-generation sequential arrangement. Such organization of data is optimum only for *some* program processing time and subjects the programmer to grave problems in setup, maintenance, and overflow. Credit is due your staff when it is able to work with random files to any extent and make the machine operate like the business.

5. The higher level languages offer documentation, control, and flexibility not available with lower order languages.

6. This is the most expensive kind of data processing; you pay dearly for each line of code. You must justify the expense by an urgent demand for results. But you must also ask yourself two questions. First, how did the crisis arise? Where was the management planning, direction, and data processing staff training and retention program to avoid the crisis? Second, can you live with the

consultant's solution? These persons are necessarily "results now" oriented. Was the system studied? Was the program documented? Will it stand up to the test of years of processing? Probably not, and your own retained staff will not be able to decipher the consultant's notes and program logic.

If you've answered "Yes" and consultants do write programs, subtract 5 from the score.

Hardware

7. A "Yes" to this question indicates your computer salesman wins the prizes in *his* company's sales contest—thanks to you!

8. A "Yes" to this question demonstrates lack of requirements planning and/or a zealous computer salesman again. Can he *really* solve problems with more hardware? It is possible that your configuration planning is so good that five or more additions are actually appropriate and economical? Such exceptional cases will find that their scores are over 115 without this question. The proof is in the final score.

9. A score over 3 again indicates poor long-range planning and/or capable computer salesmen.

10. Meter-hours are lost for several reasons such as operator error, machine malfunction, and a faulty sequence of data or programs. All sources should not total more than 4% of total meter-hours.

11. This type of equipment is older in design and function then most of your organization personnel. It is also very expensive. Your

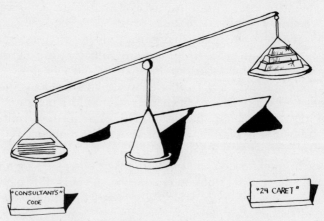

Figure 30   Weighing the cost of Consultants code.

requirements for these pieces of equipment are somewhat proportional to the capabilities of the entire operation. In the 1970s information processing environment you need NONE of it. To use it is like riding a horse to work on a freeway—it will get you there, but very slowly!

Documentation and Organization

12. The question on program folders (or whatever you choose to call the documentation of a computer program) allows you to select one of six possible numeric ratings. Select only one.

    Since the program folder explains HOW a particular job is run on your computer, it is extremely important to your operation. If you cannot understand some portion of it, you must employ a specialist to decipher it. If no program folder exists or the one that does can't be easily explained to you, the problem gets worse. Imagine running the Accounting Department without an updated Chart of Accounts? Or, even worse, no chart at all? What then of the documentation of vital business routines now submerged in a vast complex machine! A score of less than 8 indicates you've lost control of your organization systems! What happens in that machine, how it happens, whether or not it was correct is anybody's guess.

13. Master flowcharts indicate interrelationships between programs. Like an audit trail, they indicate how information develops from program to program. Master flowcharts also serve as a safety device for program changes. By tracing the uses of proposed changed information or structures of data through a series of programs, we can detect the impact of the changes on other facets of the data processing product.

14. Whereas question 12 looked for relevant documentation of computer solutions, this question seeks suitable recording of the structured information that machines process.

    Information organized in a computer is commonly called a file. Files in turn have elements of information commonly called fields. Exact, up-to-date record layouts of files are essential to accurate information processing. If labels do not indicate field content, decimal placement, or the meaning of codes, you are in trouble. How can the programmer (or his next replacement) figure out what the unlisted codes mean? How can he treat dollar and cent or percent fields accurately? How can you rely on your report data?

15. The master Reports Book indicates what information is available on a standard basis. In a vital, growing organization, with frequent promotions and turnover, information requests are duplicated over and over as new people request information contained in old reports. But the new people are not aware of the old reports or of similar versions of a particular report. We find also that long-term stable organization managers will request what appears to be new information. A master Reports Book frequently can provide existing report sources or the basis for easy modification without extensive and expensive reprogramming.

Planning

18. This is a very expensive resource. Books have been written on how to formulate plans and establish priorities. If you answered "No," it may be the appropriate time to get a planning manual and a formal program.
19. New requests and demands cannot always be planned for. You must have a system that will accommodate continual change.
20. Once the user sees what the output costs, he may decide he can operate successfully without it. A "free" computer installation is an expensive luxury.
21. The comments for question 10 pointed out several reasons for unproductive meter-hours. If you know how many hours are lost, a firm positive reporting system is a strong tool to eliminate repetitive errors. Be aware that, regardless of your answer, it may be possible to do better! Both hardware devices and software are available to measure productive hardware meter-hour utilization.

Testing

This entire section of questions offers a guideline to the speed and accuracy of program implementation. Consider your own impatience when you read what you've written. Frequently, you think so fast (and know what you mean) that you write and proofread through your own errors. The programmer is just as impatient and frequently is pressed as hard as you are. Verification before actual program testing is essential and must be done by or with someone other than the principal program writer.

A programmer will normally test all proper solutions and all calculations in his program. Quite frequently, however, he will not test all possible real-world business conditions or sequences of conditions that will actually take place in his program. Failure to test a wide variety of line organization transactions means eventual program deficiency. Failure to test all possible error conditions will cause innumerable delays and even quicker program problems.

Personnel

28. A good programmer is a person dedicated to the development of perfect problem solutions in terms of computer equipment utilization. Such a programmer is invaluable. He must, however, be balanced by an organization generalist—a systems analyst.

This systems analyst is similar to an internal consultant. He too is dedicated, but to total organization success. He seeks success in the form of efficient results for human beings—sometimes at the expense of the machine.

It is not possible to have the best of both worlds. The organization generalist (systems analyst) and the dedicated programmer cannot be the same person. Do your draftsmen also do your product development engineering? If you allow machine specialists (programmers) to design your business systems, then beware! You've placed the very life blood of your organization—your information—in the hands of dedicated technicians.

30. Promotion from machine operations to programming to programmer/analyst to systems analyst is *not* a normal individual growth pattern. Each area requires certain talents which are not necessarily requirements for admission to another level. A good accounting clerk can, but normally does not, become controller. The close association of work does not normally make a clerk into an accountant. The same is true in data processing. High percentages of upward mobility within the Data Processing Department suggests low potential from the current incumbents.

32. A poor score on this question and low scores on questions 30 and 31 normally indicate an unwillingness to meet the salary standards of the computer profession. Sometimes a supervisor's abrasive personality causes an equally bad score on this question.

Protection

Society and our environment are a hazard to data processing. Big glass windows facing the street, a disgruntled data processing employee, or a carelessly abandoned cigarette all pose a danger to this vital organization function.

Summary

How does your organization stack up? Don't be surprised if the score is not as high as you might like it to be. The Data Processing Department is not the technician's playground filled with ego building contraptions. It is, rather, a vital resource frequently used in the most unsophisticated ways available in order to produce the blandest possible products.

What we need, perhaps, is a doctor of business to cure our informational ills.

Bibliography

Ansoff, H. I., *Corporate Strategy*. New York: McGraw-Hill, 1965.

Archer, S. H. and C. A. D'Ambrosio, *Business Finance Theory and Management*. New York: Macmillan, 1972.

Batten, J. D., *Developing a Tough-Minded Climate . . . for Results*. New York: American Management Association, 1965

Baumol, W. J., *Economic Theory and Operations Analysis*. Englewood Cliffs, N.J.: Prentice-Hall, 1965.

Bayless, W. H., "Management by CSROEPM," *Harvard Business Review,* March–April 1969.

Beckett, J. A., "Systemation: The Advent of Systematic Management," keynote address, 17th International Systems Meeting, Philadelphia, Pa.: Oct. 12, 1964.

Berne, E., *Games People Play*. New York: Grove Press, 1964.

Blake, R. R., J. S. Mouton, and A. C. Bidwell, "The Managerial Grid: A Comparison of Eight Theories of Management," *Advanced Management Journal*, 1962.

Blau, P. M. and W. R. Scott, *Formal Organizations*. San Francisco: Chandler, 1962.

Burns, T., "The Directions of Activity and Communication in a Departmental Executive Group," *Human Relations* No. 7, 1954.

Burns, T., "Management in Action," *Operational Research Quarterly,* No. 8, 1957.

Caldwell, J., "The Effective Reports Crisis," *Journal of Systems Management,* June 1975.

Carlson, S., *Executive Behaviour: A Study of the Work Load and the Working Methods of Managing Directors*. Stockholm: Strombergs, 1951.

Chapin, N., *Flowcharts*. Princeton, N.J.: Auerback, 1971.

Chow, J. V., "What You Need to Know about DBM," *Journal of Systems Management,* May–June 1975.

Cleland, D. I., "Project Management," *Air University Review,* January–February 1966.

Clifton, H. D., *Systems Analysis for Business Data Processing*. Princeton, N.J.: Auerbach, 1969.

Cohan, A. B., *Financial Decision Making—Theory and Practice*. Englewood Cliffs, N.J.: Prentice-Hall, 1972.

Collins, O. F. and D. G. Moore, *The Organization Makers*. New York: Appleton, 1970.

Coman, E. T., Jr., *Sources of Business Information*. New York: Prentice-Hall, 1949.

Dale, E., *The Great Organizers*. New York: McGraw-Hill, 1960.

250   BIBLIOGRAPHY

Dale, E. and L. F. Urwick, *Staff in Organization.* New York: McGraw-Hill, 1960.

Dale, M., *Men Who Manage.* New York: Wiley, 1957.

Davis, K. R. and G. W. Taylor, "Systems Design through Gaming," *Journal of Systems Management,* September 1975.

De Newfville, R. and D. Marks, *Systems Planning and Design.* Englewood Cliffs, N.J.: Prentice-Hall, 1974.

Di Roccaferrera, G. M.; *Operations Research Models for Business and Industry.* Cincinnati, Ohio: Southwestern, 1964.

Drucker, P. F., *The Practice of Management.* New York: Harper & Row, 1954.

Drucker, P. F., *The Effective Executive.* New York: Harper & Row 1967.

Edwards, M. O., "Creativity Solves Management Problems," *Journal of Systems Management,* June 1975.

Ewing, D. W., *The Managerial Mind,* New York: Free Press, 1964.

Fahey, R. J., D. A. Love, and P. F. Ross, *Computer Science and Management Dynamics.* New York: Financial Executives Research Foundation, 1969.

Filley, A. C. and R. J. House, *Managerial Process and Organizational Behavior.* Glenview, Ill.: Scott, Foresman, 1967.

Galbraith, J. K., *The New Industrial State.* Boston: Houghton-Mifflin, 1967.

Gattis, M., "How Not to Succeed in Management by Being Really Trying," *Machine Design,* May 11, 1967.

Grayson, C. J., Jr., "Management Science and Business Practice," *Harvard Business Review,* July–August 1973.

Guest, R. H., "Of Time and the Foreman," *Personnel* No. 32, 1955–1956.

Hacker, A., "The Making of a (Corporation) President," *The New York Times Magazine,* April 2, 1967.

Haire, M., ed., *Modern Organization Theory.* New York: Wiley, 1959.

Hall, D. M., *The Management of Human Systems.* Cleveland, Ohio: Association for Systems Management, 1971.

Handbook of Successful Operating System and Procedures, with Forms. Englewood Cliffs, N.J.: Prentice-Hall, 1964.

Haslett, J. W., "Streaking Is Not for the Analyst," *Journal of Systems Management,* May 1974.

Head, R. F., *A Guide to Packaged Systems.* New York: Wiley, 1971.

Helmer, O., *Analysis of the Future: The Delphi Method.* Santa Monica, Calif.: Rand Corporation, 1967.

Hertzberg, F., B. Mausner, and B. Snyderman, *The Motivation to Work.* New York: Wiley, 1959.

Homans, G. C., *The Human Group.* New York: Harcourt Brace Jovanovich, 1950.

Jennings, E. E., *An Anatomy of Leadership.* New York: Harper & Row, 1960.

Joslin, F., *Analysis, Design and Selection of Computer Systems.* Arlington, Va.: College Readings, Inc., 1971.

Katz, D. and R. L. Kahn, *The Social Psychology of Organizations.* New York: Wiley, 1966.

Kelly, J., *Organizational Behavior.* Homewood, Ill.: Irwin-Dorsey, 1974.

Kozmetsky, G. and P. Kircher, *Electronic Computers and Management Control*. New York: McGraw-Hill, 1956.

Lason, L., *Optimization Theory for Large-Scale Systems*. New York: Macmillan, 1970.

Lawrence, P. R., "How to Deal with Resistance to Change," *Harvard Business Review*, January–February 1969.

Lewis, R. and R. Stewart, *The Boss*. London: Phoenix House, 1958.

Light, H. R., *The Business Executive*. London: Pitman, 1961.

Likert, R., *New Patterns of Management*. New York: McGraw-Hill, 1961.

Livingston, J. S., "Myth of the Well-Educated Manager," *Harvard Business Review*, January–February 1971.

Mackenzie, R. A., "The Management Process in 3-D," *Harvard Business Review*, November–December 1967.

Madnick, S. E., "Future Use of Computers," *Technology Review*, July–August, 1973.

Mager, R. F. and P. Pipe, *Analyzing Performance Problems or "You Really Oughta Wanna."* Belmont, Calif.: Fearon, 1970.

March, J. G. and H. A. Simon, *Organizations*. New York: Wiley, 1958.

Martino, R. L., "Creating the Integrated Management System," *Computers & Data Processing*, April 1964.

Maslow, A. H., *Motivation and Personality*. New York: Harper & Row, 1954.

Matthies, L. H., *The Playscript Procedure: A New Tool of Administration*. Stamford, Conn.: Office Publications, Inc., 1961.

McGregor, D., *The Human Side of Enterprise*. New York: McGraw-Hill, 1960.

McGregor, D., *The Professional Manager*. New York: McGraw-Hill, 1967.

McKinsey and Company, Inc., "Unlocking the Computer's Profit Potential," *The McKinsey Quarterly*, Fall 1968.

Mills, C. W., *The Power Elite*. New York: Oxford University Press, 1956.

Mintzberg, H., *The Nature of Managerial Work*. New York: Harper & Row, 1973.

Morris, D. *The Naked Ape*. New York: McGraw-Hill, 1967.

Myers, M. S., "Who Are Your Motivated Workers?" *Harvard Business Review*, January–February 1964.

Nadler, G., *Work Simplification*. New York: McGraw-Hill, 1957.

Neustadt, R. E., *Presidential Power: The Politics of Leadership*. New York: Wiley, 1960.

Newcomer, M., *The Big Business Executive*. New York: Columbia University Press, 1955.

Optner, S. L., *Systems Analysis for Business Management*. Englewood Cliffs, N.J.: Prentice-Hall, 1968.

Orlicky, J., *The Successful Computer System*. New York: McGraw-Hill, 1969.

Paretta, R. L. The Frequency of Information Flows: A Misunderstood Management Variable," *Management Adviser*, July–August 1974.

Parkinson, C. N., *Parkinson's Law*. Boston: Houghton-Mifflin, 1957.

Porter, S., *Money Book*. Garden City, N.Y.: Doubleday, 1975.

Ramlow, D. E. and E. H. Wall, *Production Planning and Control*. Englewood Cliffs, N.J.: Prentice-Hall, 1967.

Ramsgard, W. C., "Operational Control of Total Effort," *NAA Bulletin*, July 1964.

Ramsgard, W. C., "Evaluate Your Computer Installation," *Management Service,* January–February 1971.

Ramsgard, W. C., "The Systems Analyst: Doctor of Business," *Journal of Systems Management,* July 1974.

Rayburn, L. G., "Do Accounting Reports Reinforce Failure?" *Management Adviser,* May–June 1974.

Robinson, J. P. and J. D. Graviss, *Documentation Standards Manual for Computer System.* Cleveland, Ohio: Association for Systems Management, 1973.

Rockwell, W. F., Jr., *The Twelve Hats of a Company President.* Englewood Cliffs, N.J.: Prentice-Hall, 1971.

Ross, H. J., *Technique of Systems and Procedures.* Miami, Fla.: Office Research Institute, 1948.

Sackman, H., *Man–Computer Problem Solving.* Princeton, N.J.: Auerbach, 1970.

Sayles, L. R., *Managerial Behavior: Administration in Complex Organizations.* New York: McGraw-Hall, 1964.

Schon, D. A., "The Fear of Innovation," *International Science and Technology,* November 1966.

Selznick, P., *Leadership in Administration.* New York: Harper & Row, 1957.

Shephard, R. W., *Cost and Production Functions.* Princeton, N.J.: Princeton University Press, 1963.

Simon, H. A., *The Shape of Automation.* New York: Harper & Row, 1965.

Slaybaugh, C. J., "Pareto's Law and Modern Management," *Management Services,* March–April 1967.

Sloan, A. P., *My Years with General Motors.* Garden City, N.Y.: Doubleday, 1963.

Sorenson, T. C., *Decision Making in the White House.* Columbia University Press, 1963.

Spriegel, W. R., *Principles of Business Organization and Operation.* Englewood Cliffs, N.J.: Prentice-Hall, 1963.

Staples, R., "Flowcharting—an Aid to Project Management," *Research Management,* July 1972.

Starr, M. K., *Systems Management of Operations.* Englewood Cliffs, N.J.: Prentice-Hall, 1971.

Steiner, G. A., *Top Management Planning.* New York: Macmillan, 1969.

Stewart, R., *Managers and Their Jobs.* London: Macmillan, 1967.

Stryker, P., *The Men from the Boys.* New York: Harper & Row, 1960.

Taylor, F. W., *Scientific Management.* New York: Harper & Row, 1947.

"The Ten Best—Managed Companies," *Dun's,* December 1970.

"The Truth about Hoover," *Time,* December 22, 1975, pp. 14–21.

Thomas, E. J. and B. J. Biddle, *Role Theory: Concepts and Research.* New York: Wiley, 1966.

Toffler, A., *Future Shock.* New York: Random House, 1970.

Townsend, R., *Up the Organization.* New York: Knopf, 1970.

Uris, A., *The Executive Deskbook.* New York: Van Nostrand, 1970.

Urwick, L. F., *The Load on Top Management—Can It Be Reduced?* London: Urwick, Orr and Partners, Ltd., 1954.

Valentine, R. F., *Performance Objectives for Systems Men*. Cleveland, Ohio: Association for Systems Management, 1971.

Vancil, R. F., "So You're Going to Have a Planning Department!" *Harvard Business Review,* May–June 1967.

Vardamen, G. T., *Effective Communication of Ideas*. New York: Van Nostrand, 1970.

Vroom, V. H., *Work and Motivation*. New York: Wiley, 1964.

Weinburg, G. M., *The Psychology of Computer Programming*. New York: Van Nostrand, 1971.

Wight, O., *The Executive's New Computer—Six Keys to Systems Success*. Reston, Va.: Reston Publishing Company,

Willoughby, T. C. and J. A., Senn, *Business Systems*. Cleveland, Ohio: Association for Systems Management, 1975.

Withington, F. G., "Five Generations of Computers," *Harvard Business Review,* July–August 1974.

Wrapp, H. E., "Good Managers Don't Make Policy Decisions," *Harvard Business Review,* September–October 1967.

Index